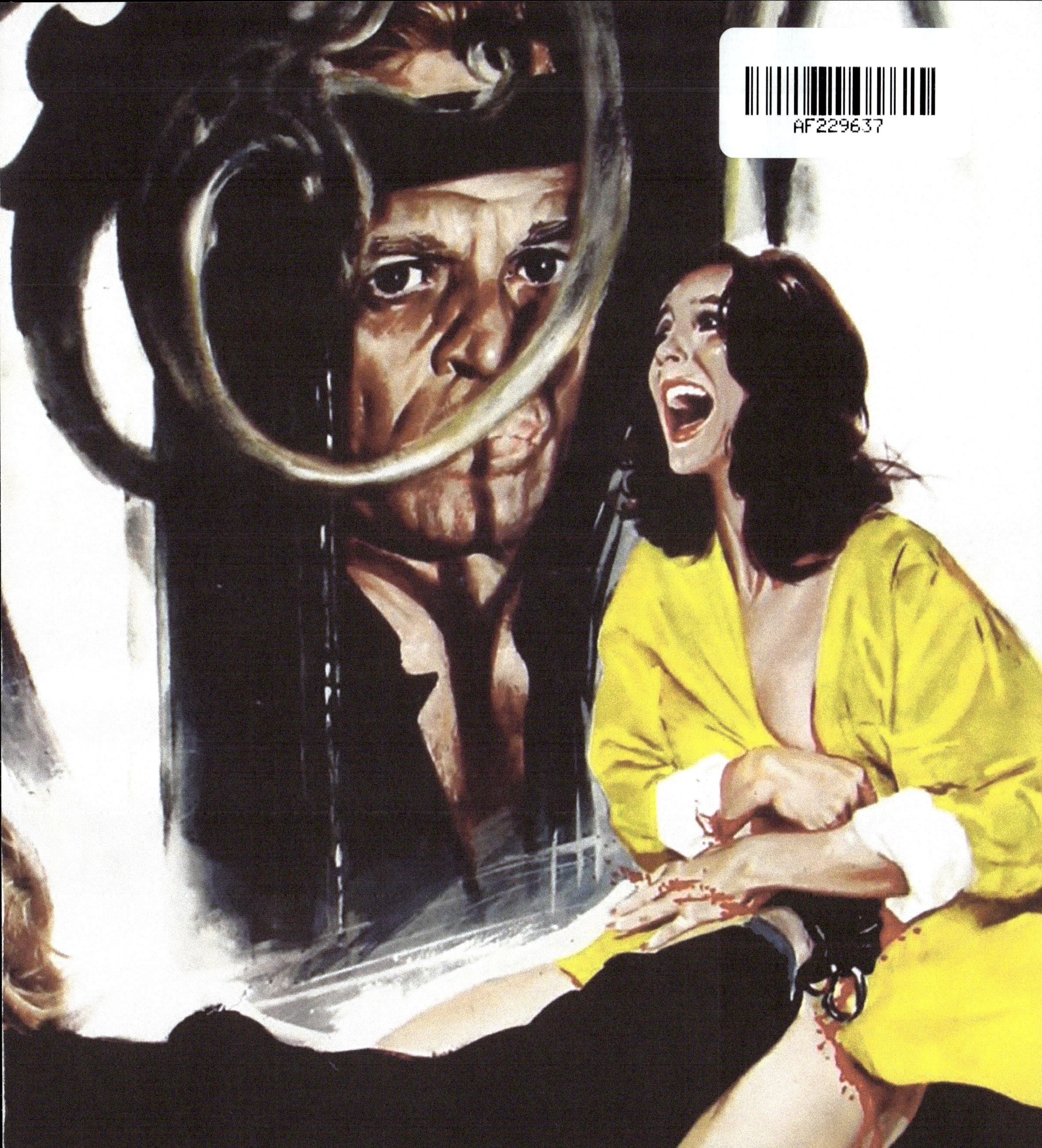

CRYPT OF CARNAL TERRORS 2

100 ARTWORKS FOR ITALIAN HORROR & GIALLO FILM POSTERS

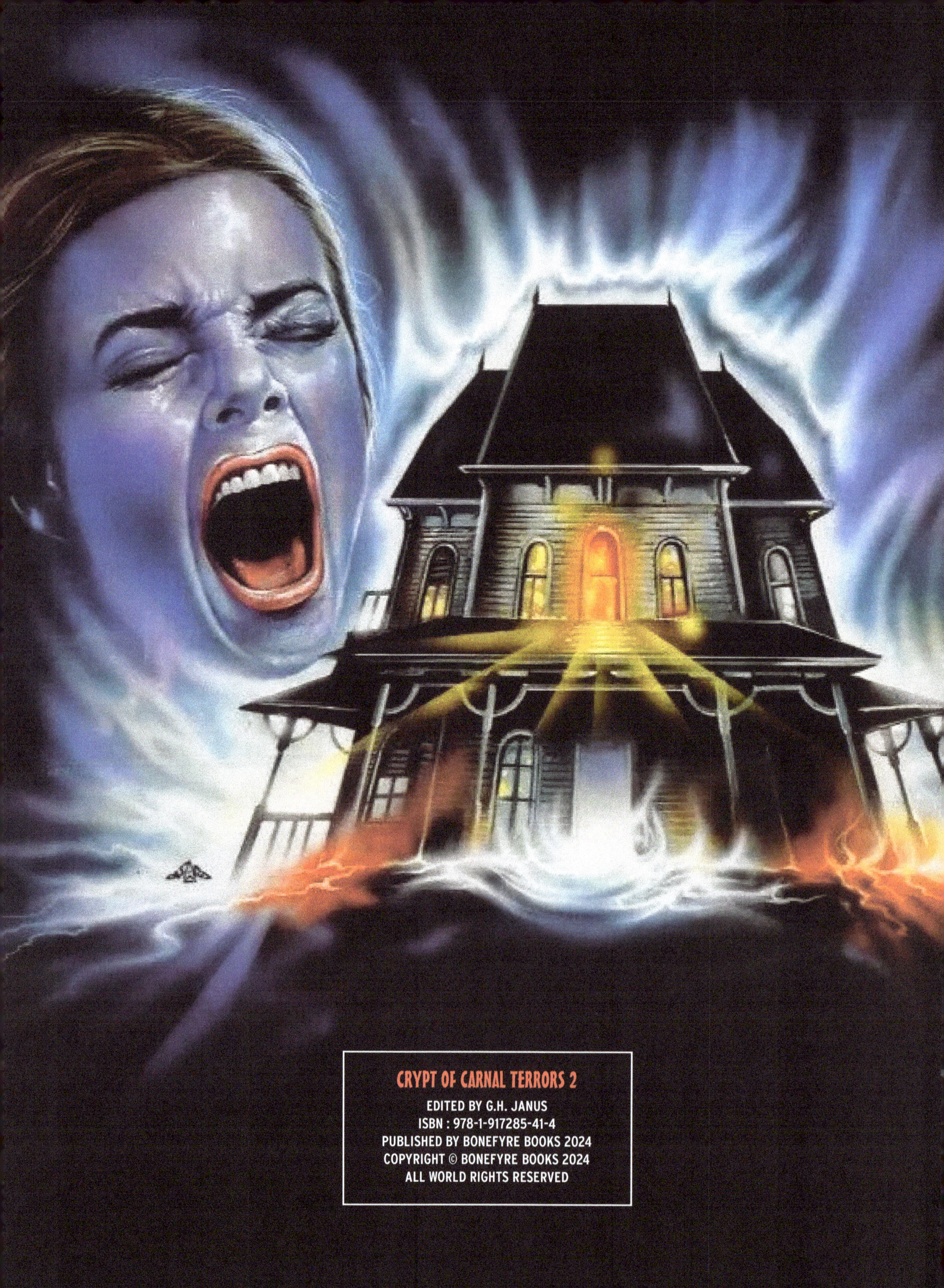
CRYPT OF CARNAL TERRORS 2
EDITED BY G.H. JANUS
ISBN : 978-1-917285-41-4
PUBLISHED BY BONEFYRE BOOKS 2024
COPYRIGHT © BONEFYRE BOOKS 2024
ALL WORLD RIGHTS RESERVED

FILMS REPRESENTED

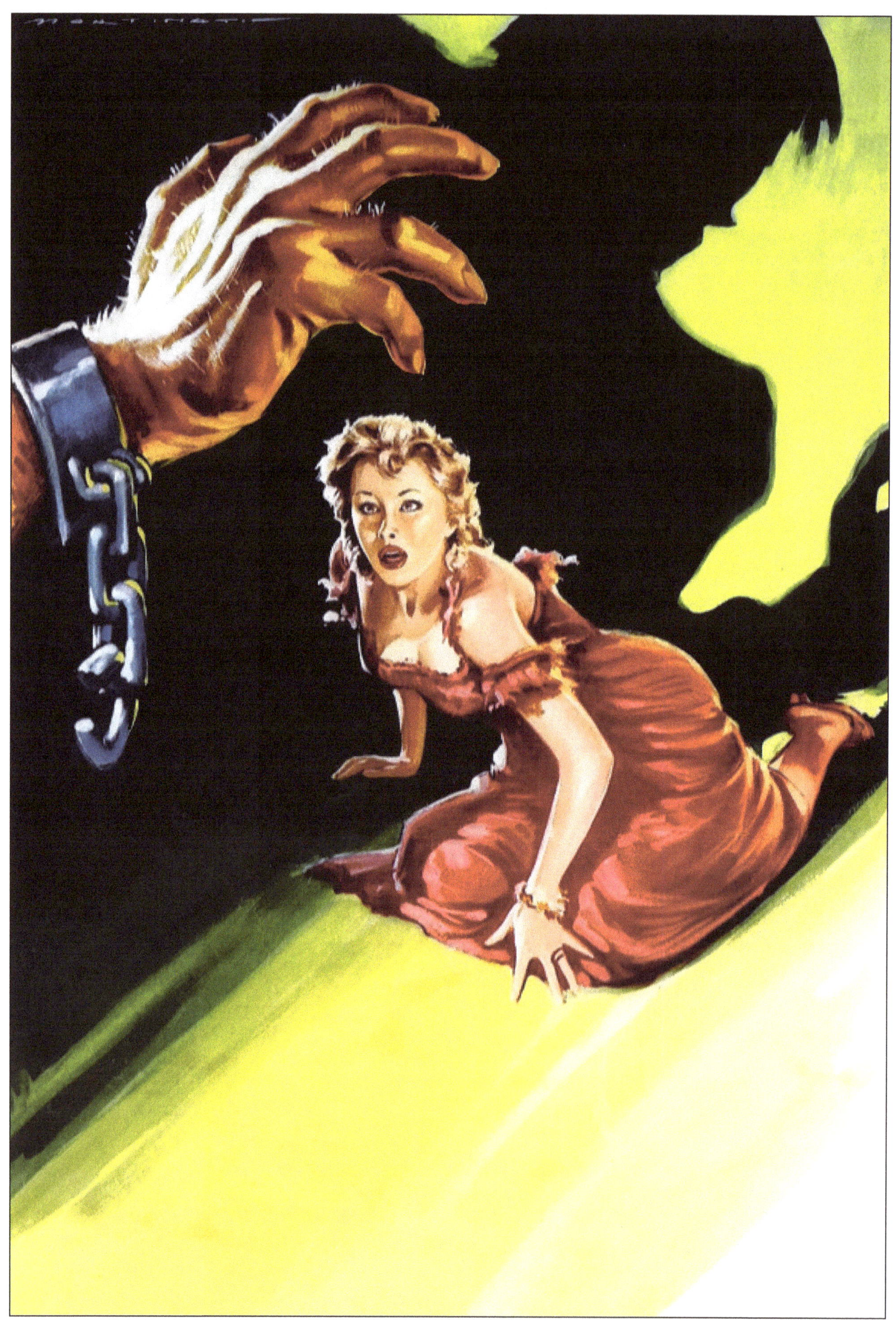

LA MASCHERA DI FRANKENSTEIN (1957). Artist: Luigi Martinati.

4

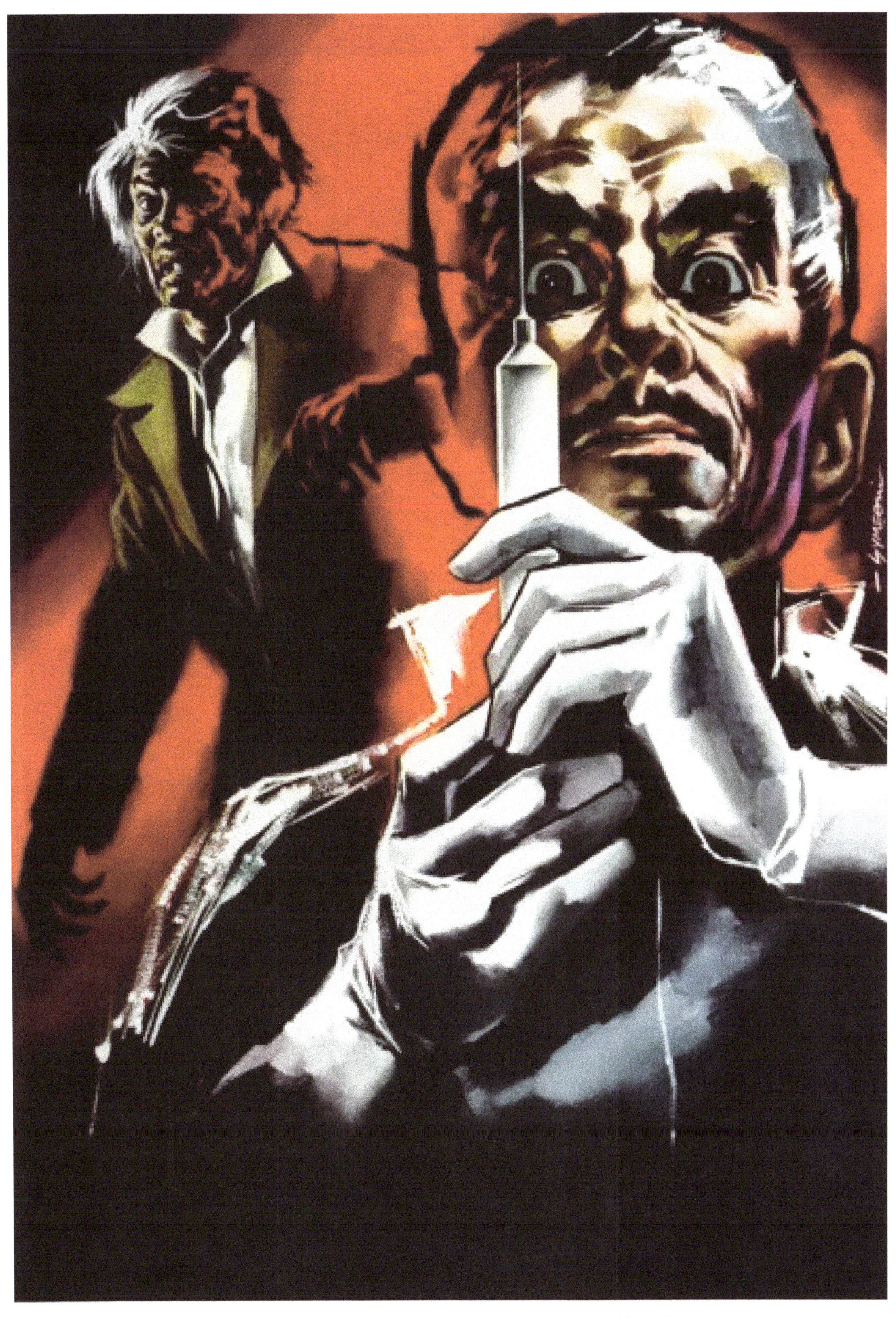

LA VENDETTA DI FRANKENSTEIN (1958). Artist: Sandro Symeoni.

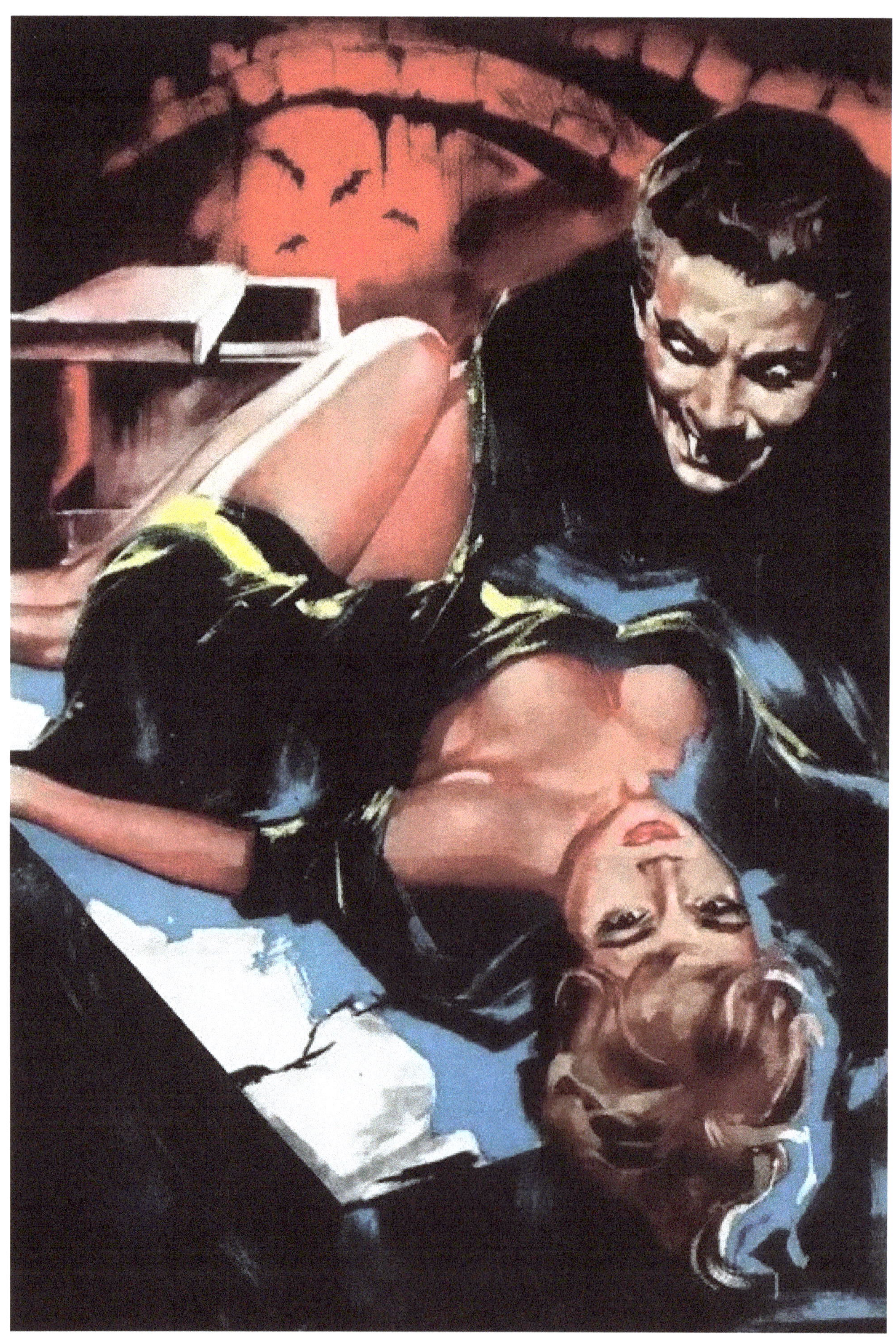

LA ULTIMA PREDA DEL VAMPIRO (1960). Artist: unsigned.

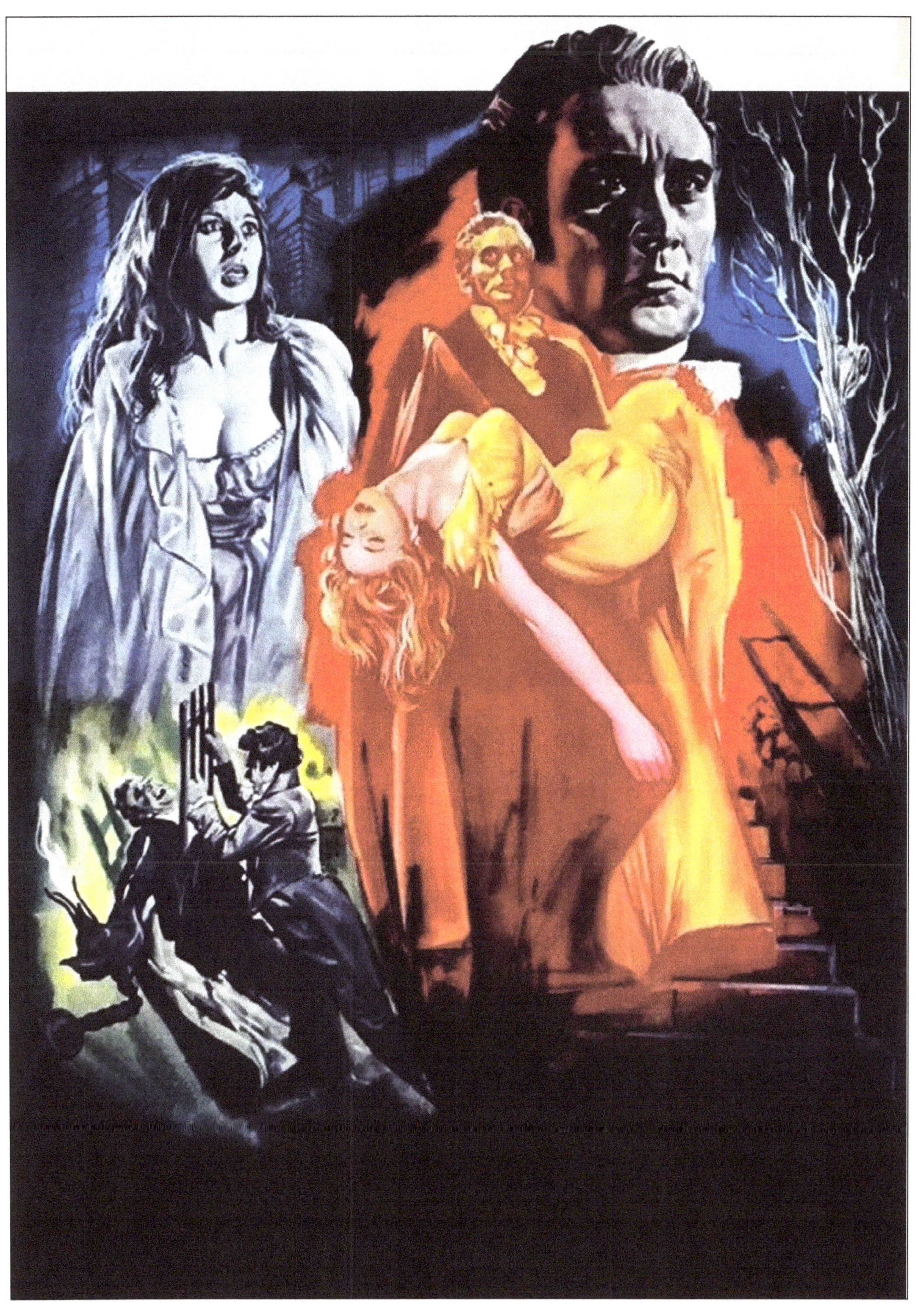

LA STRAGE DEI VAMPIRI (1962). Artist: unsigned.

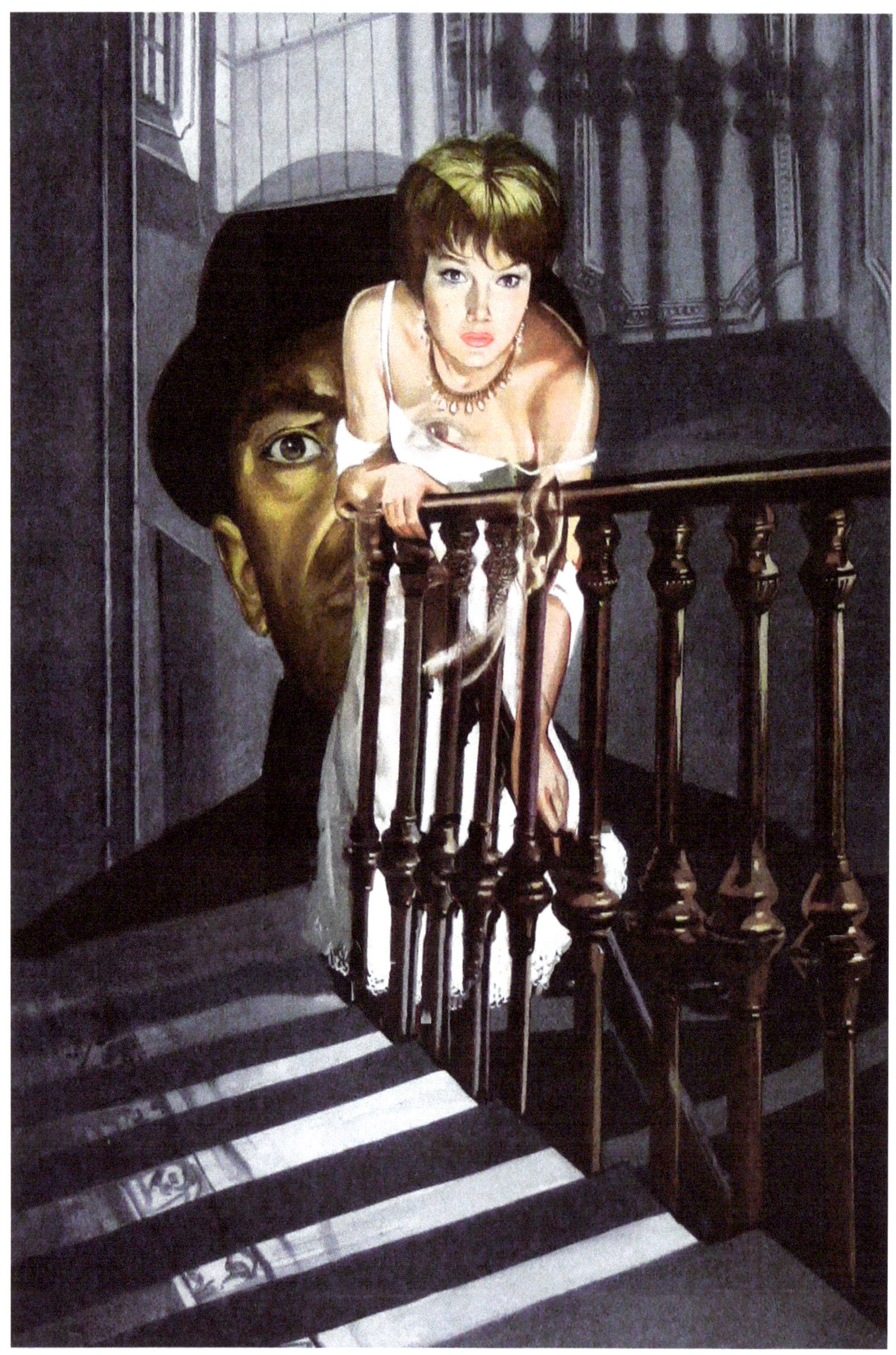

IL DIABOLICO DOTT. SATANA (1962). Artist: Mario de Berardinis.

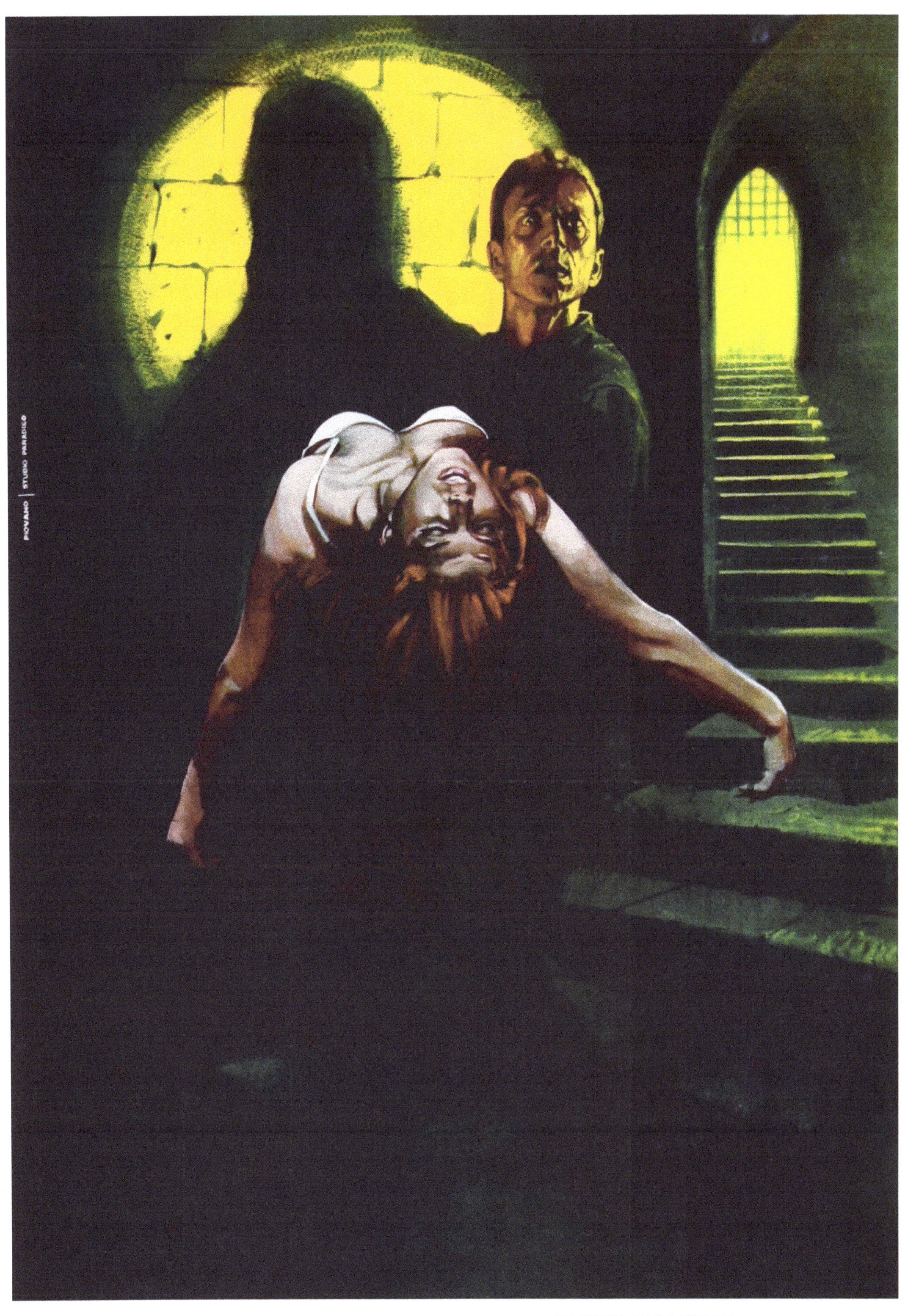

LA BESTIA DEL CASTELLO MALEDETTO (1962). Artist: Mario Piovano.

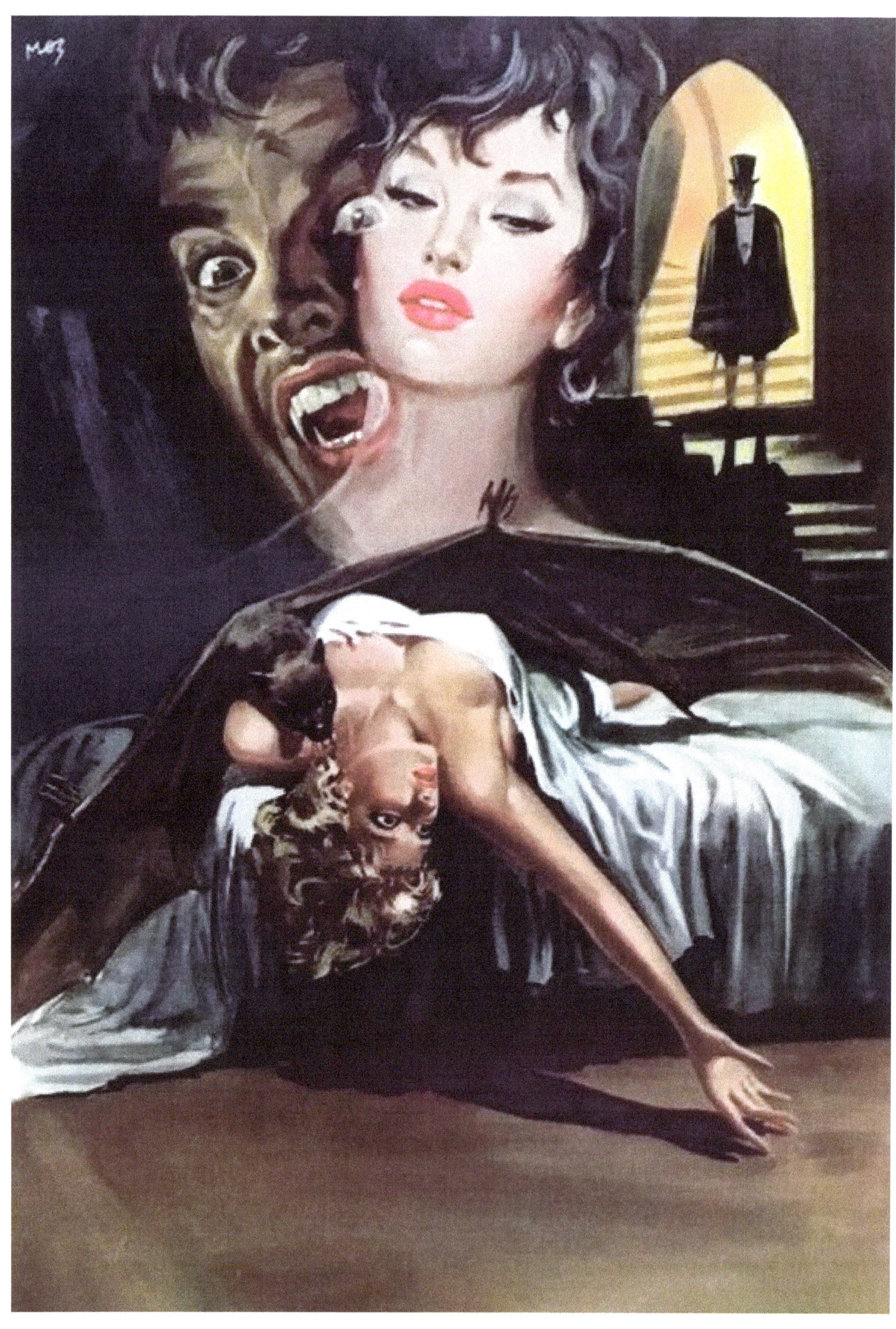

LA VENDETTA DEL VAMPIRO (1961). Artist: Mario de Berardinis.

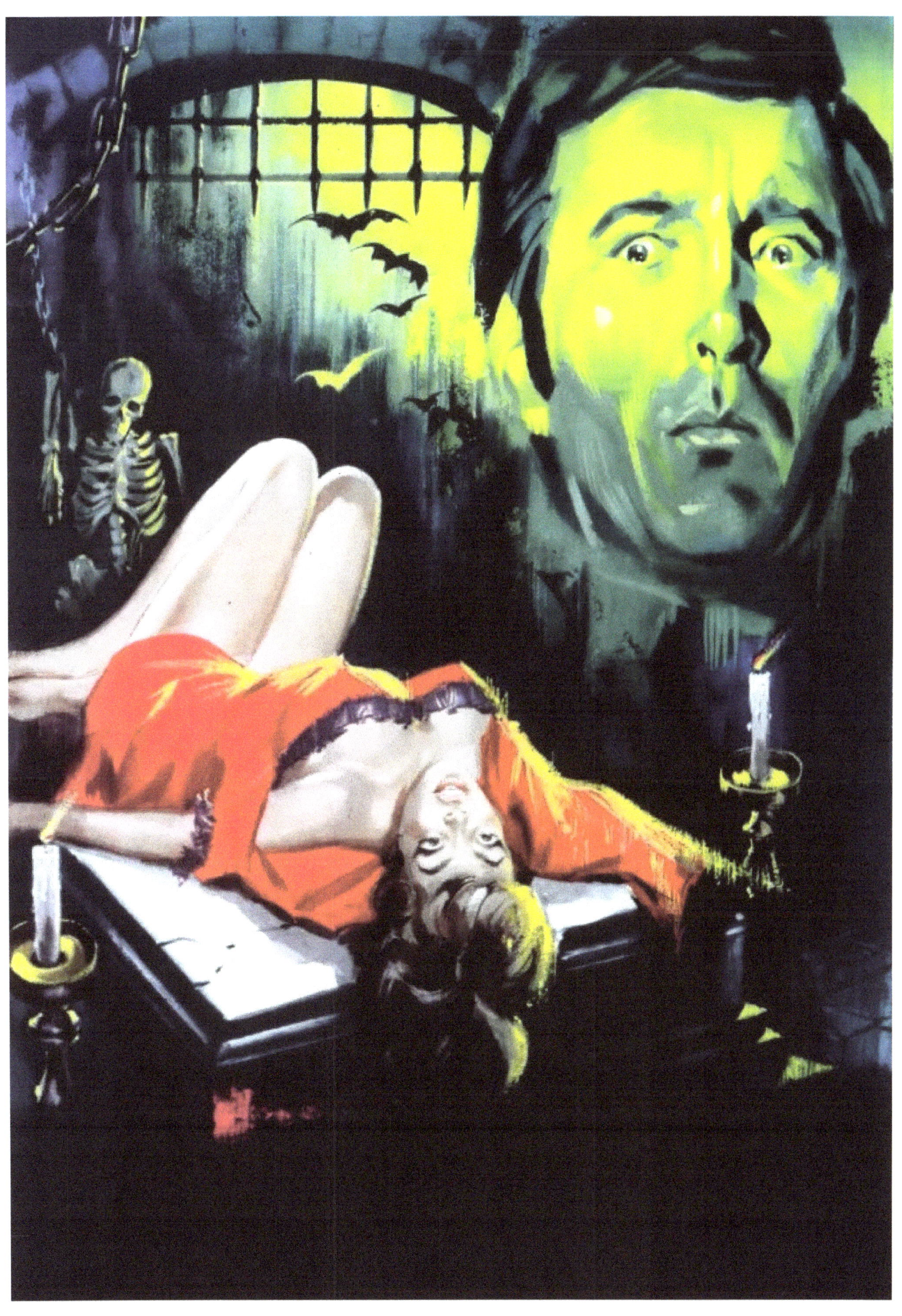

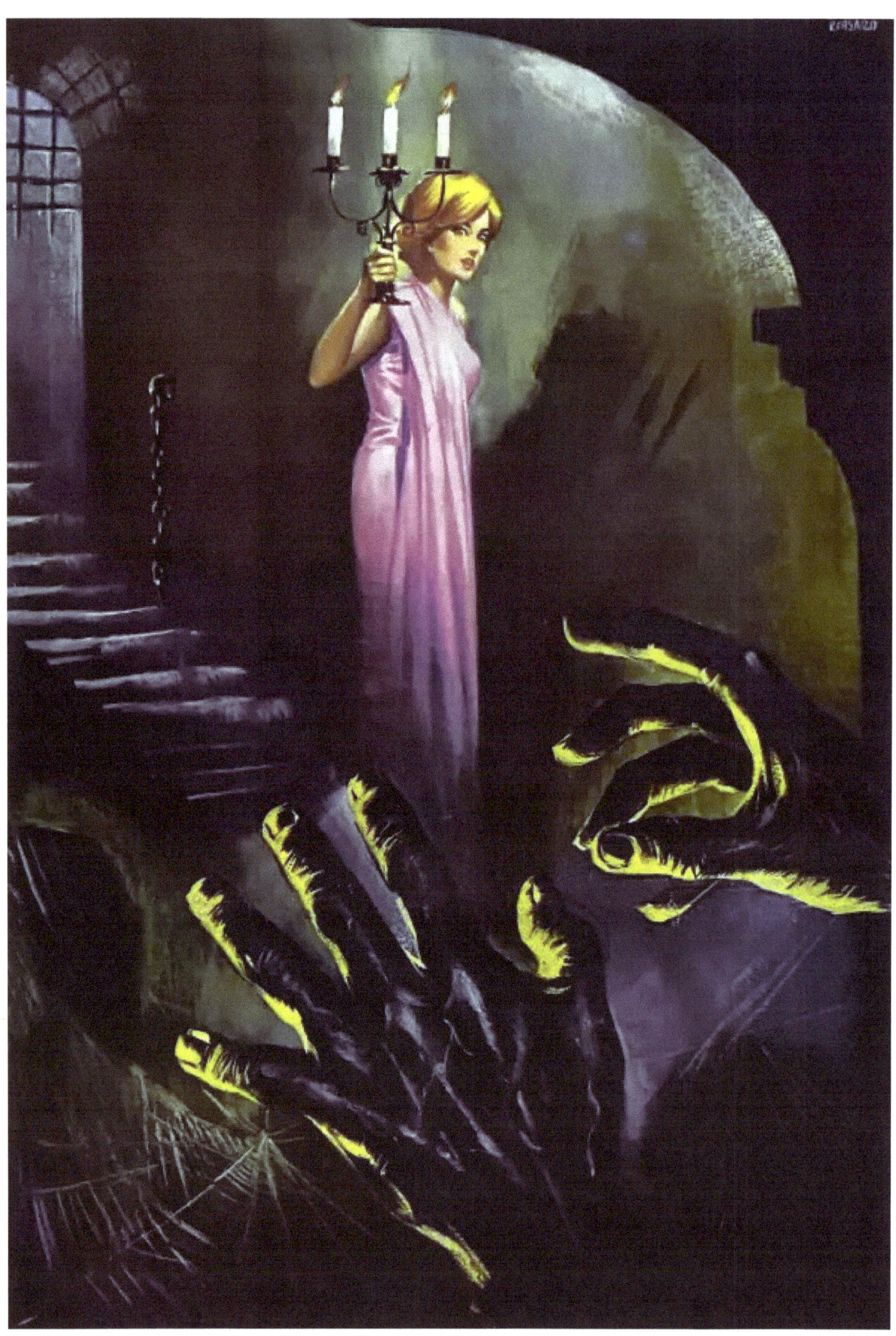

LA MORTE NERA (1964). Artist: Renato Casaro.

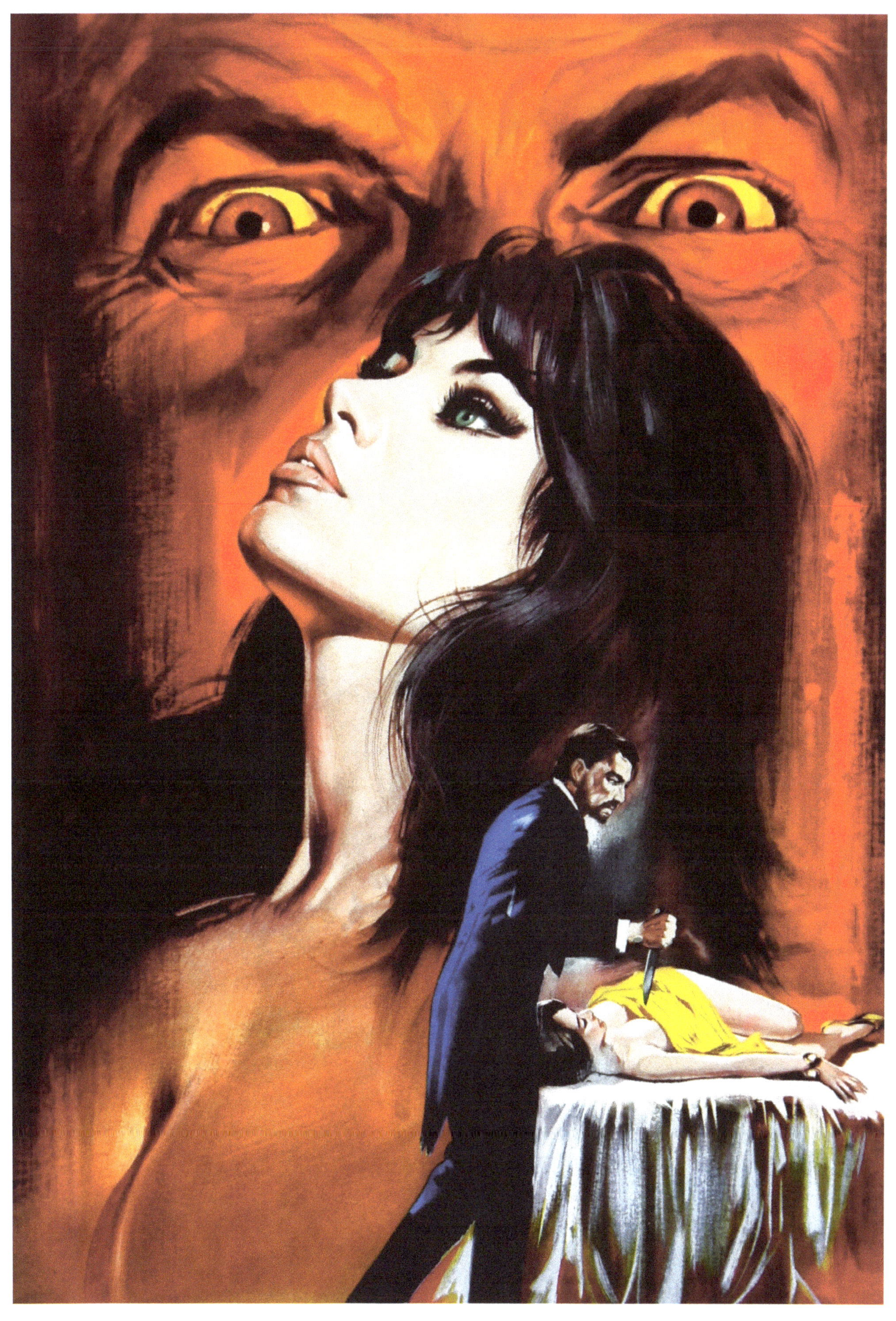

IL MOSTRO E LE VERGINI (1964). Artist: unsigned.

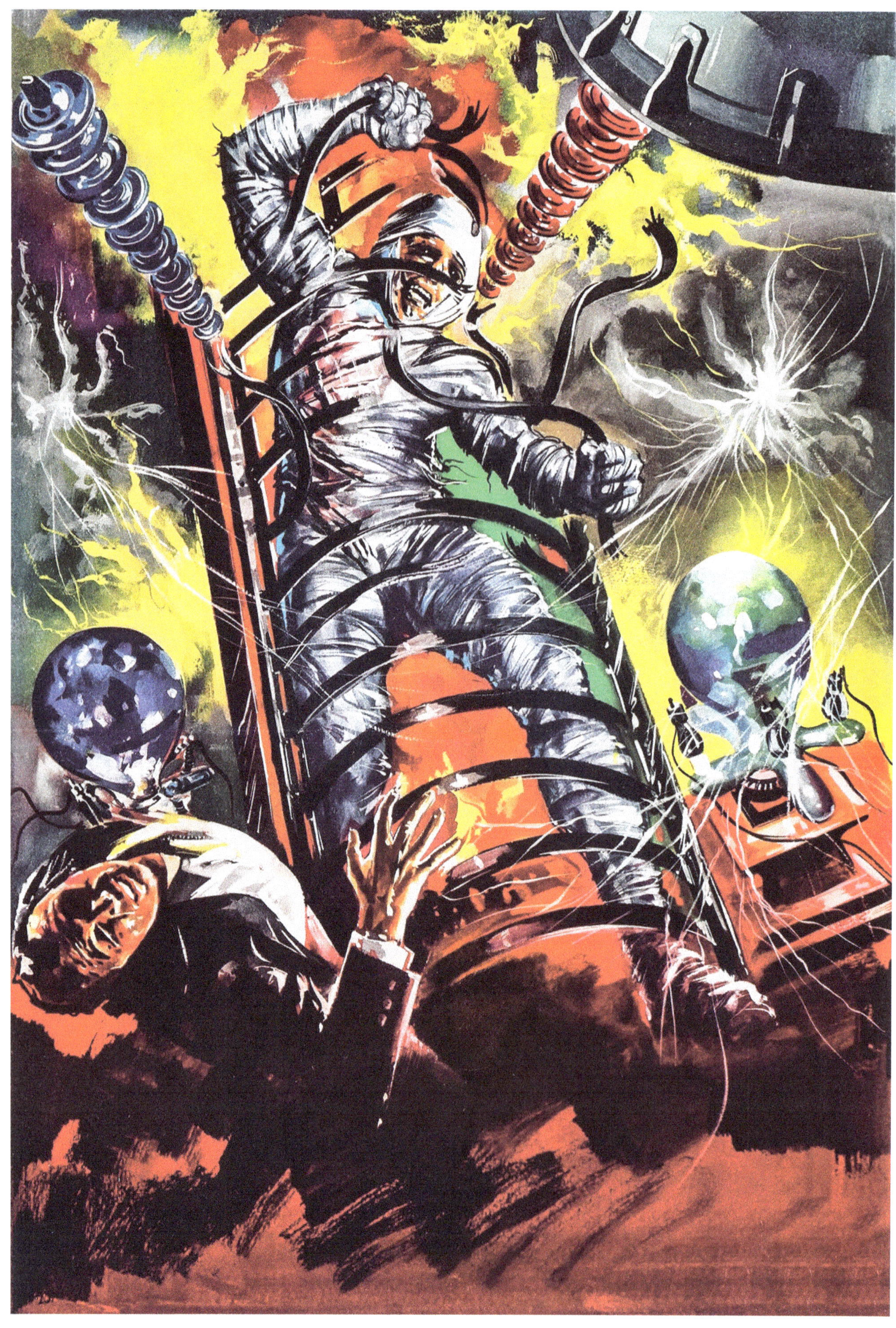

LA RIVOLTA DI FRANKENSTEIN (1964). Artist: unsigned.

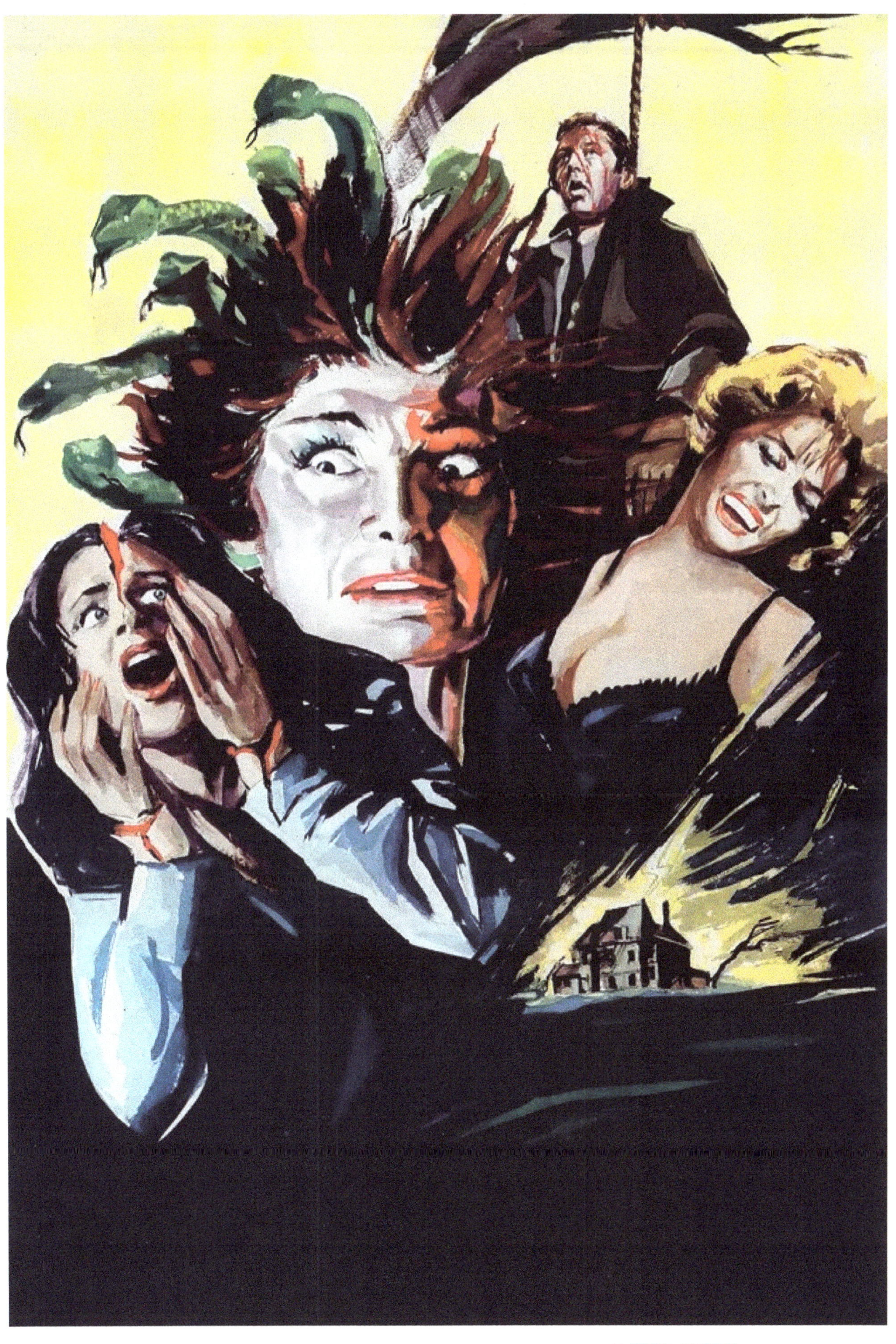

LO SGUARDO CHE UCCIDE (1964). Artist: Ercole Brini.

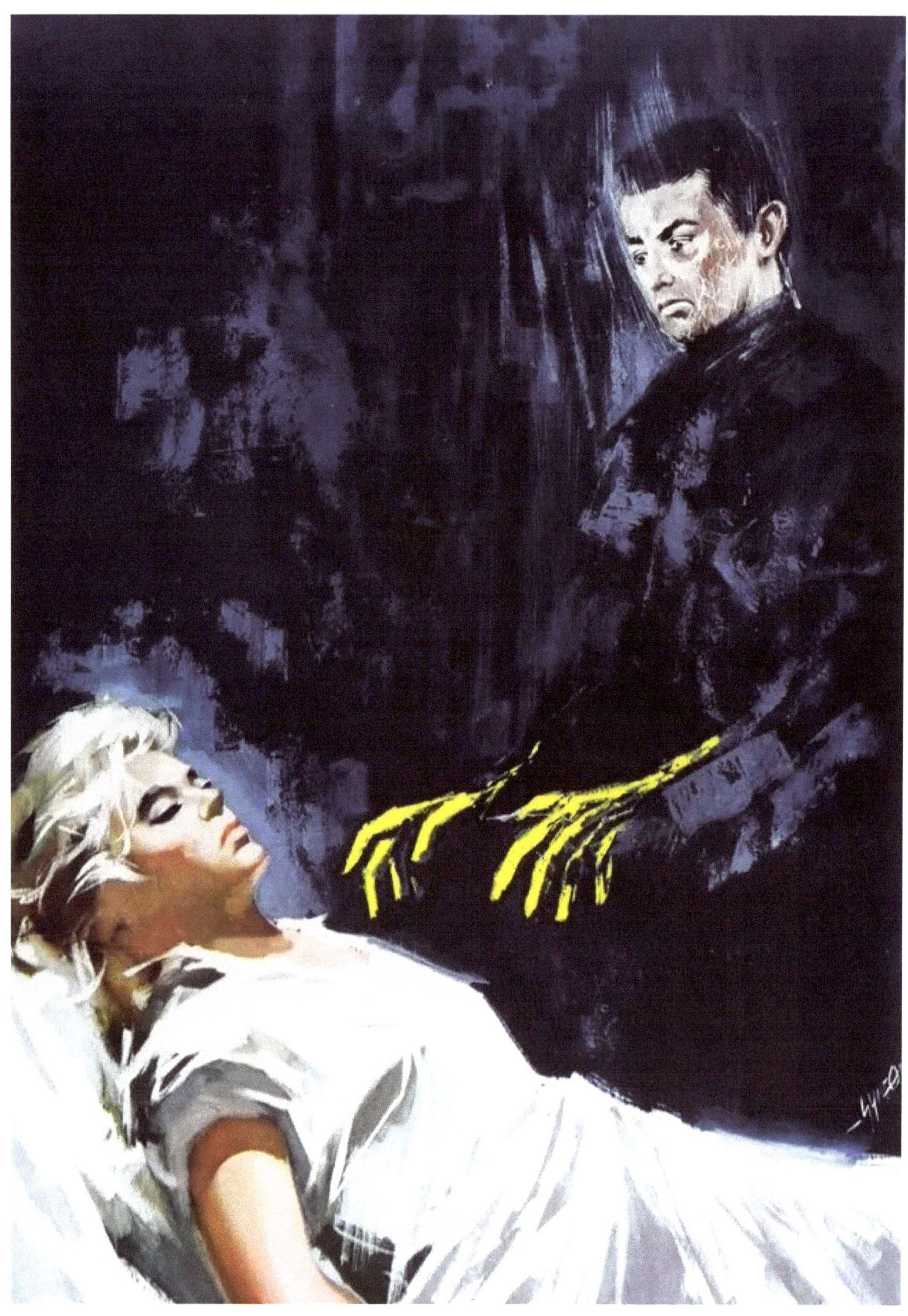

16

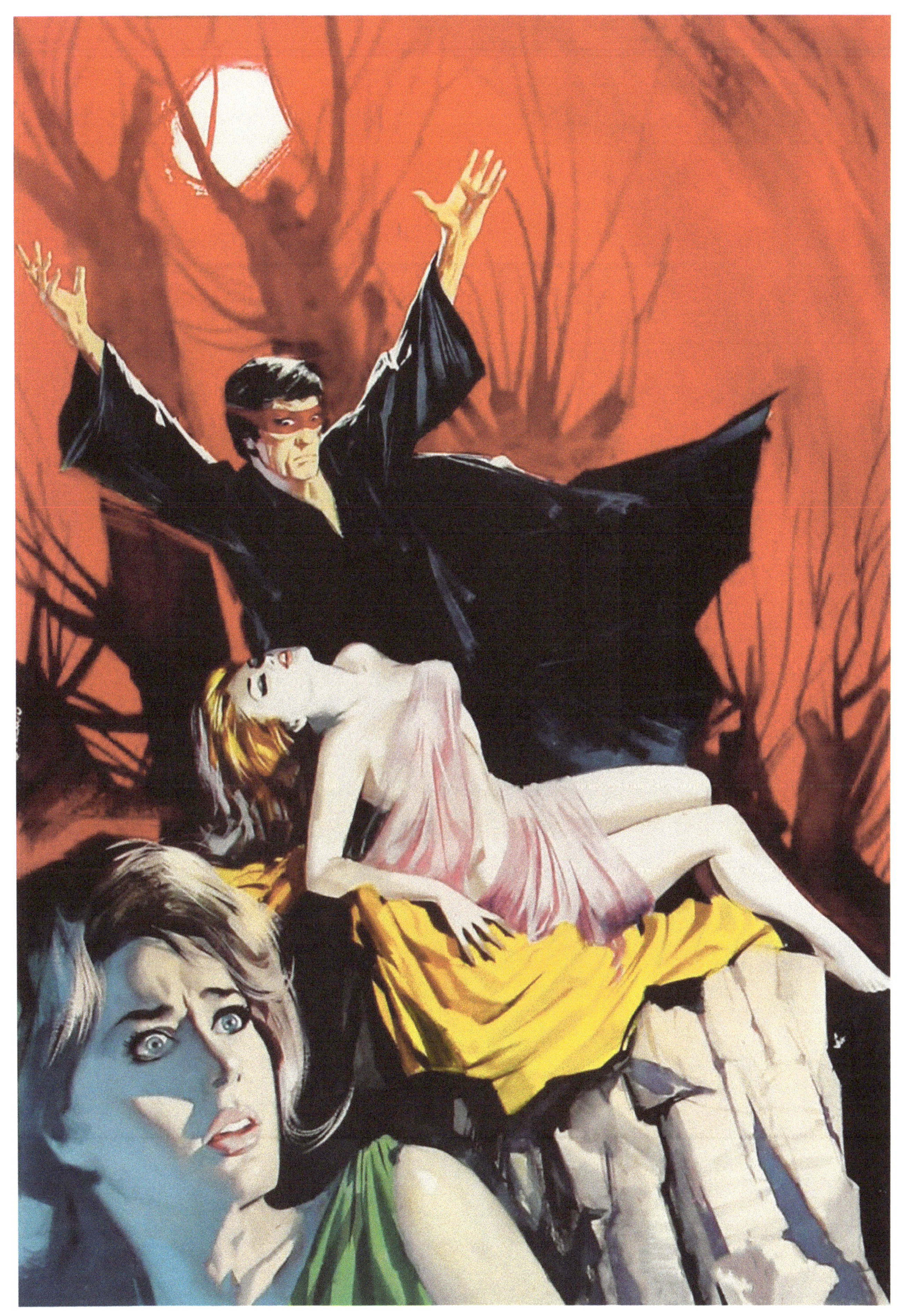

IL PRINCIPE DELLA NOTTE (1965). Artist: Reanto Casaro.

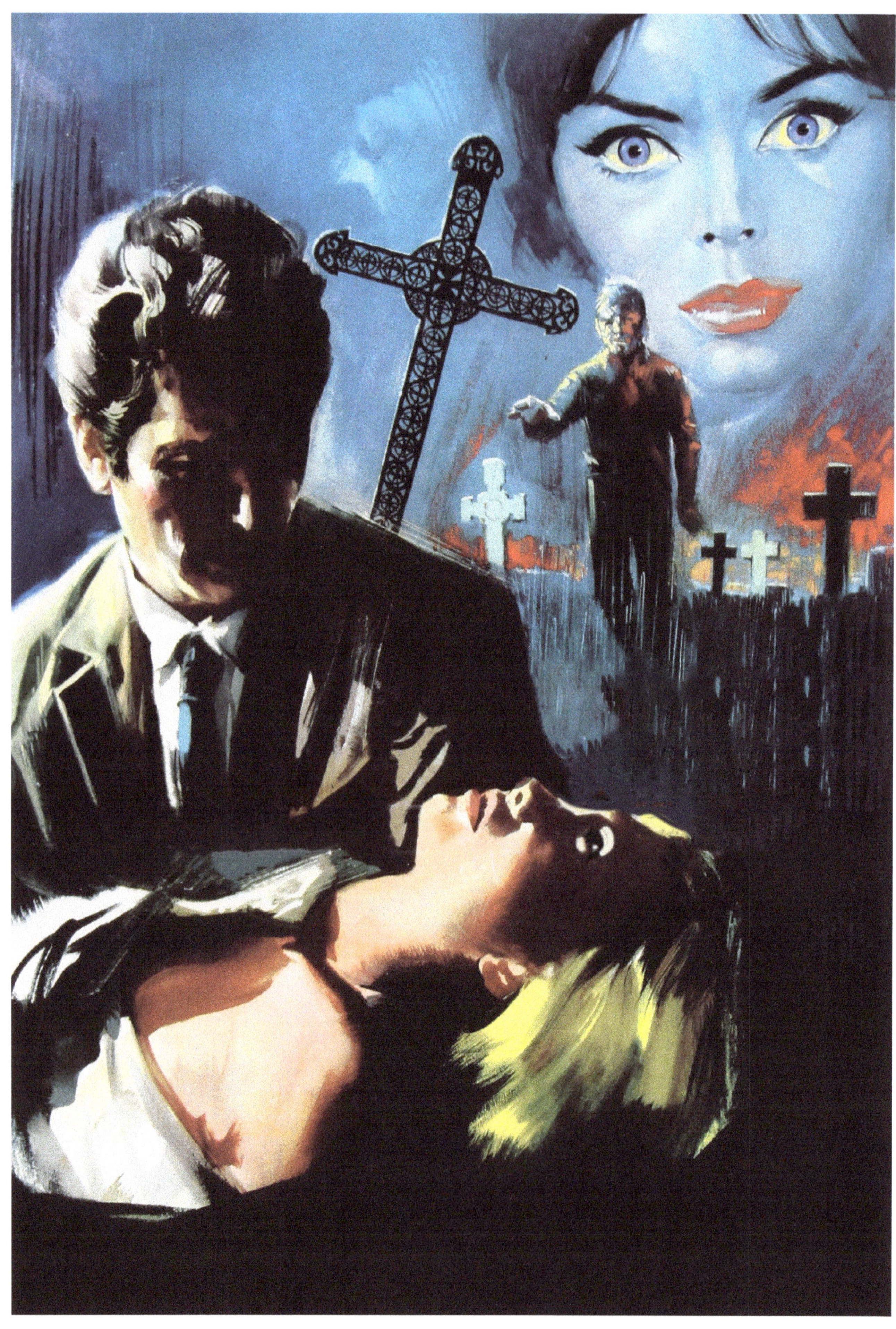

CINQUE TOMBE PER UN MEDIUM (1965). Artist: unsigned.

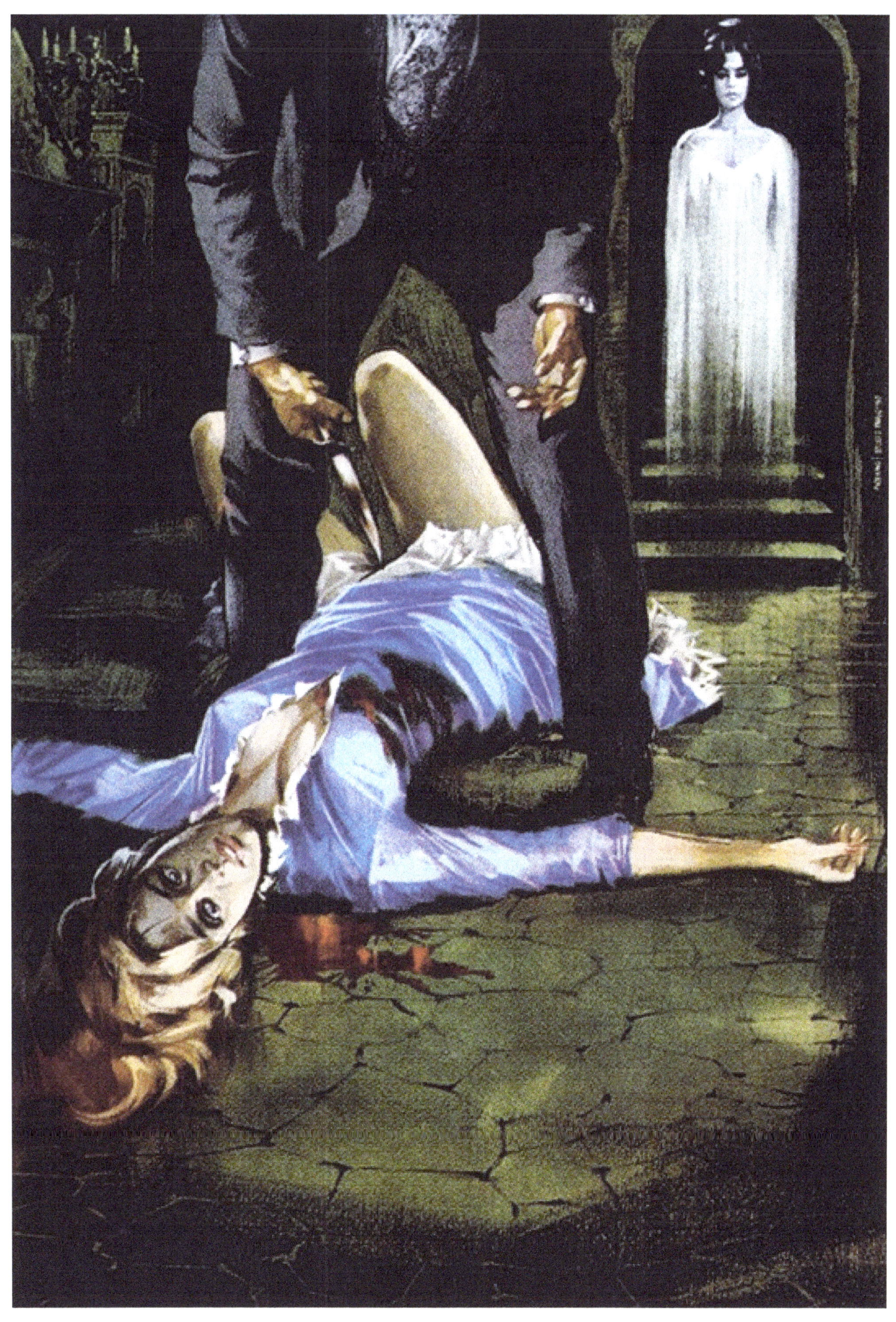

LA VENDETTA DI LADY MORGAN (1965). Artist: Mario Piovano.

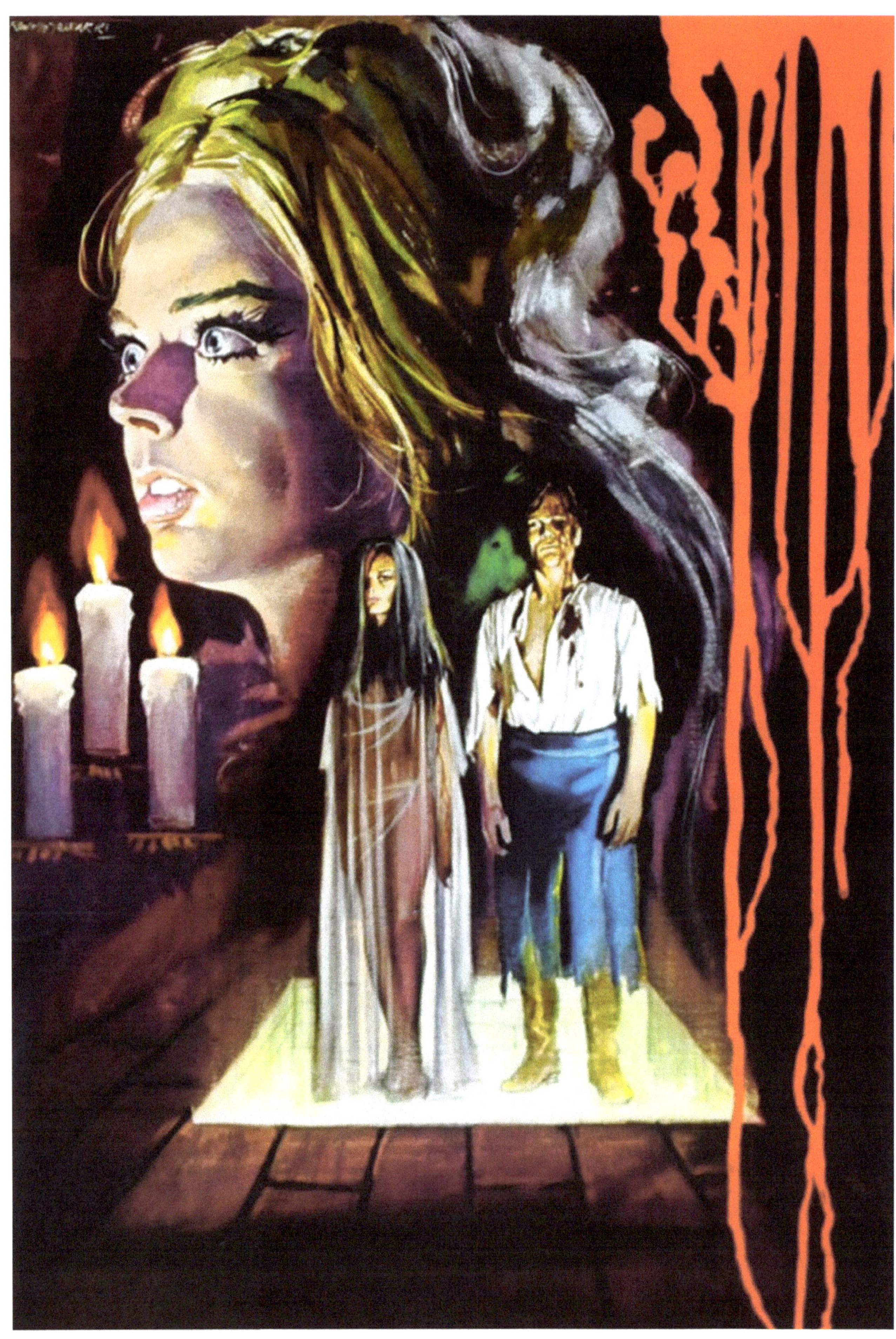

GLI AMANTI D'OLTRETOMBA (1965). Artist: Rodolfo Gasparri.

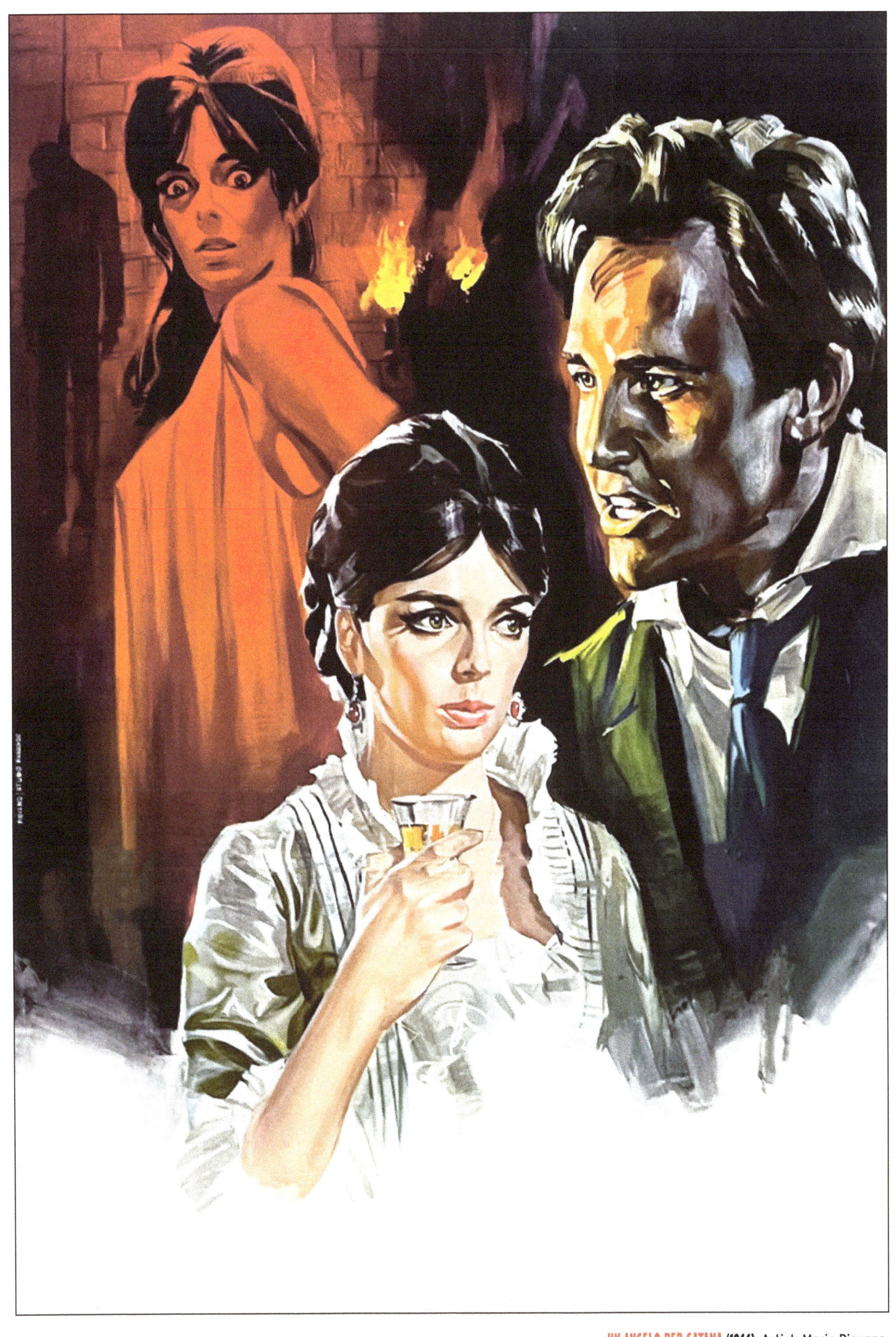

UN ANGELO PER SATANA (1966). Artist: Mario Piovano.

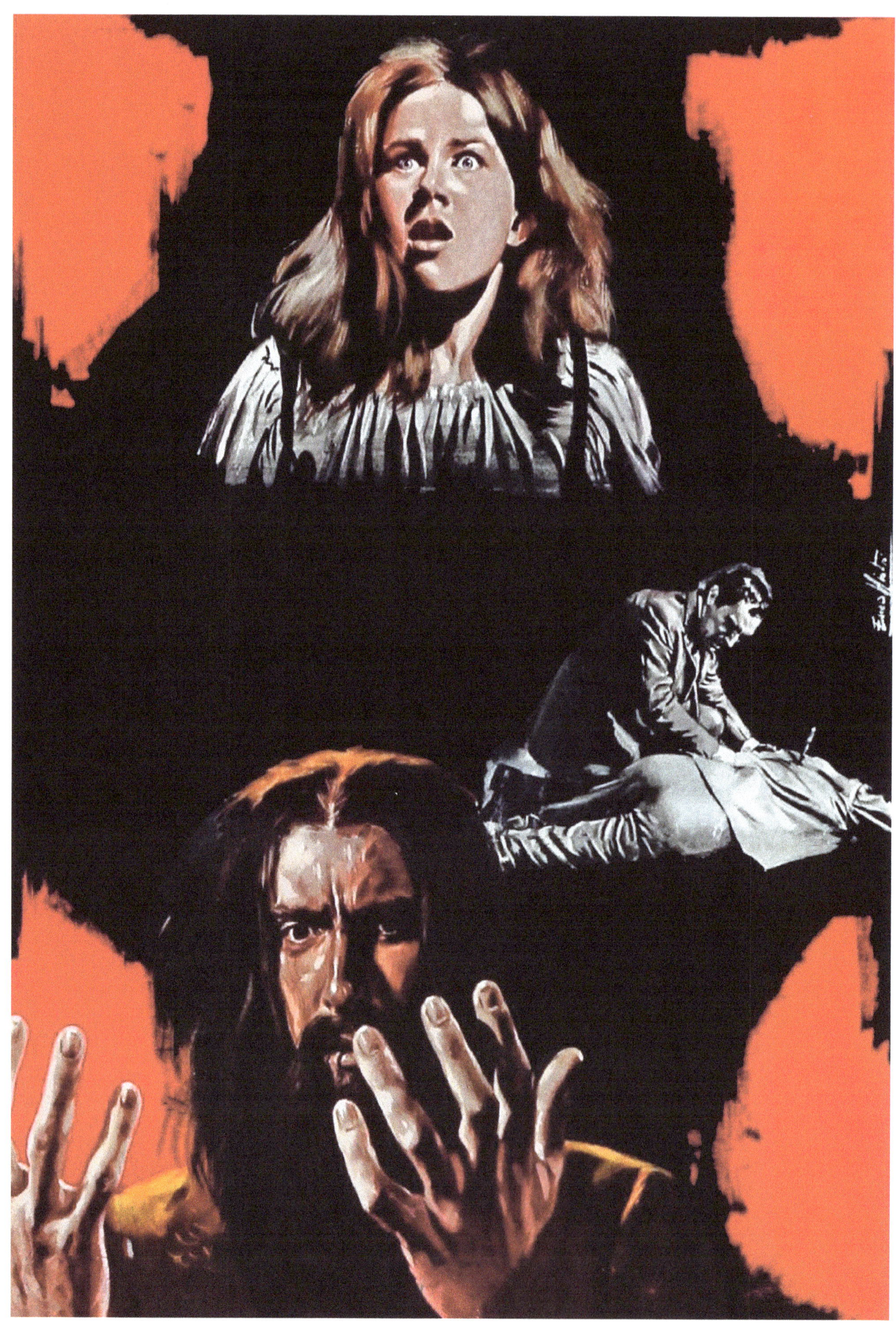

RASPUTIN IL MONACO FOLLE (1966). Artist: Enzo Nistri.

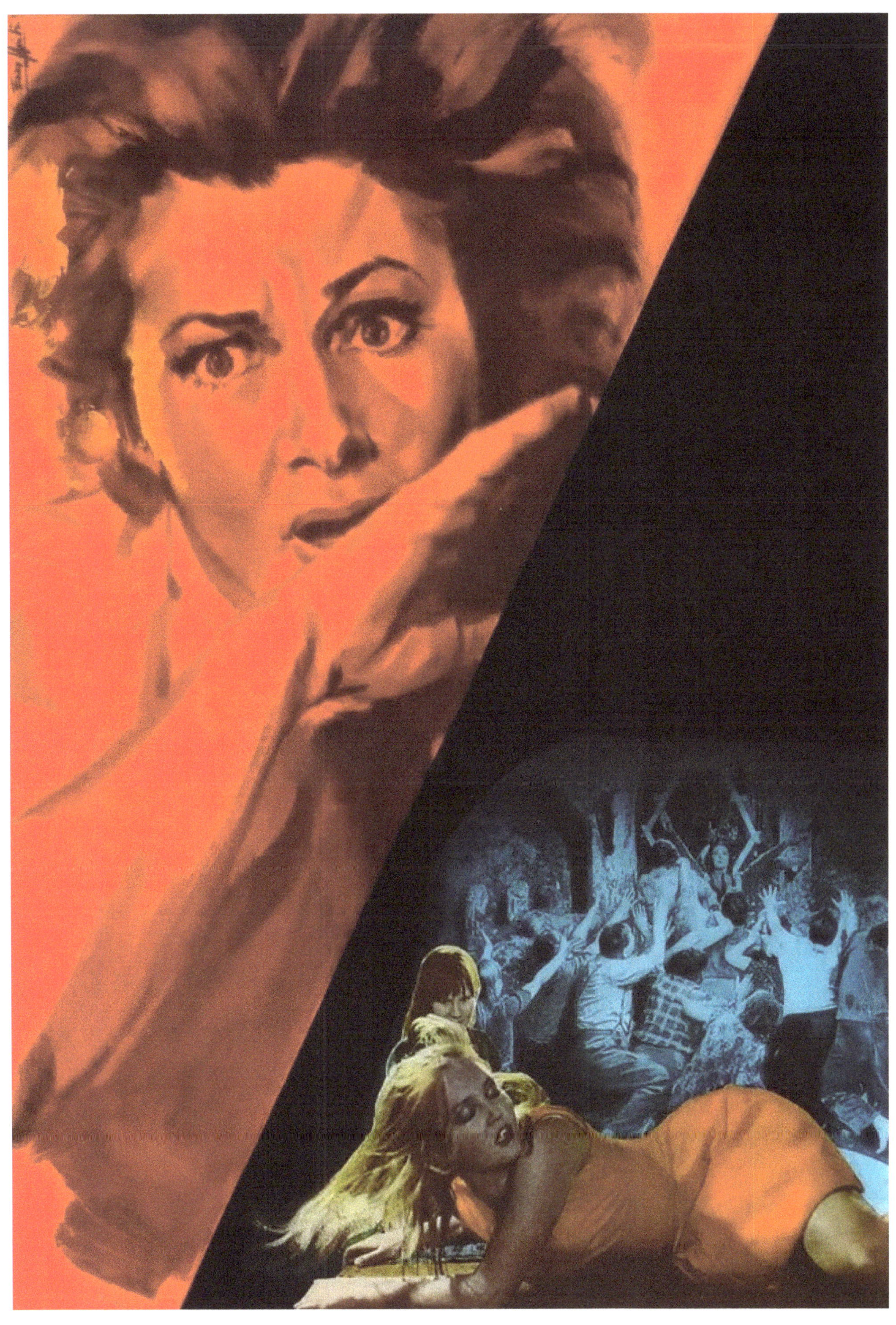

CREATURE DEL DIAVOLO (1966). Artist: Enzo Nistri.

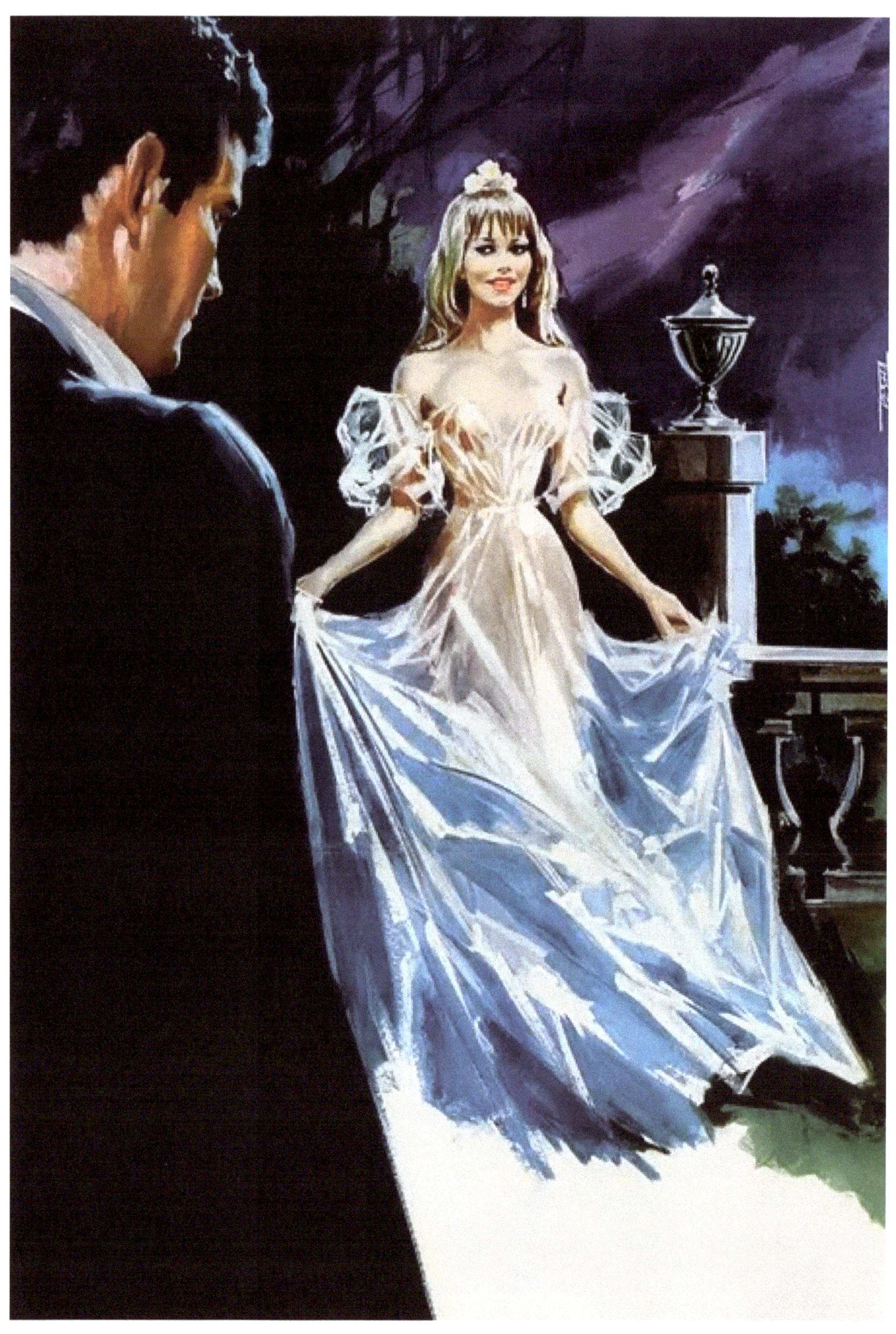

24

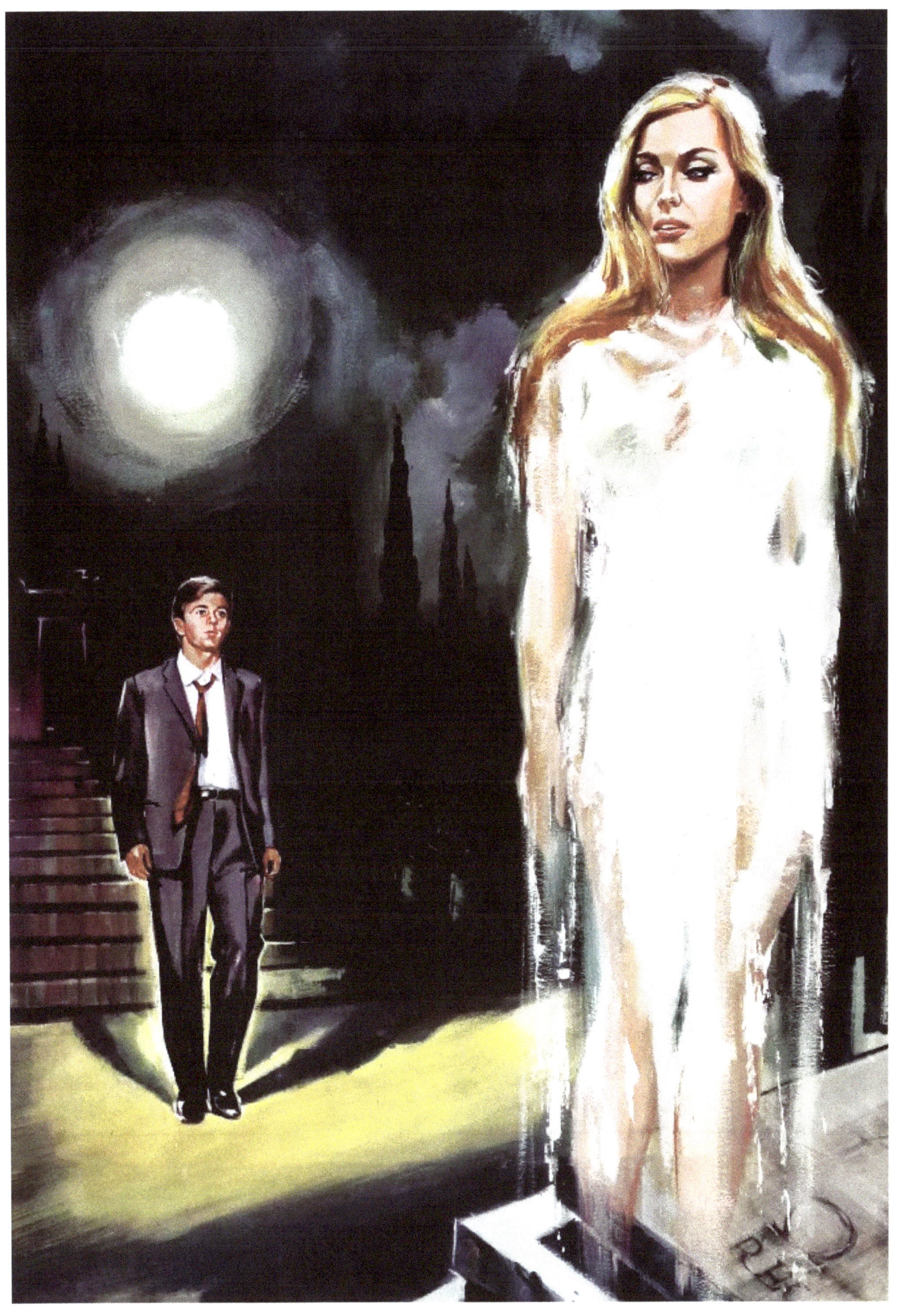

I MORTI VIVONO (1965). Artist: unsigned.

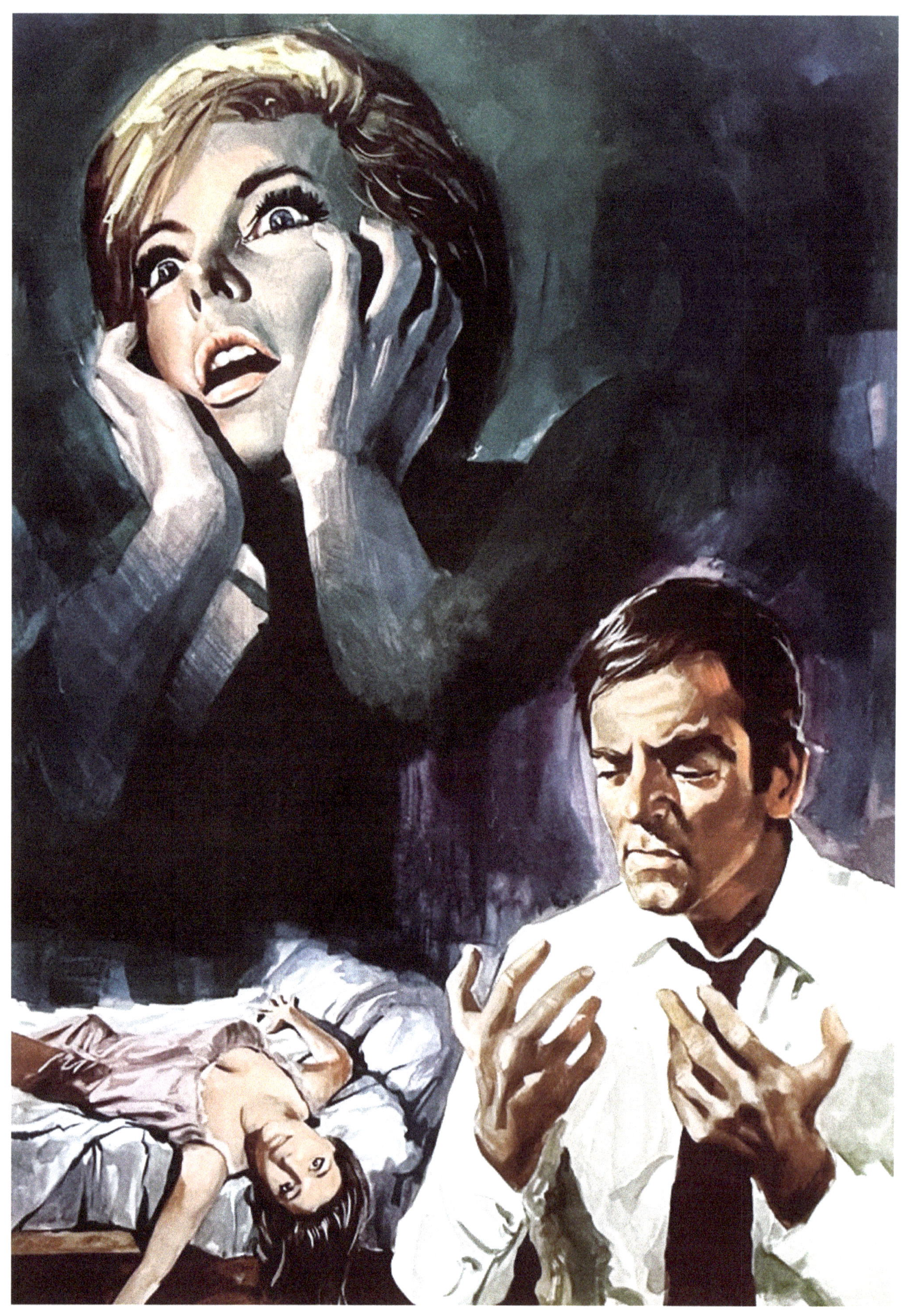

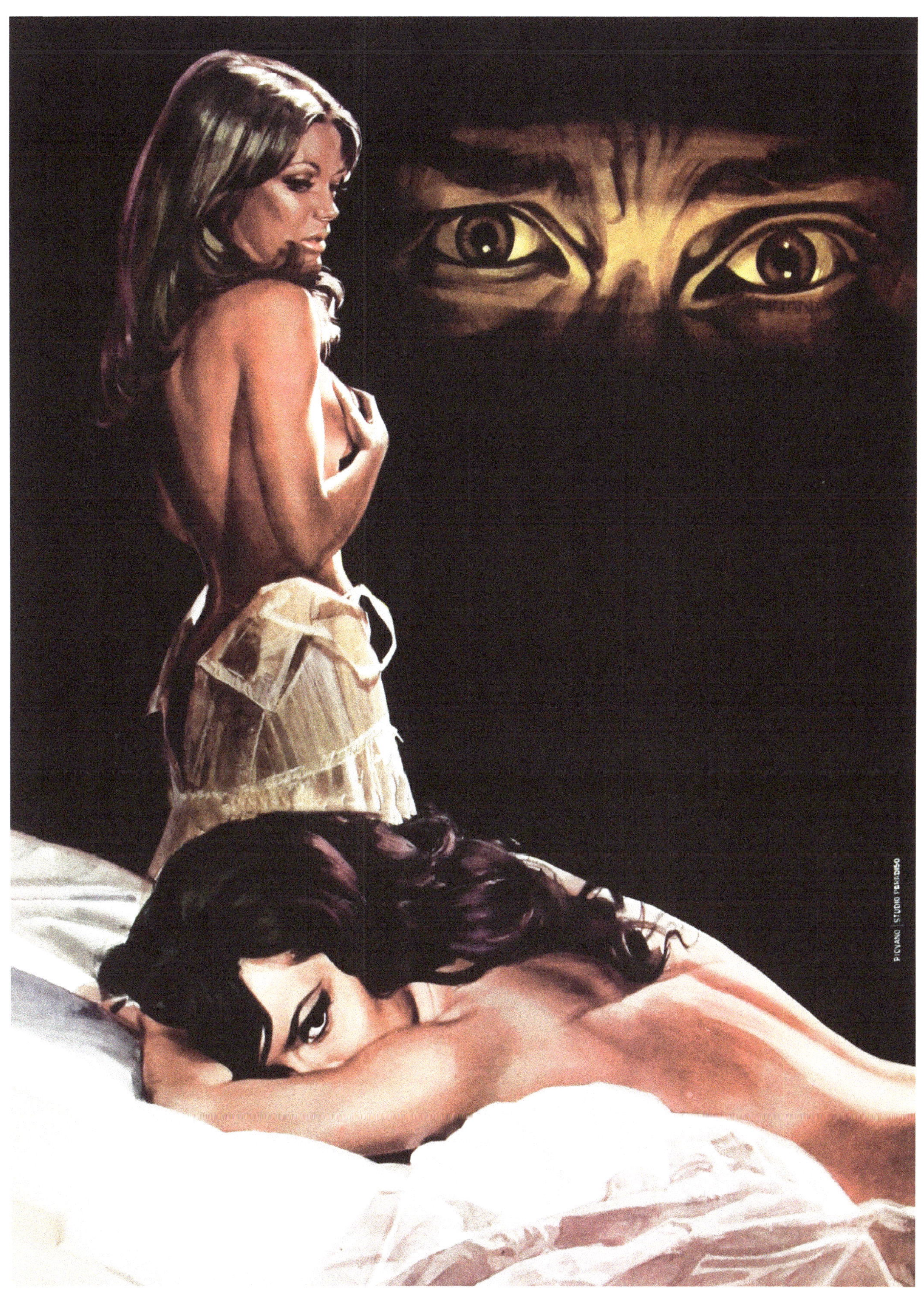

LE AMANTI PROIBITE DEL DR. SEX (1968). Artist: Mario Piovano.

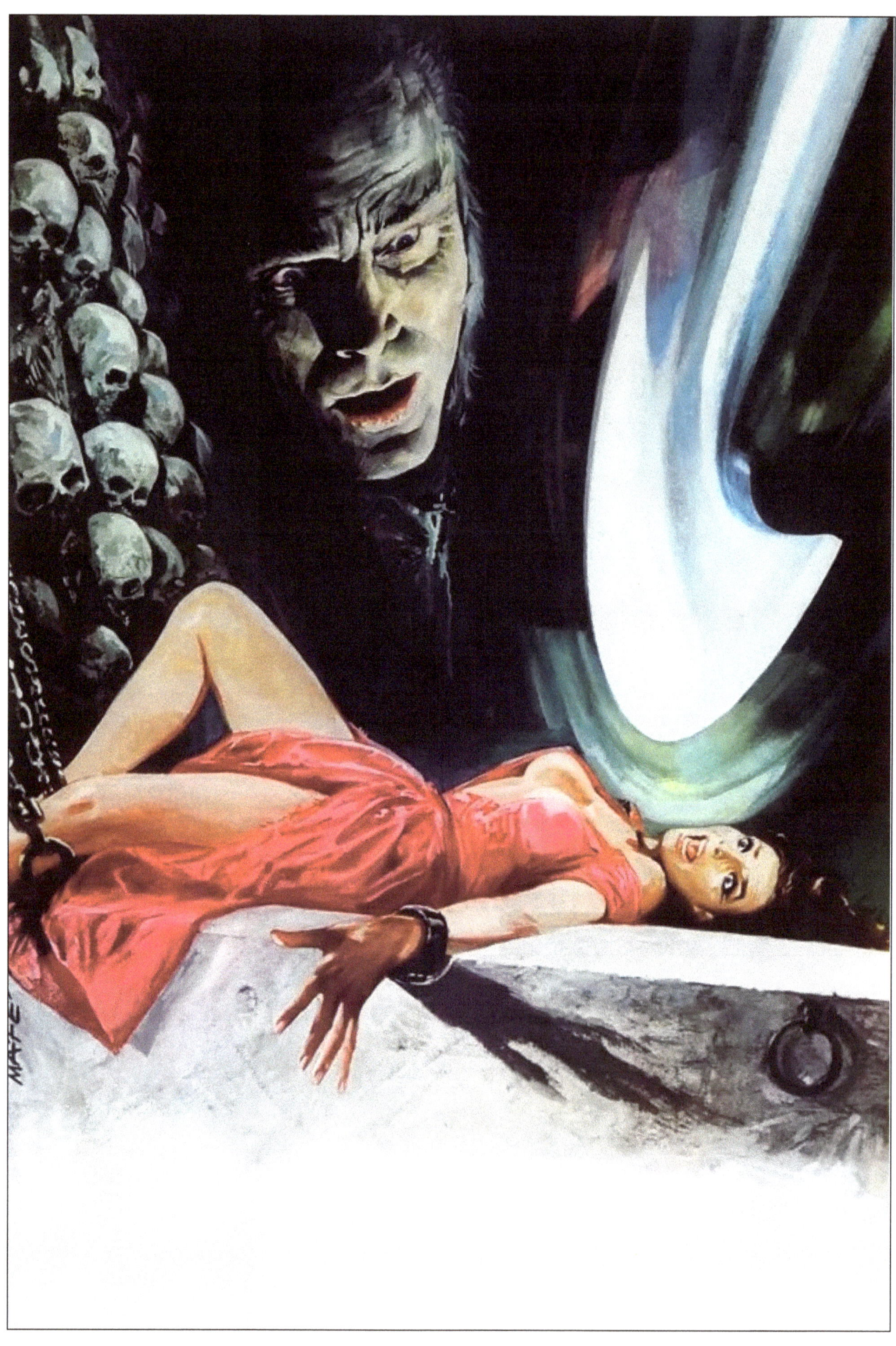

LA TREDICESIMA VERGINE (1967). Artist: Mafé.

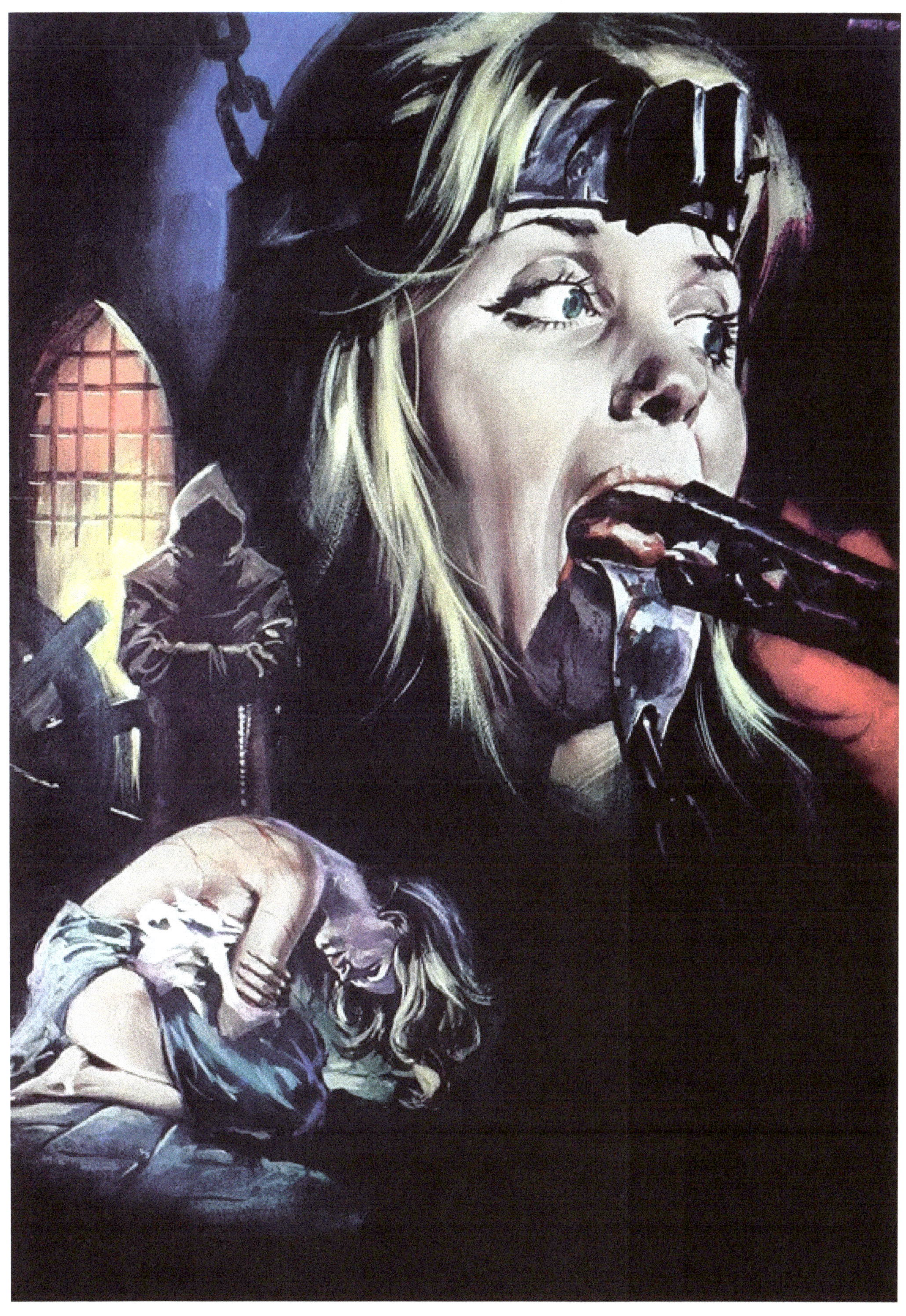

LA TORTURA DELLE VERGINI (1970). Artist: Renato Casaro.

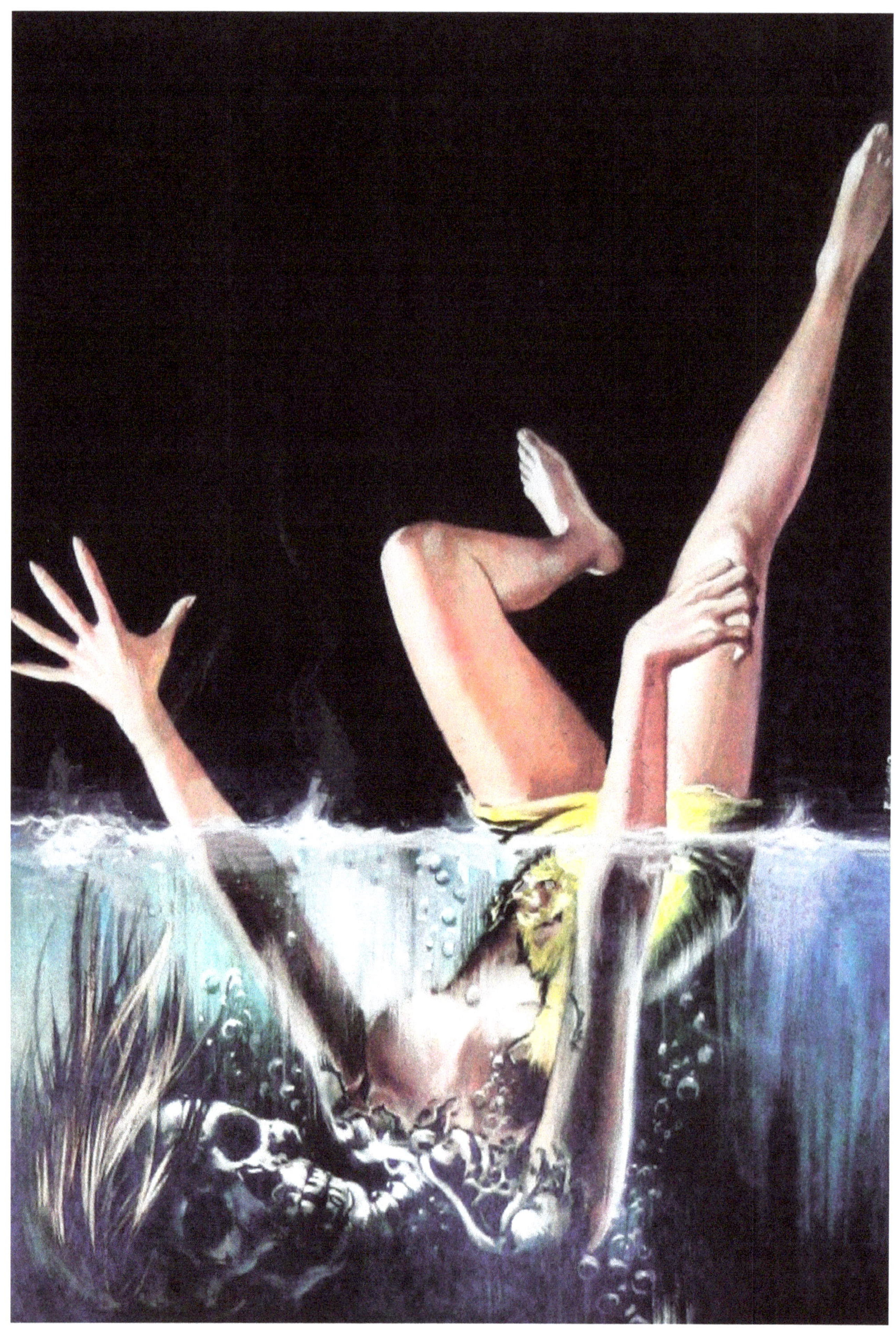

TERRORE E TERRORE (1969). Artist: Renato Casaro.

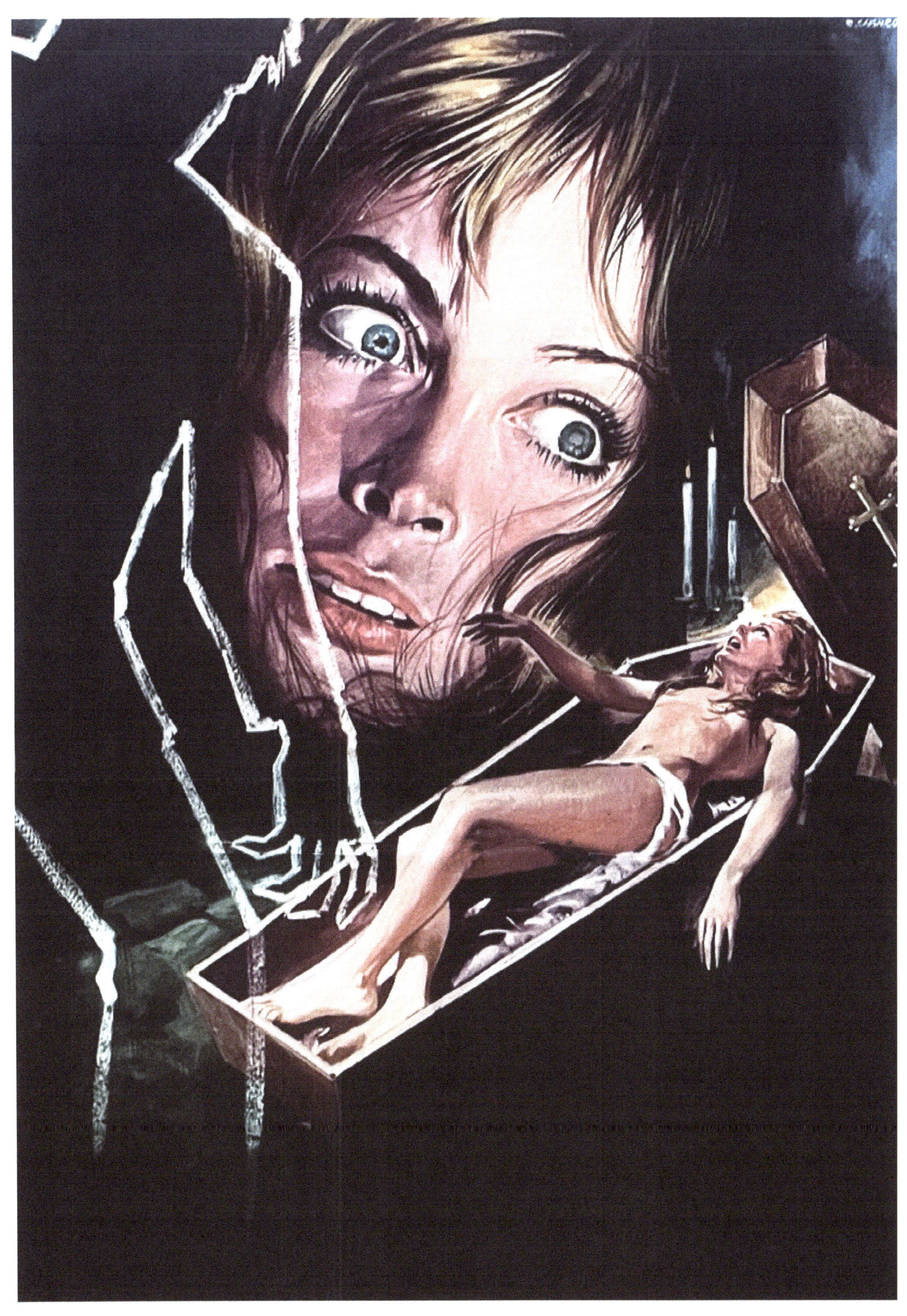

LE NOTTE EROTICHE DELL'UOMO INVISIBILE (1970). Artist: Renato Casaro.

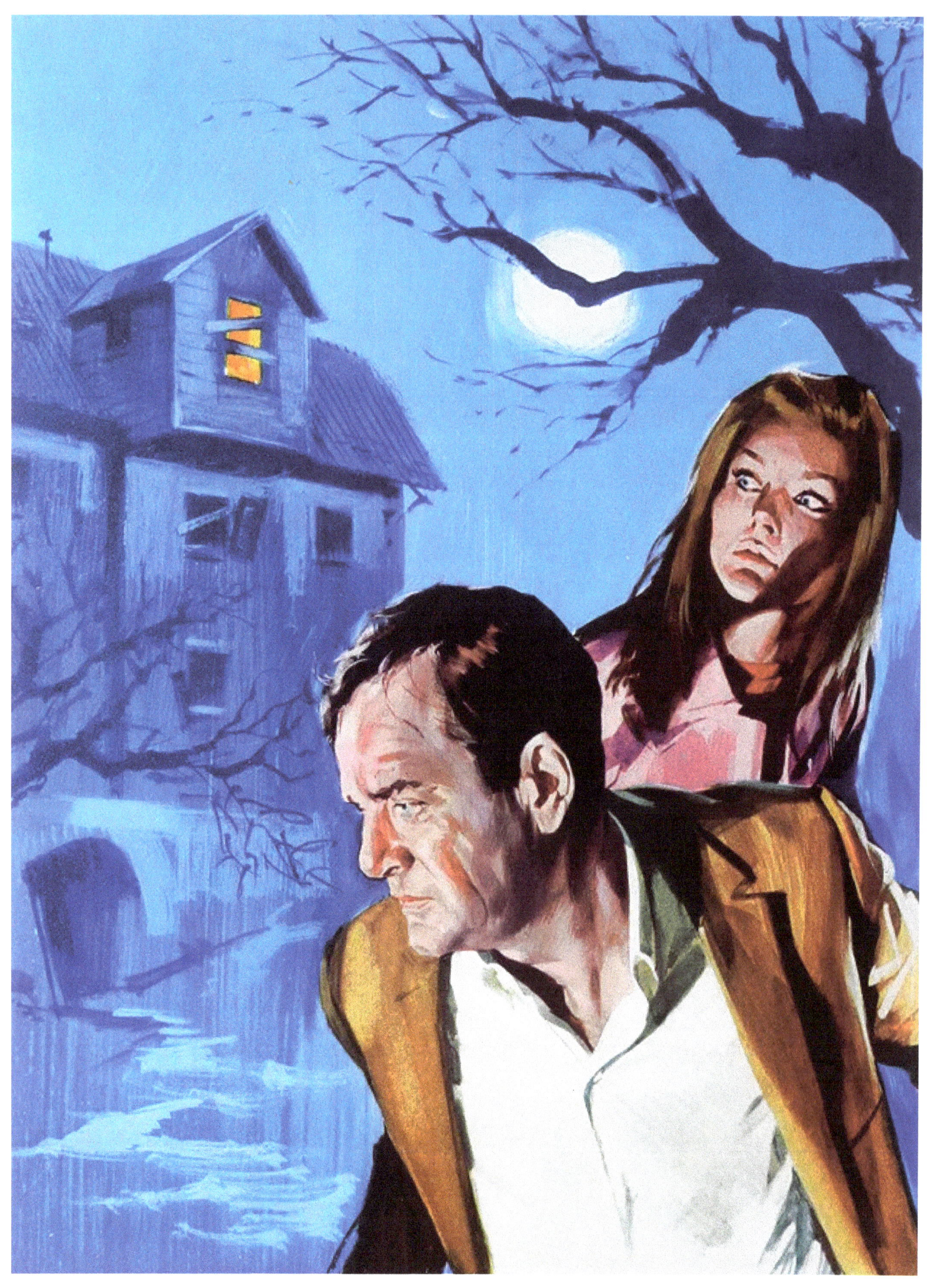

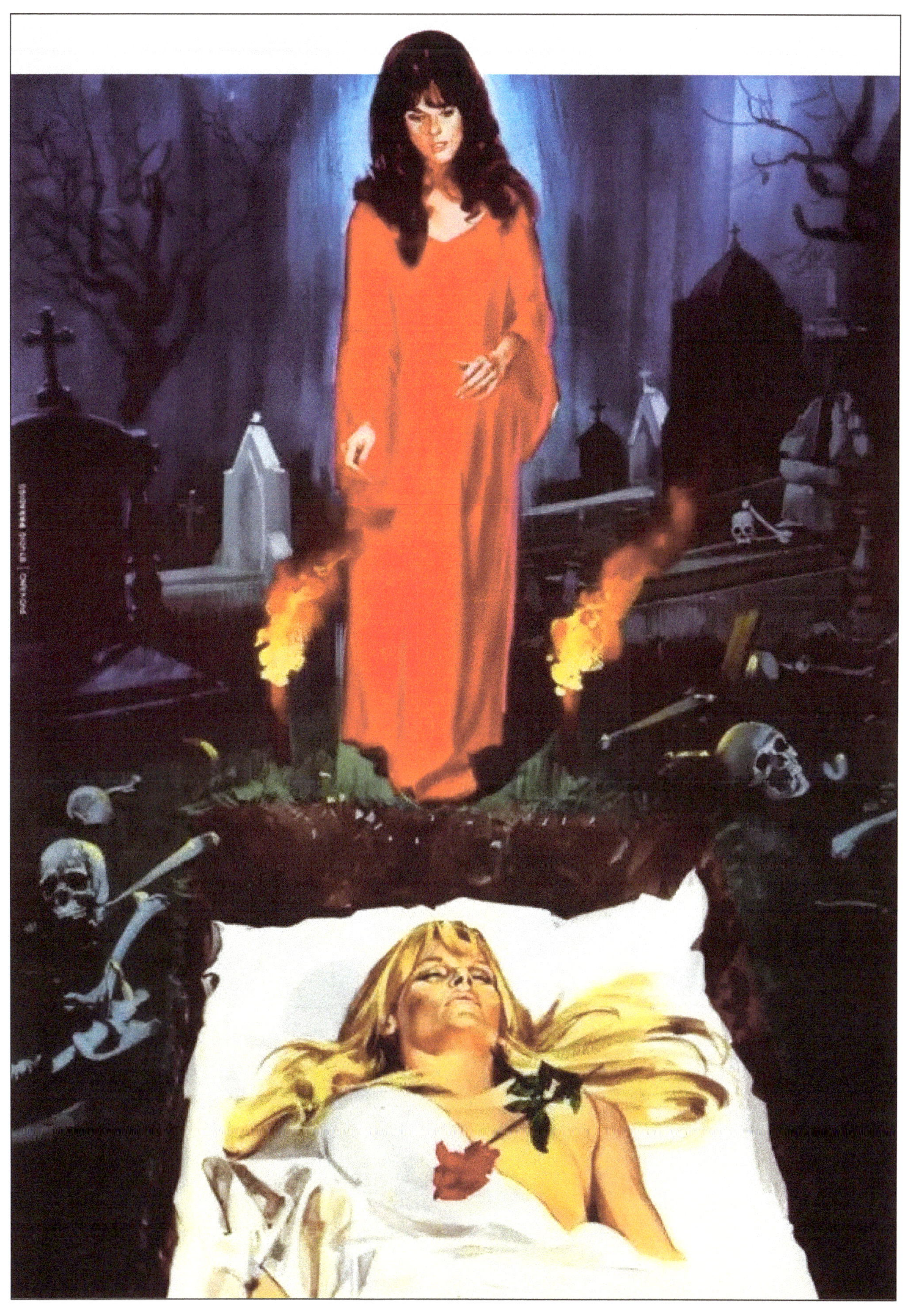

TRE GOCCE DI SANGUE PER UNA ROSA **(1969)**. Artist: Mario Piovano.

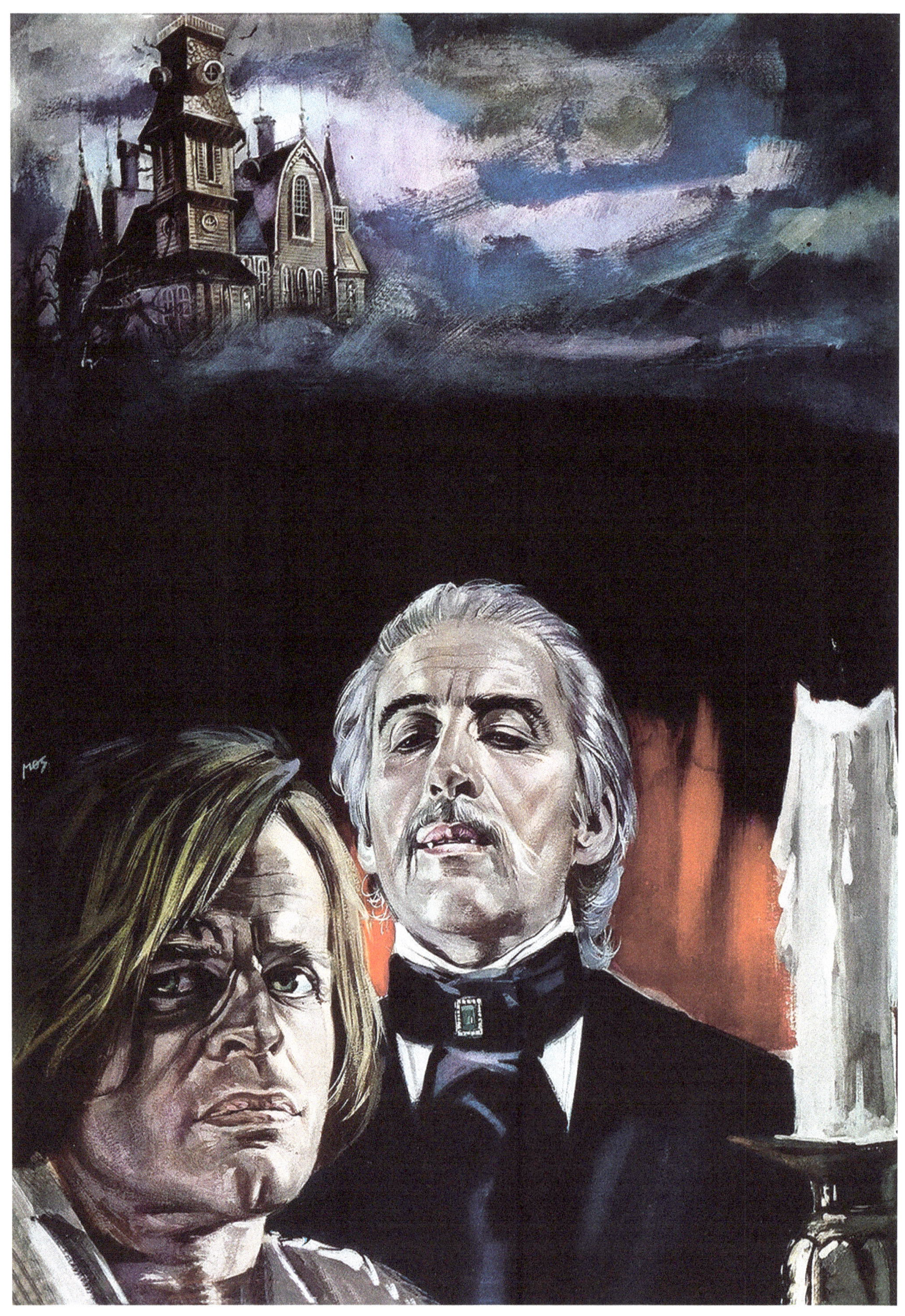

IL CONTE DRACULA (1970). Artist: Mario De Berardinis.

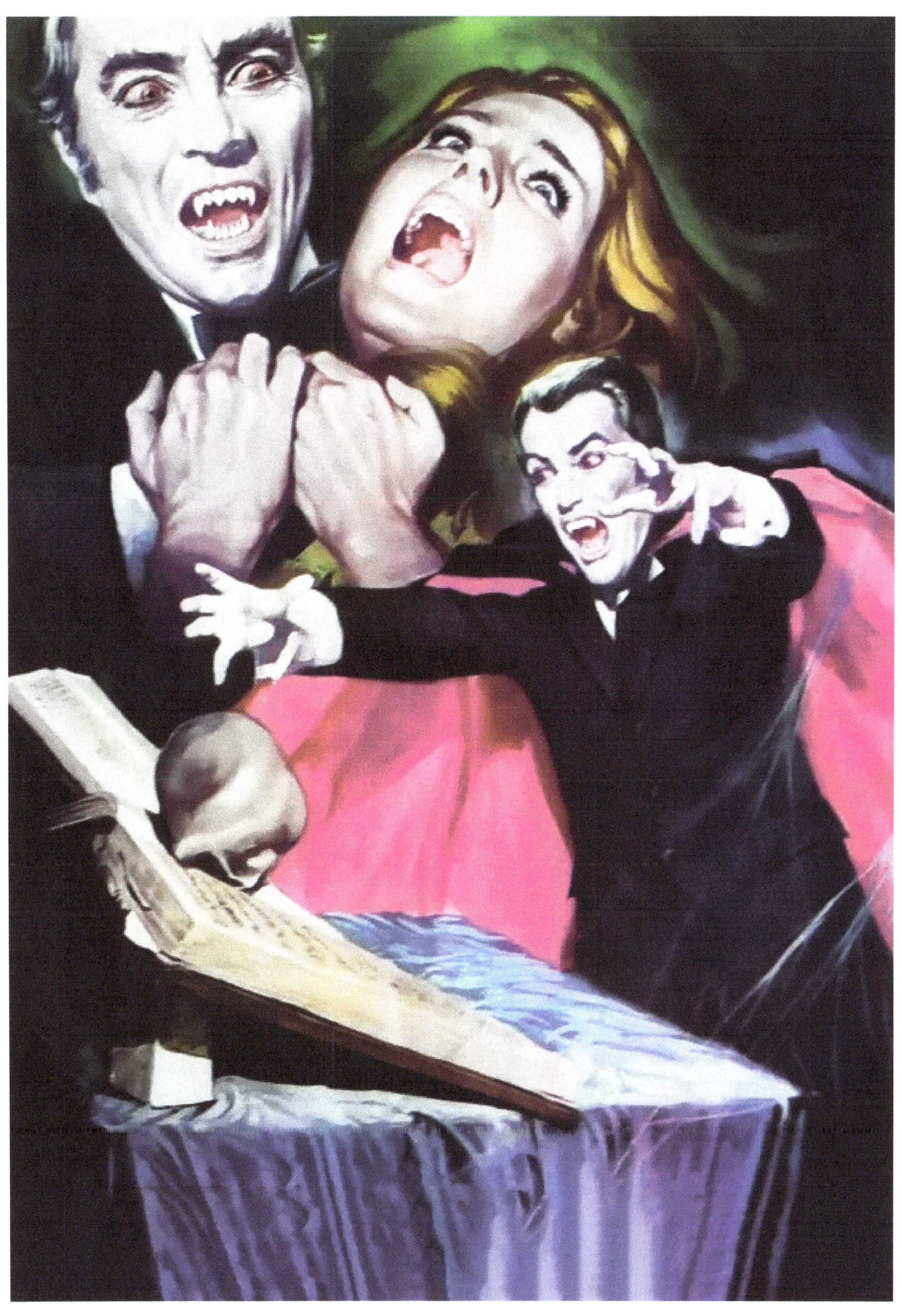

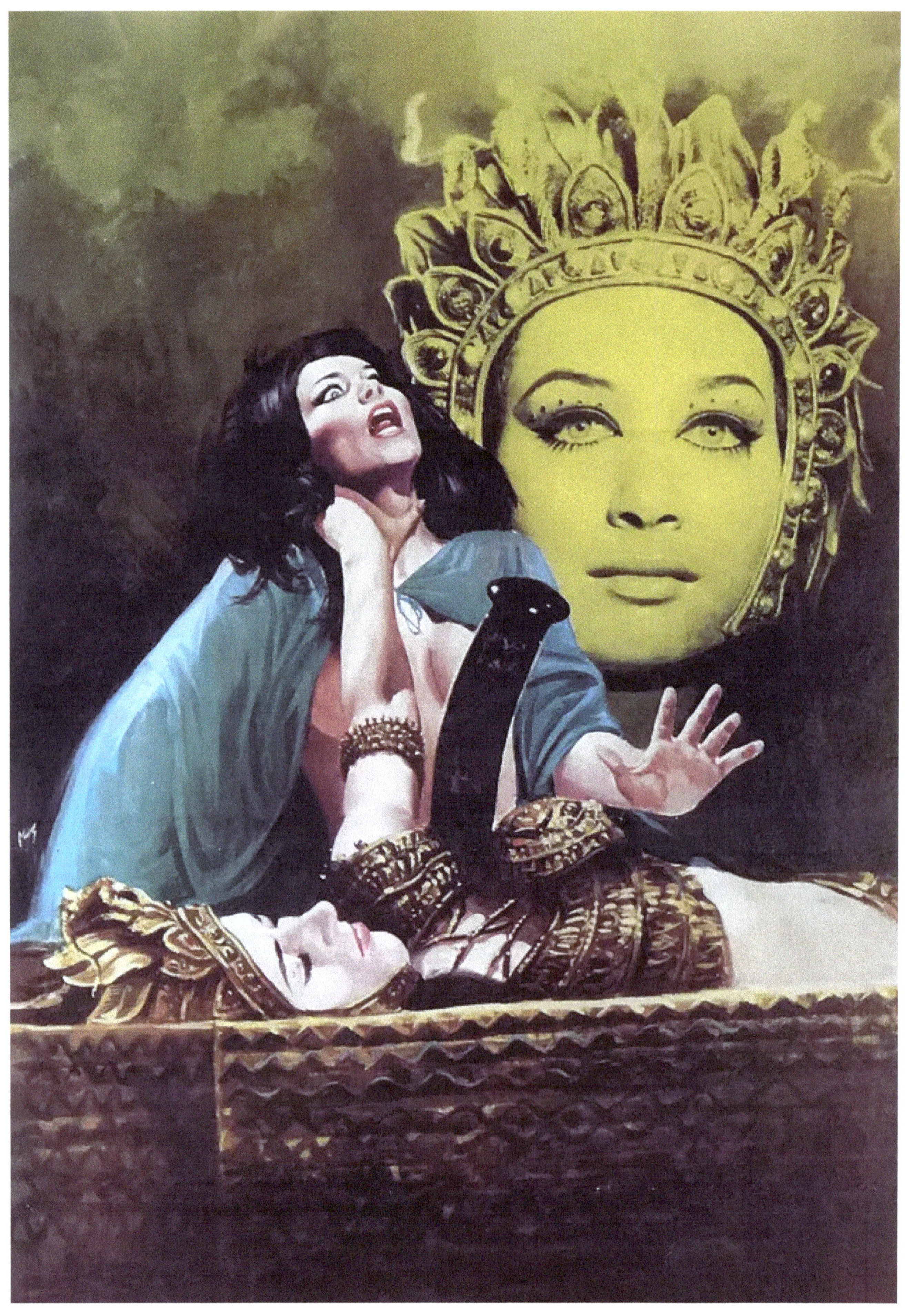

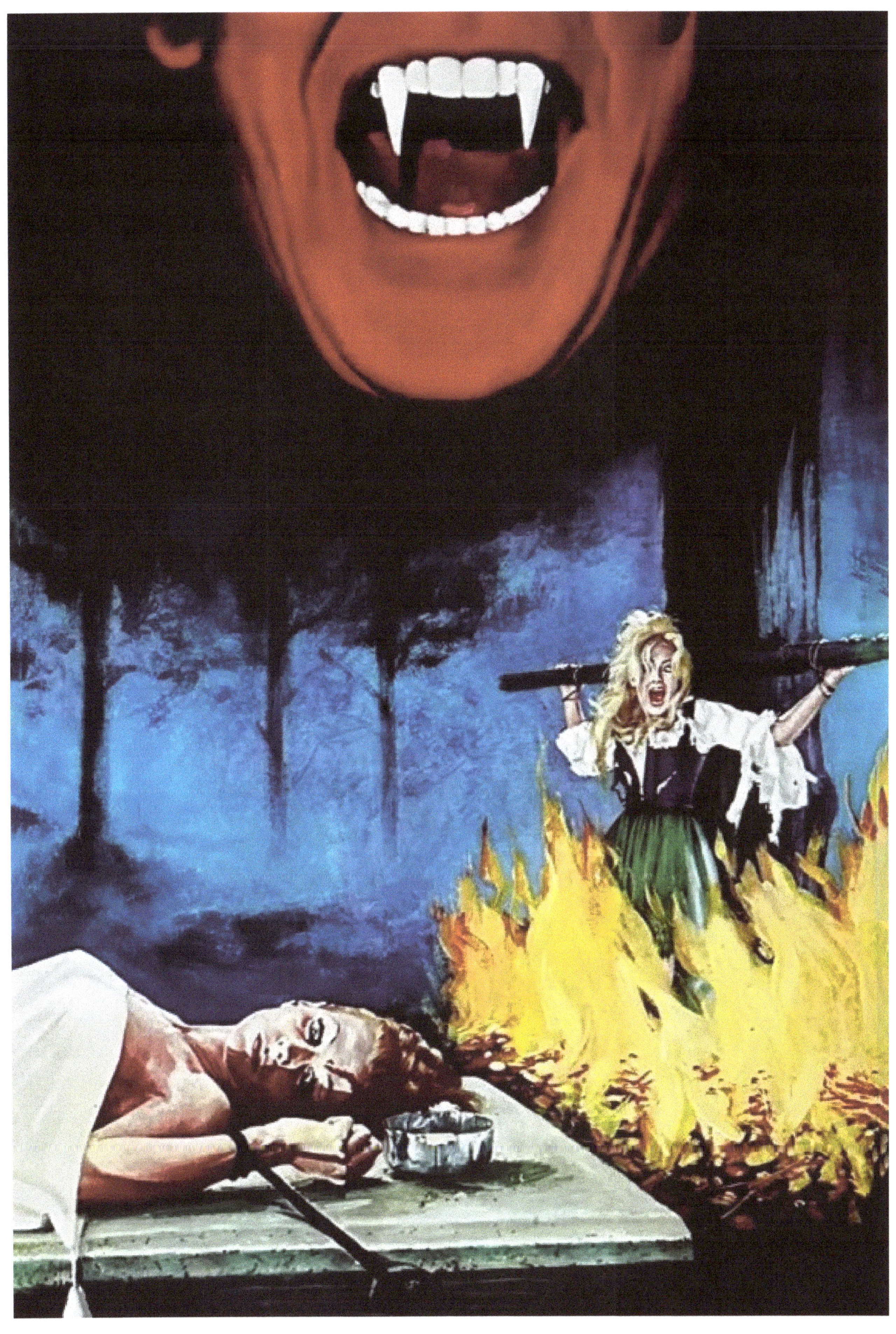

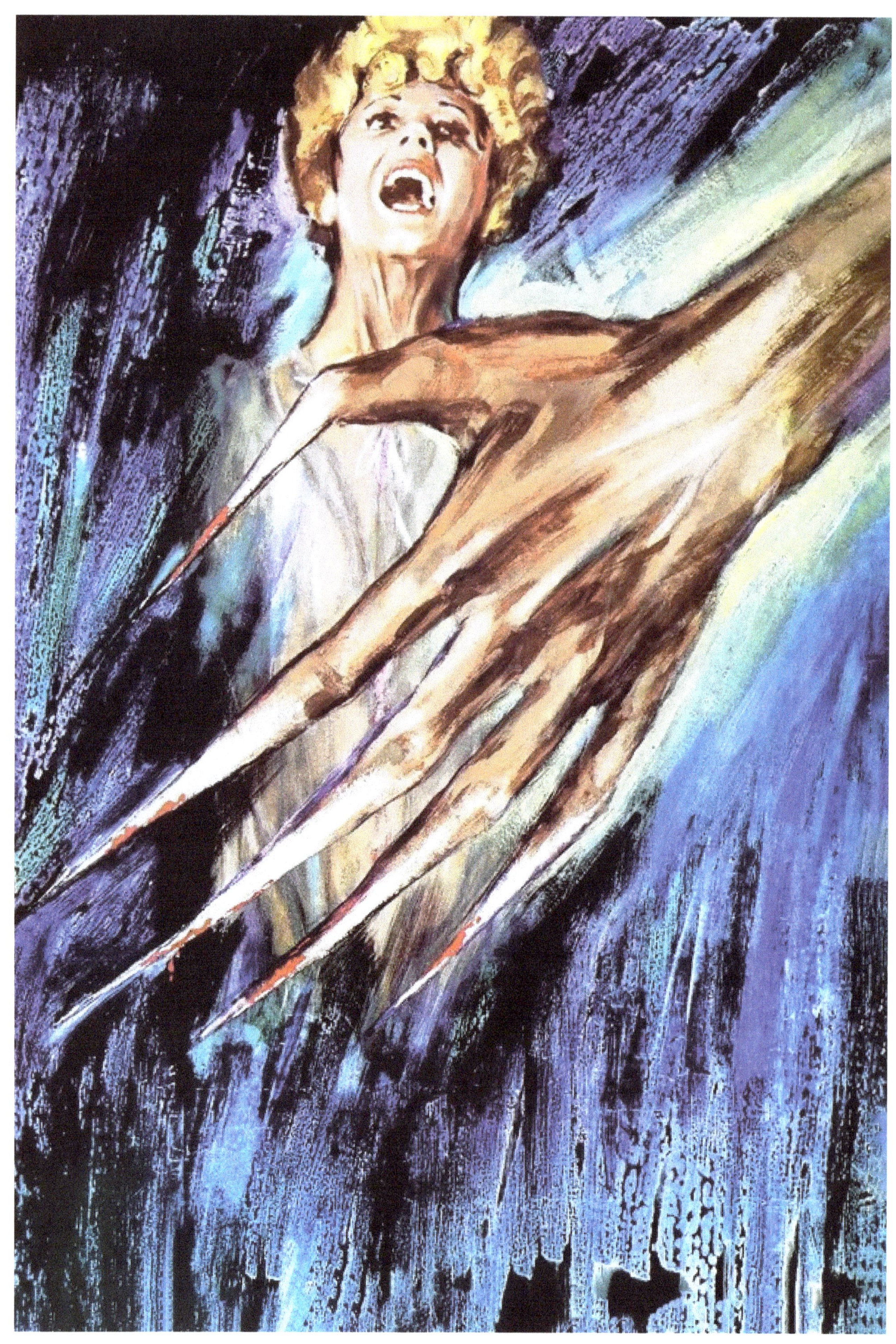

GLI ARTIGLI DELL SQUARTATORE (1971). Artist: unsigned.

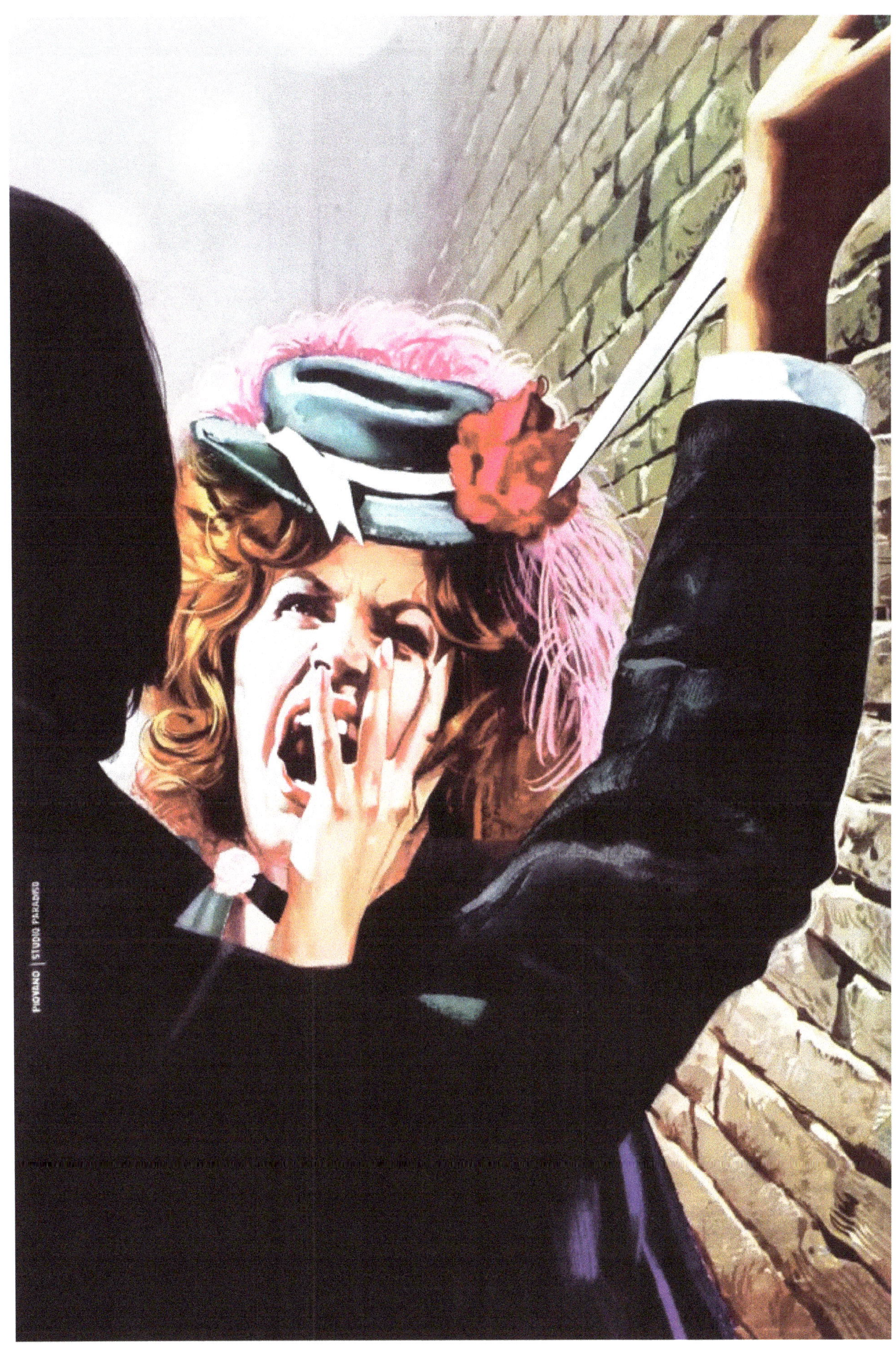

BARBARA IL MOSTRO DI LONDRA (1971). Artist: Mario Piovano.

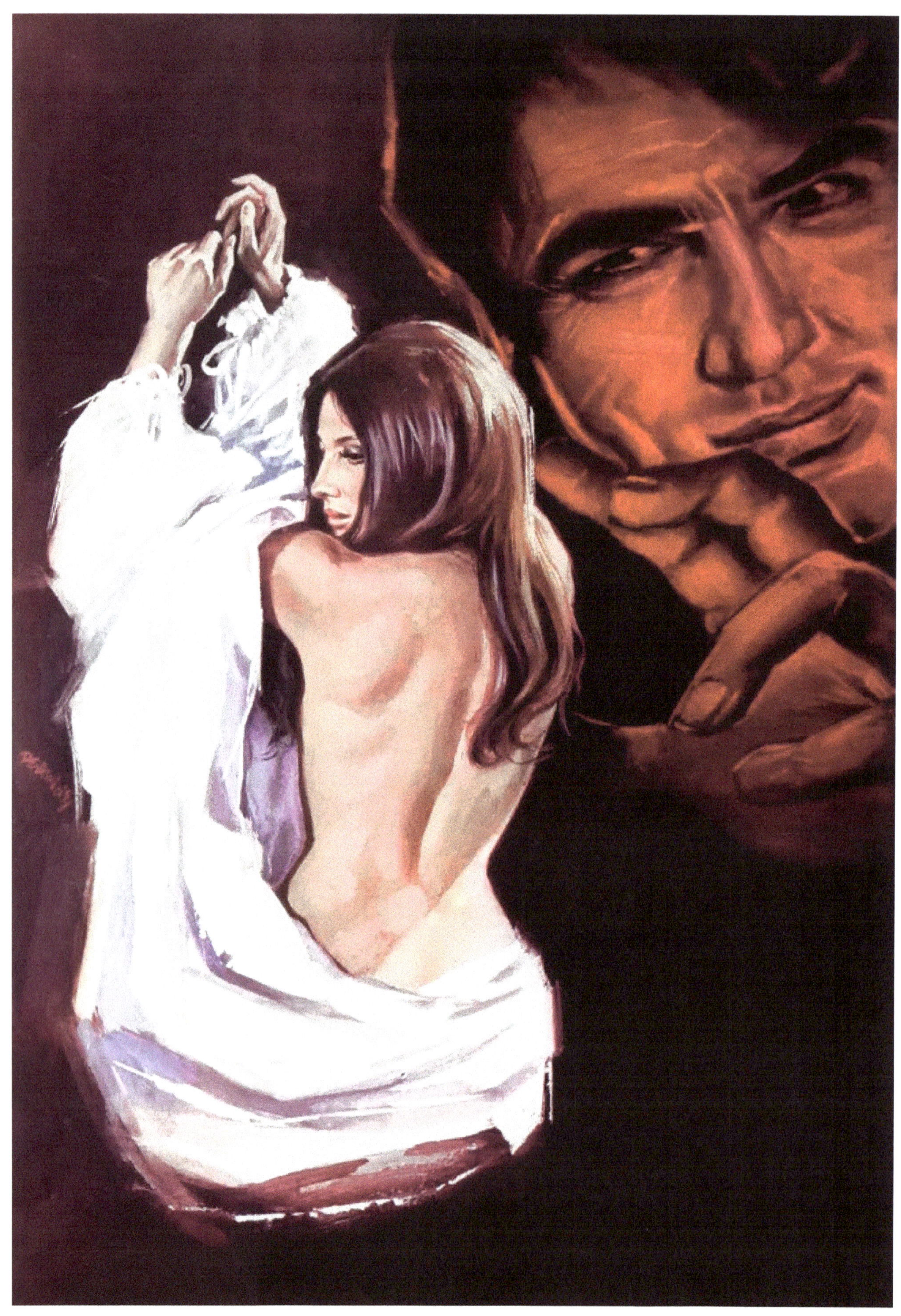

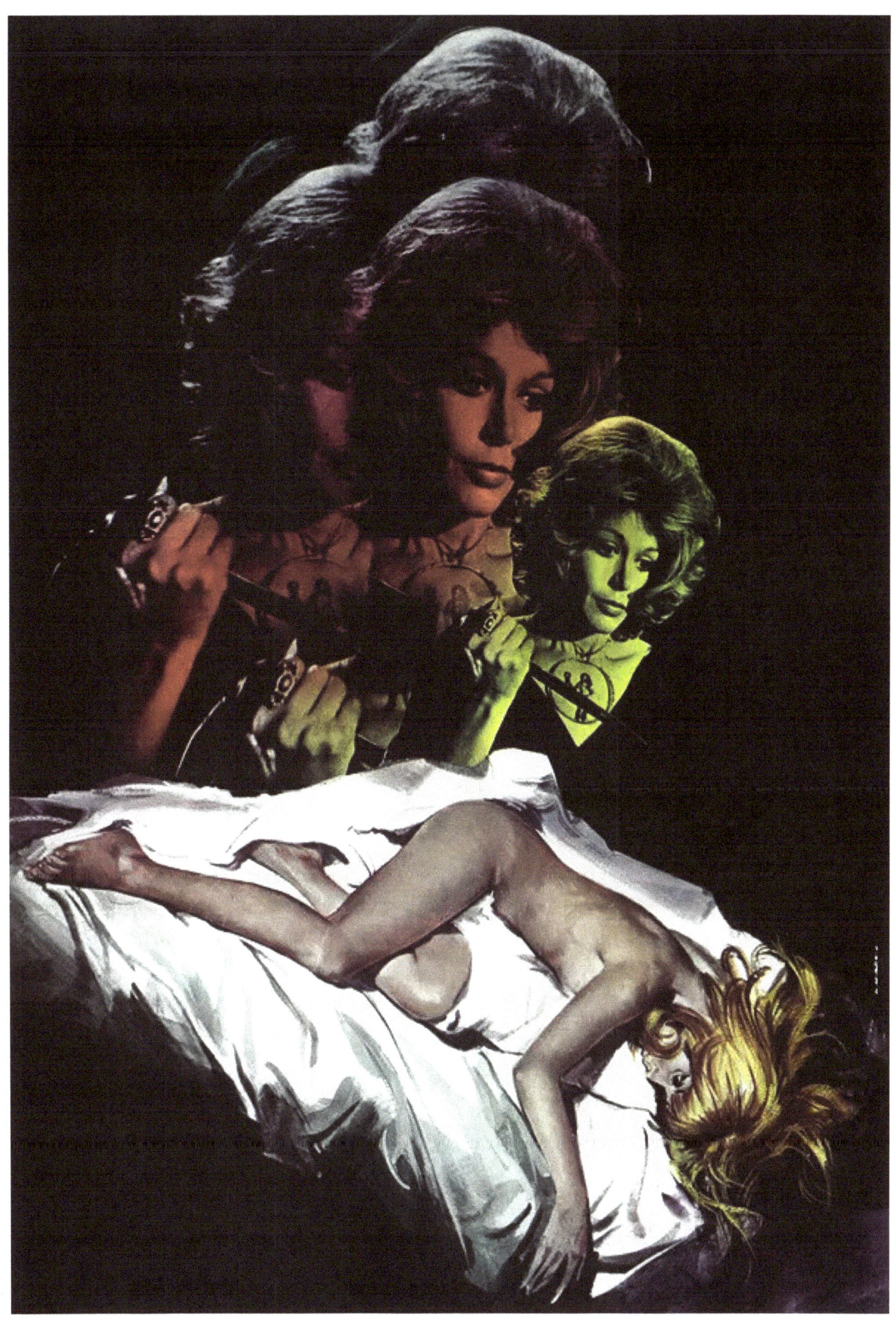

I DIABOLICI CONVEGNI (1971). Artist: Renato Casaro.

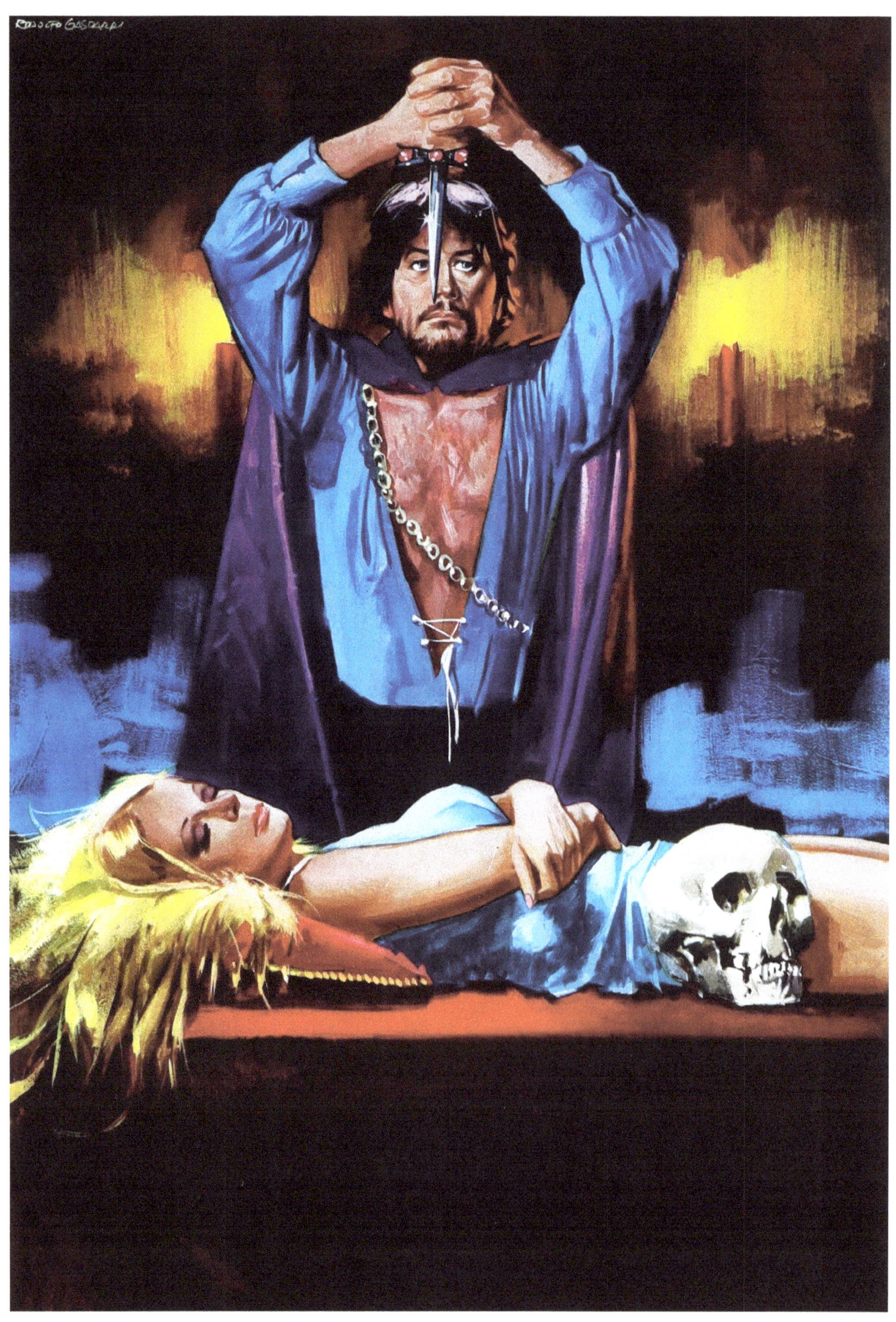

42

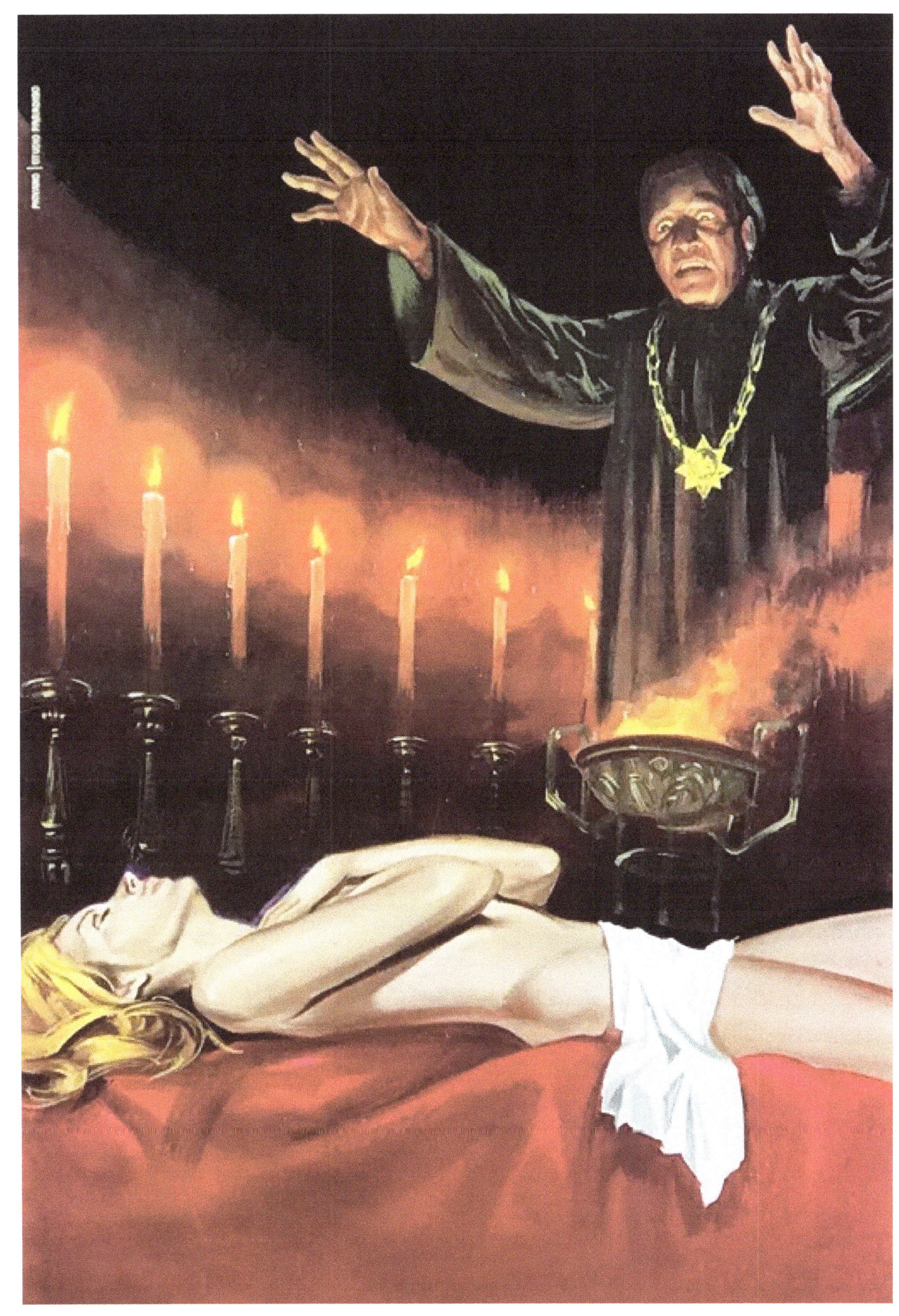

LA VERGINE E L'ESORCISTA (1972). Artist: Mario Piovano.

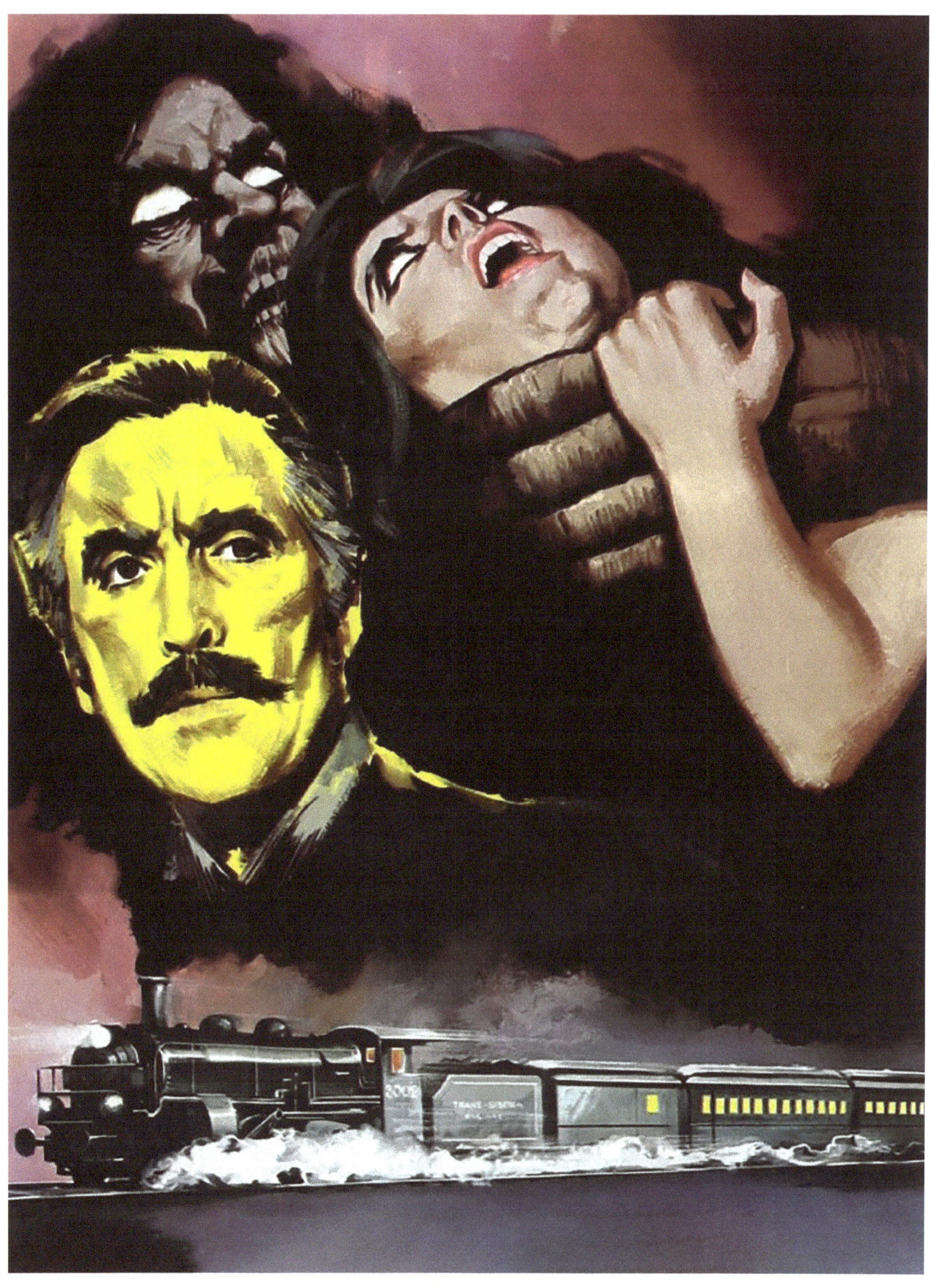

HORROR EXPRESS (1972). Artist: unsigned.

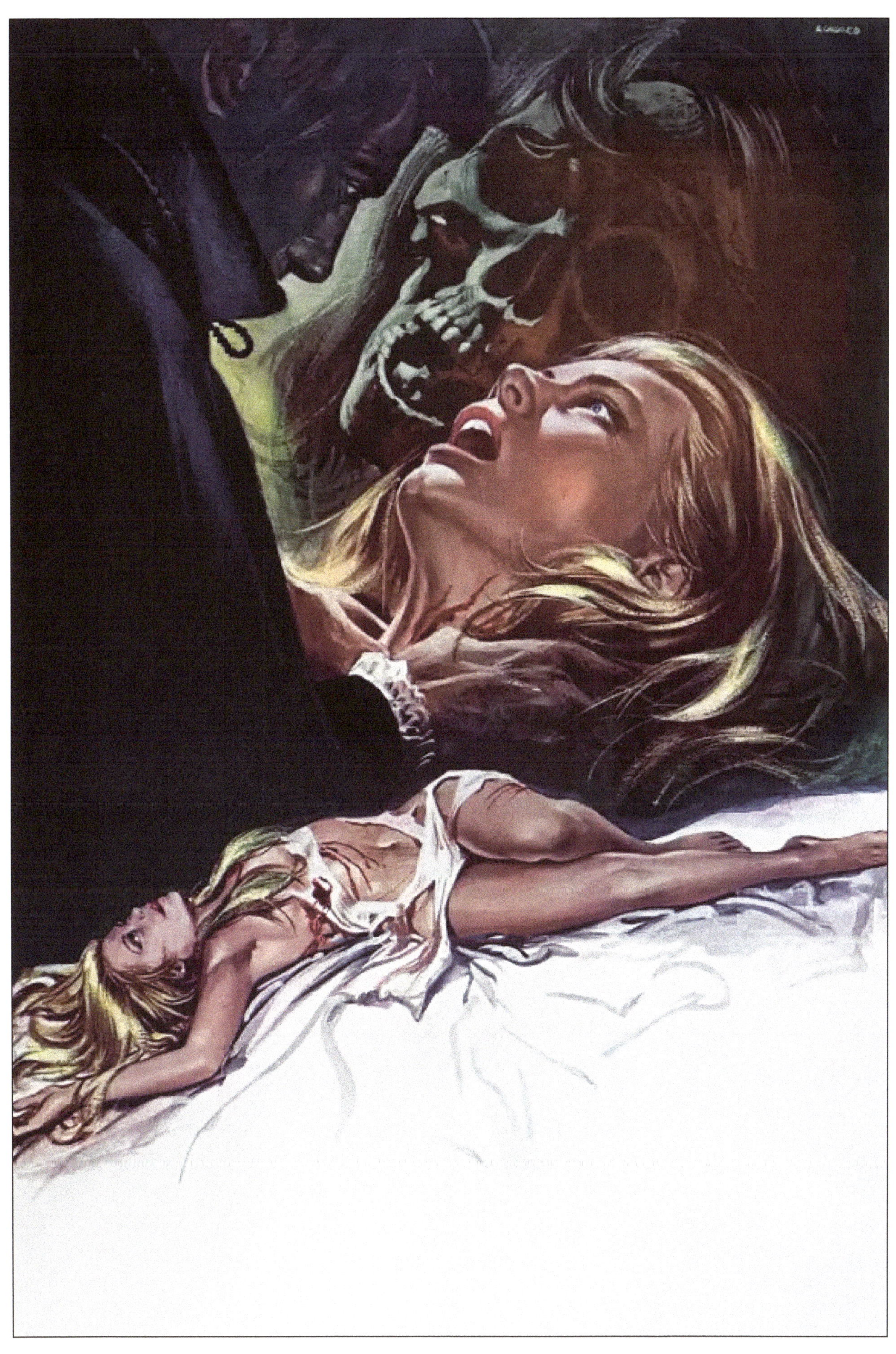

LE MANIE DI MR. WINNINGER OMICIDA SESSUALE (1970). Artist: Renato Casaro.

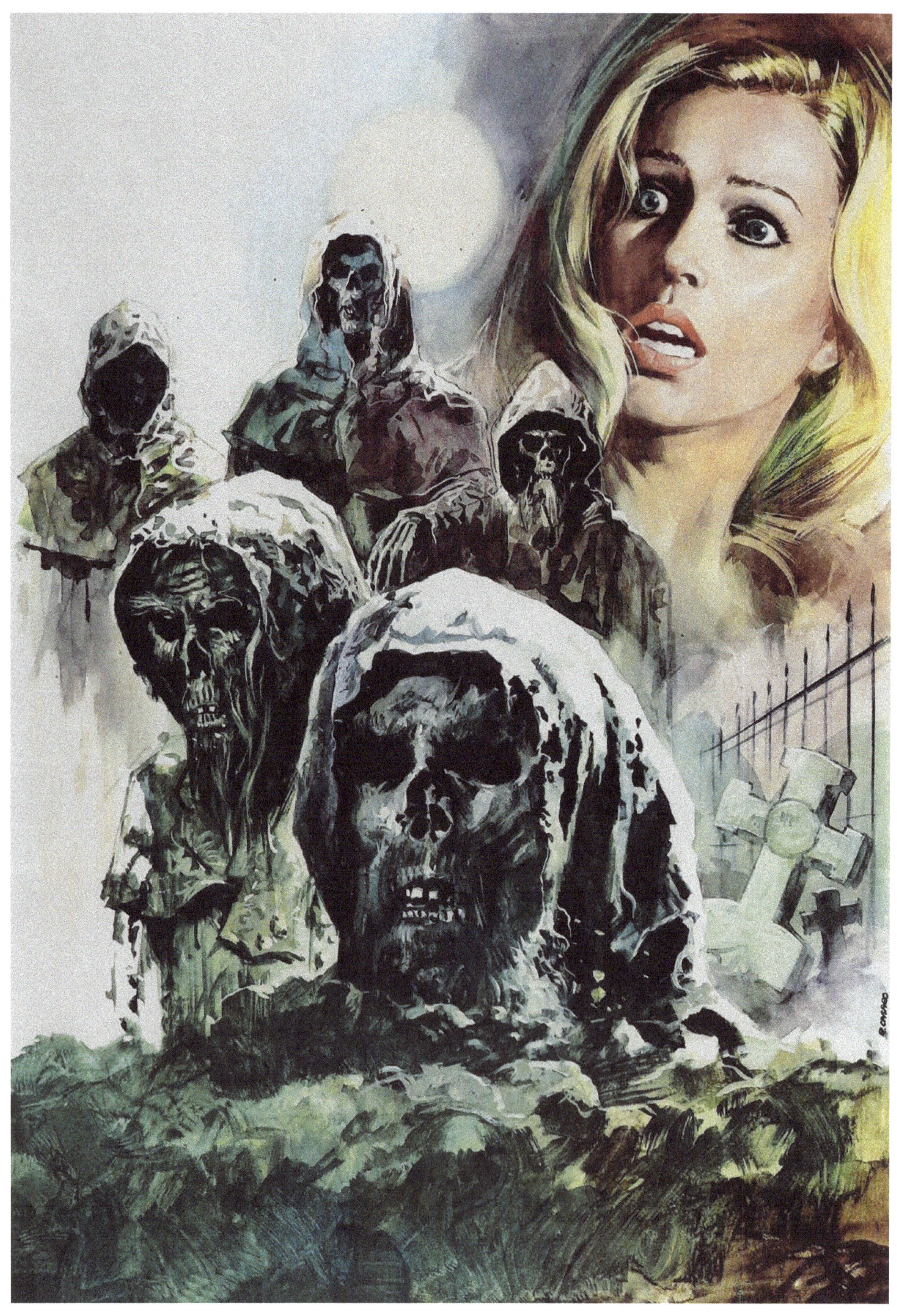

LE TOMBE DEI RESUSCITATI CIECHI (1972). Artist: Renato Casaro.

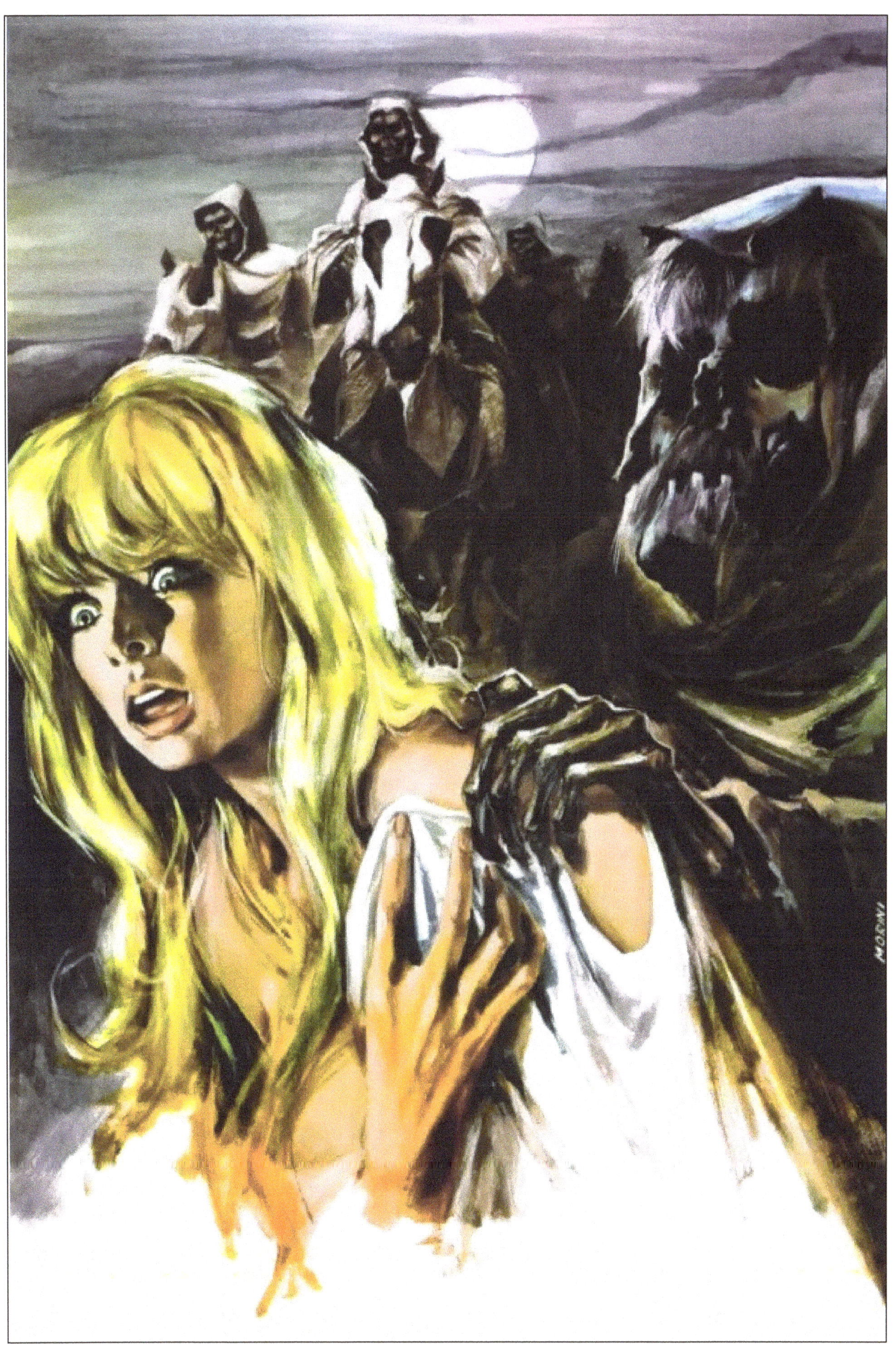

LA CAVALCATA DEI RESUSCITATI CIECHI (1973). Artist: Morini.

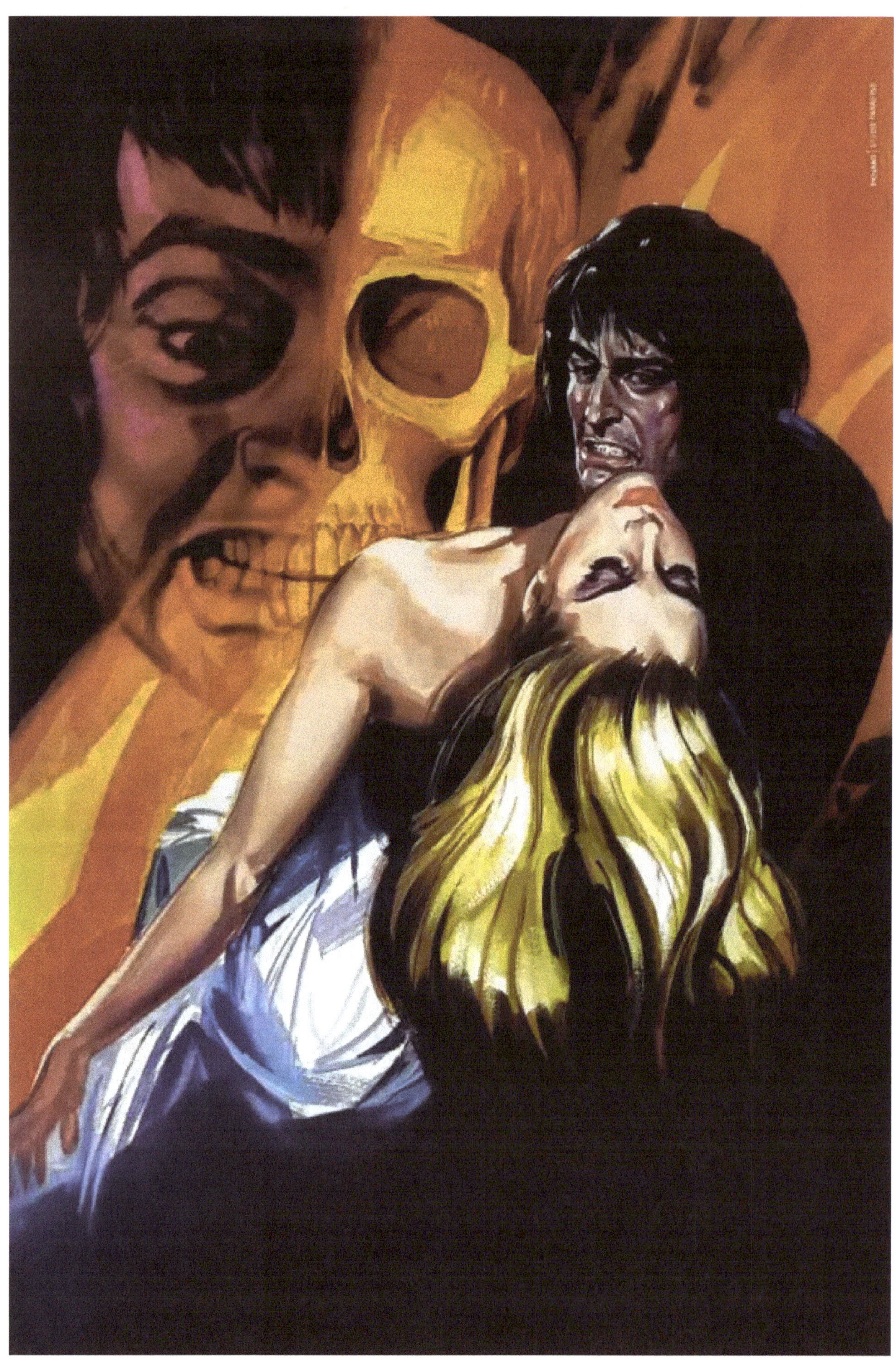

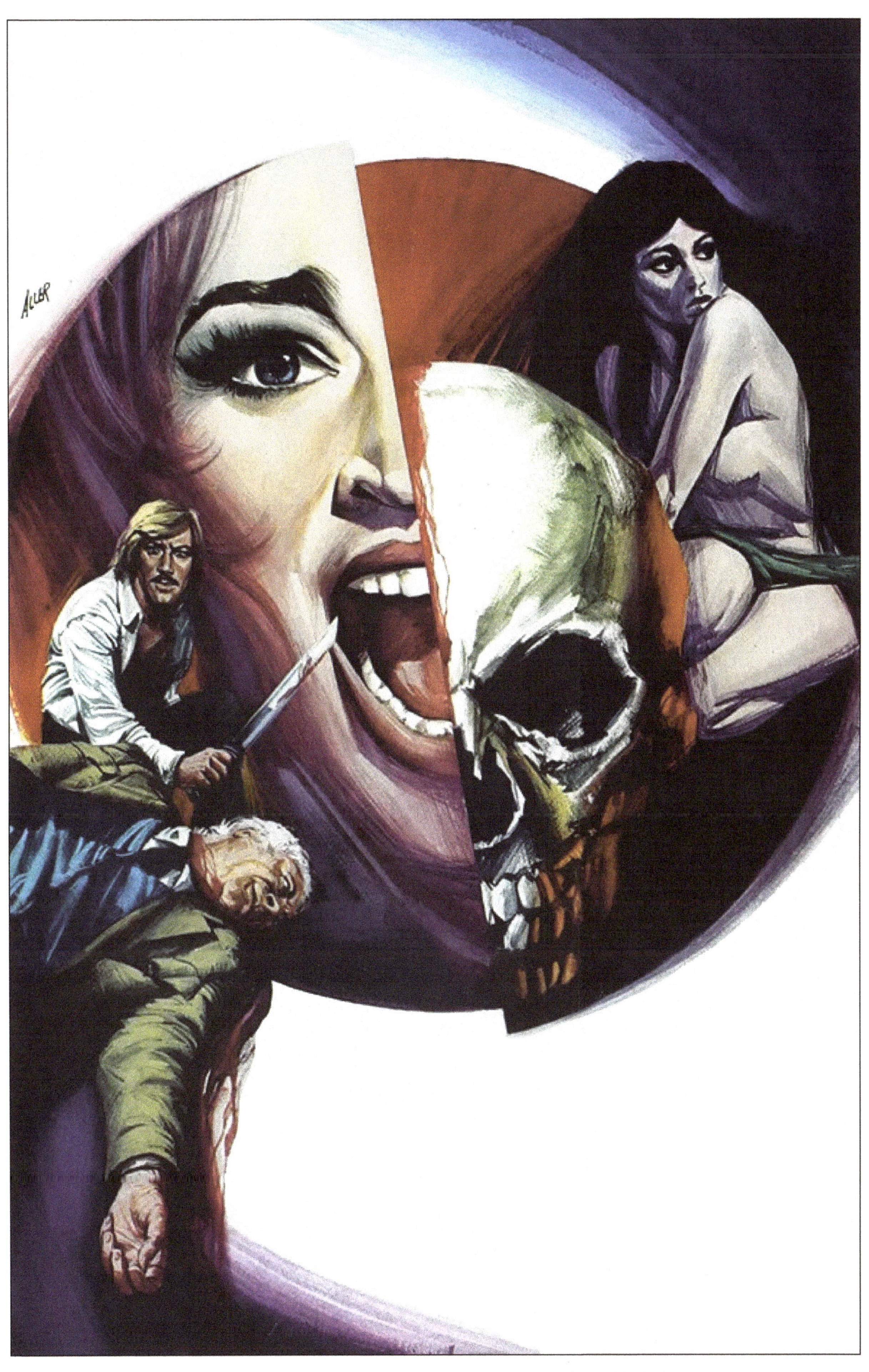

L'ORGIA DEI MORTI (1973). Artist: Carlo Alessandrini.

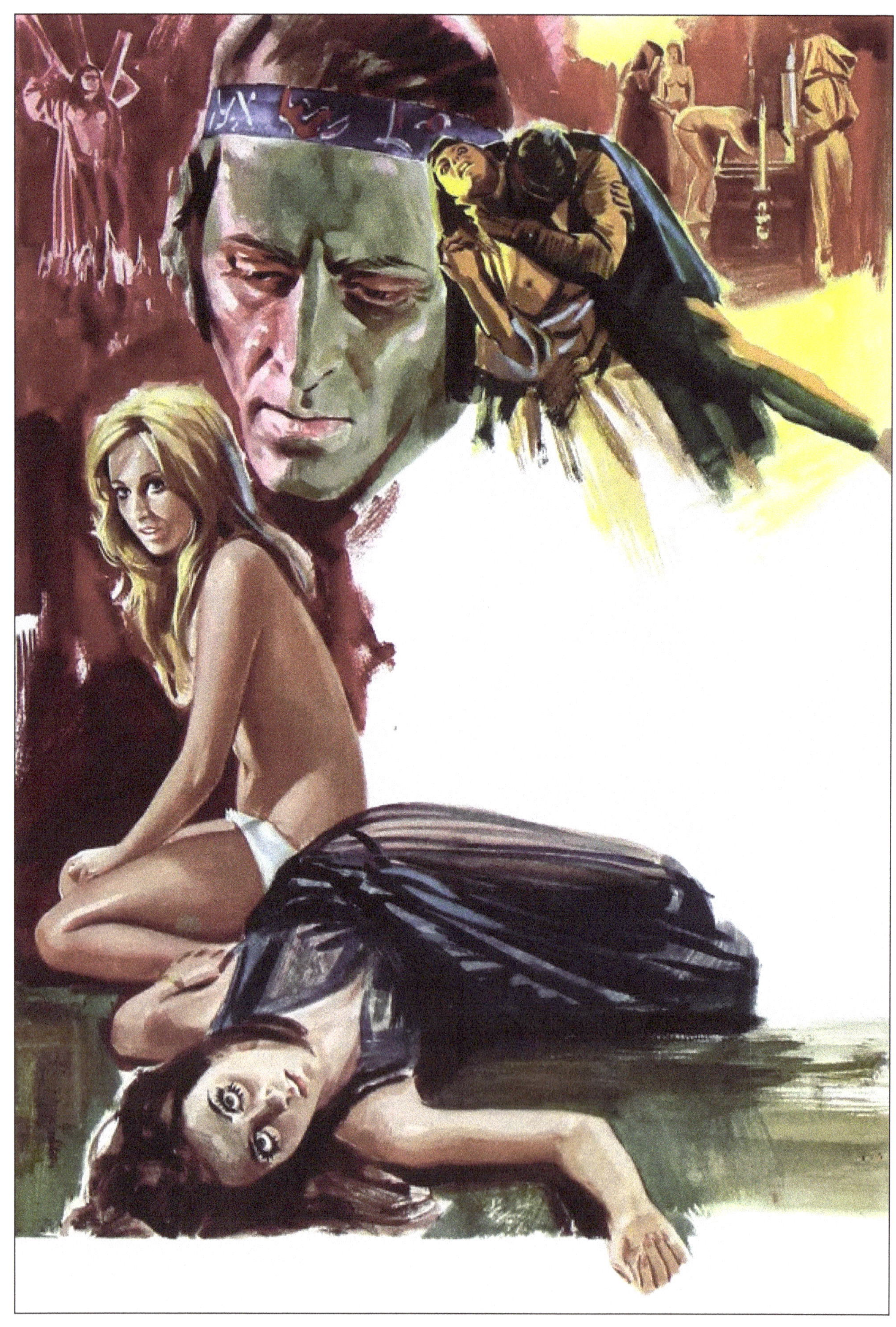

RITI, MAGIE NERE E SEGRETE ORGE NEL TRECENTO (1973). Artist: unsigned.

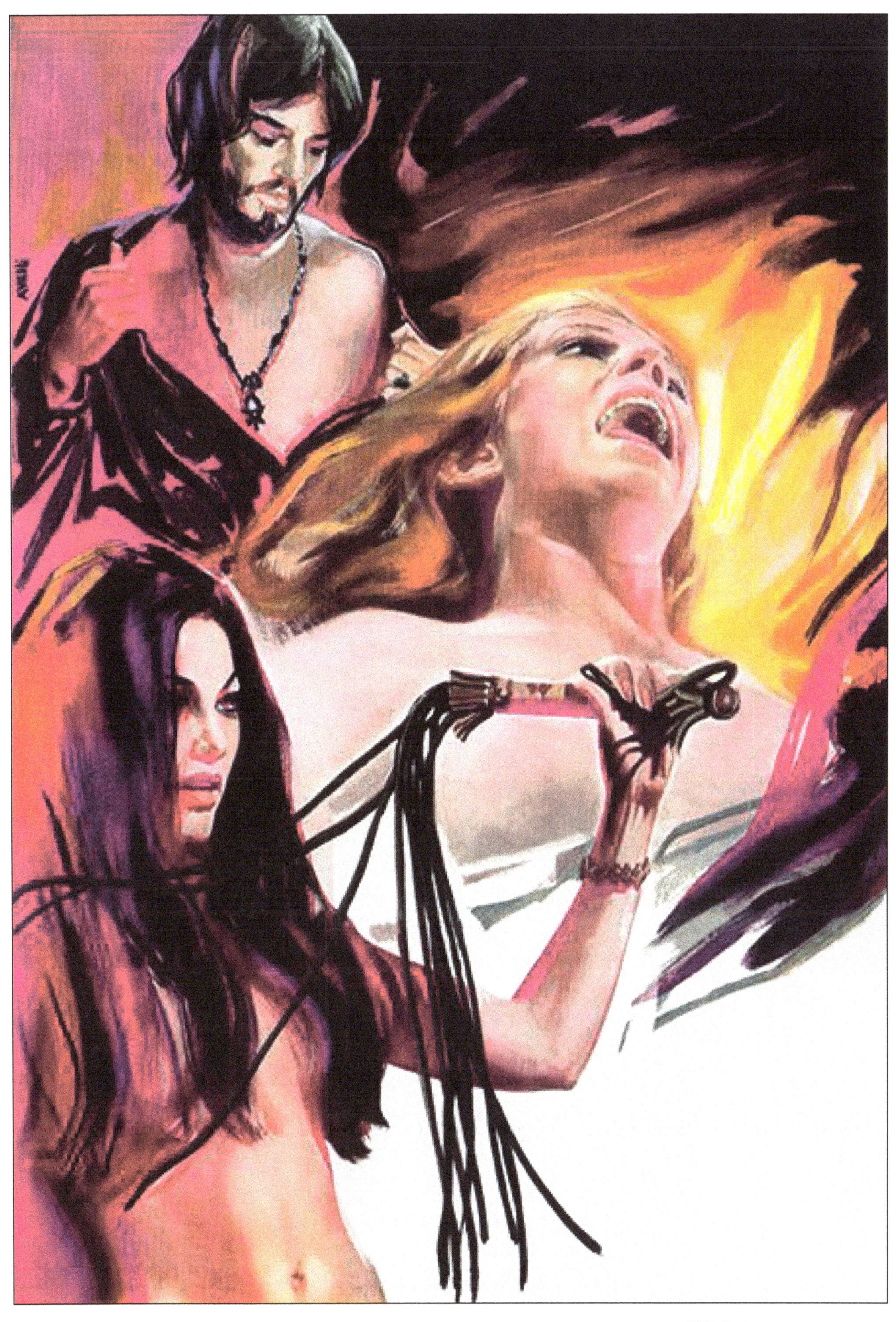

OMBRE ROVENTI (1970). Artist: Tino Avelli.

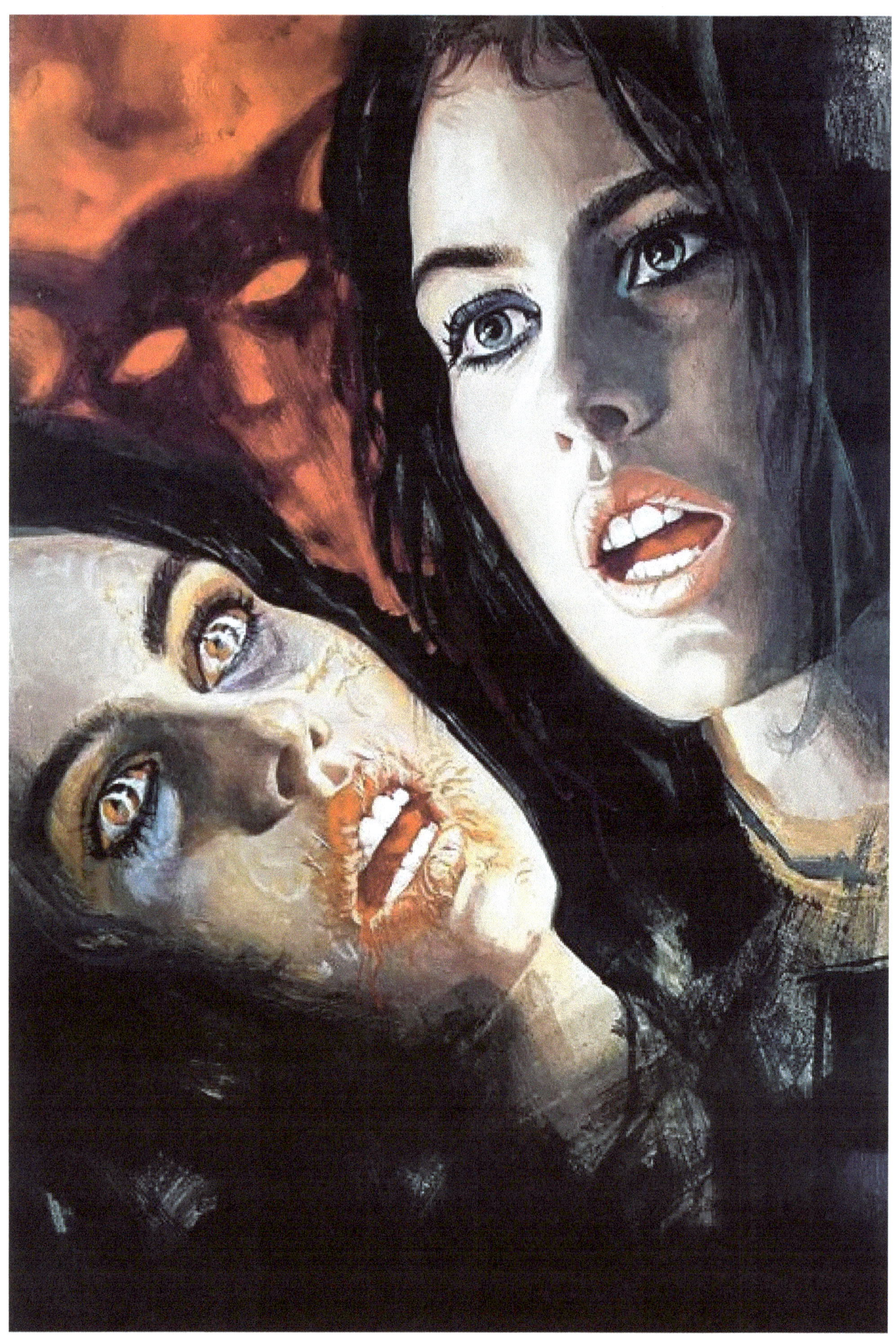

L'OSSESSA (1974). Artist: unsigned.

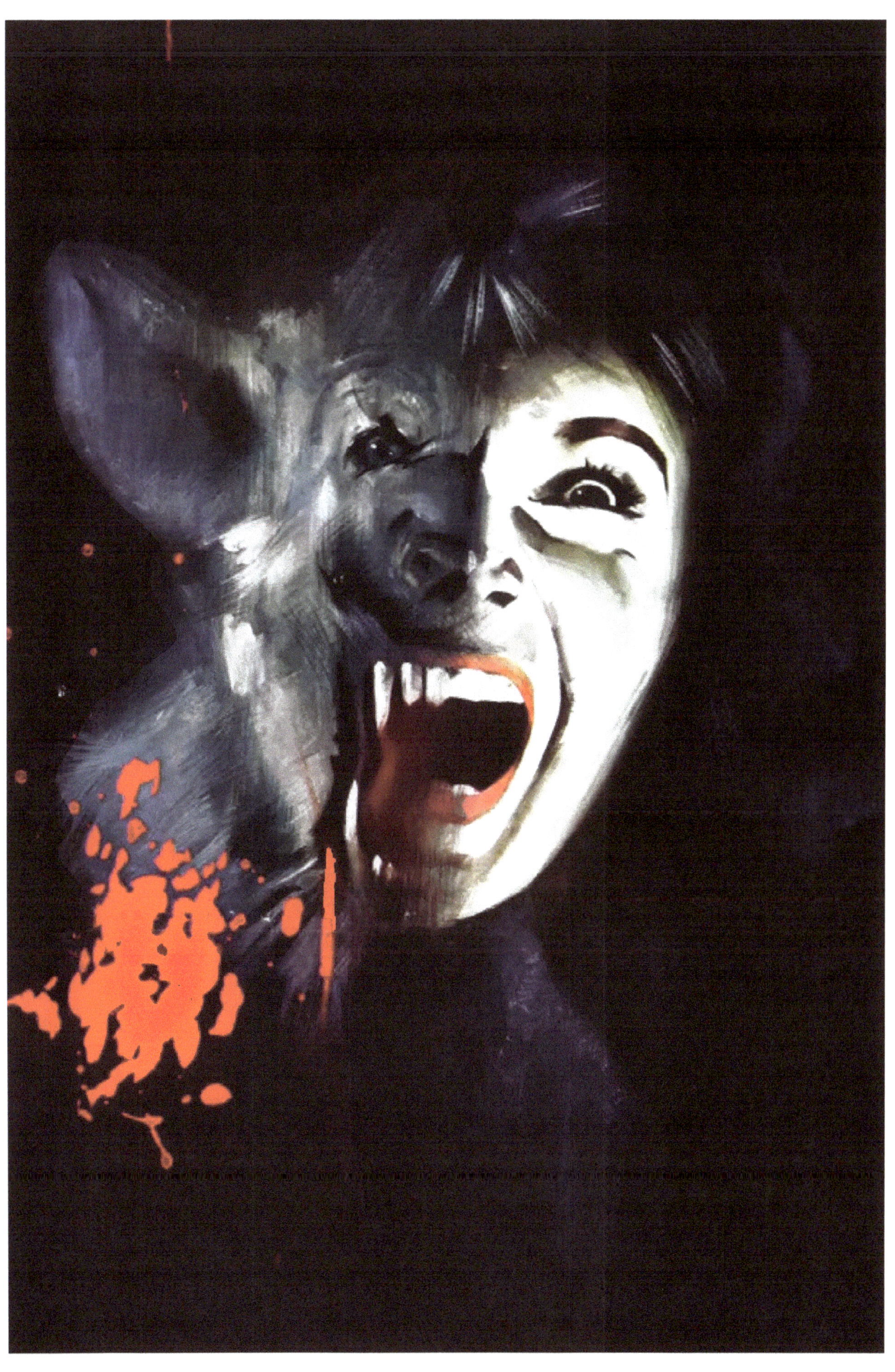

LE NOTTI DI SATANA (1975). Artist: unsigned.

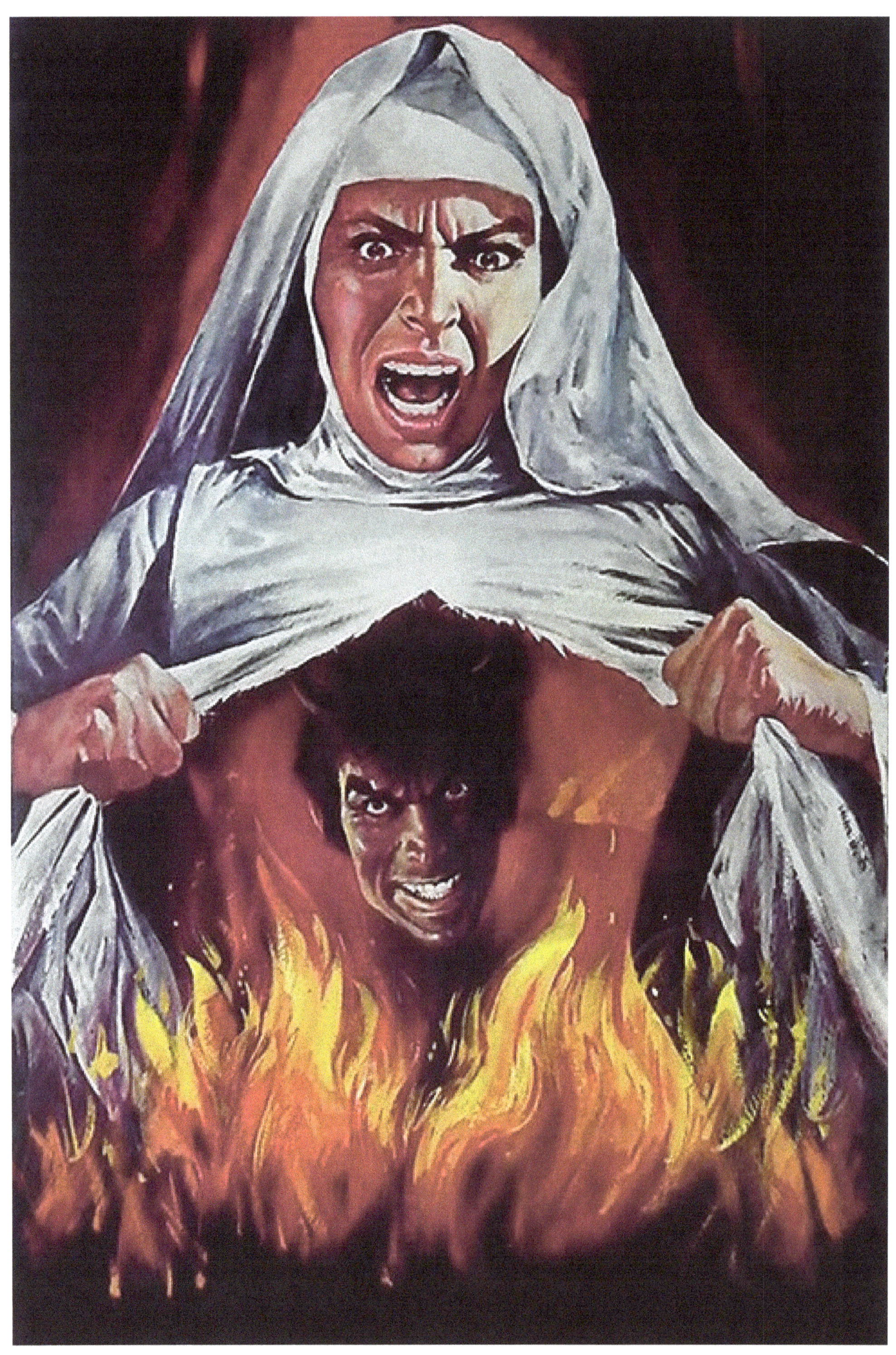

LA NOVIZIA INDEMONIATA (1975). Artist: unsigned.

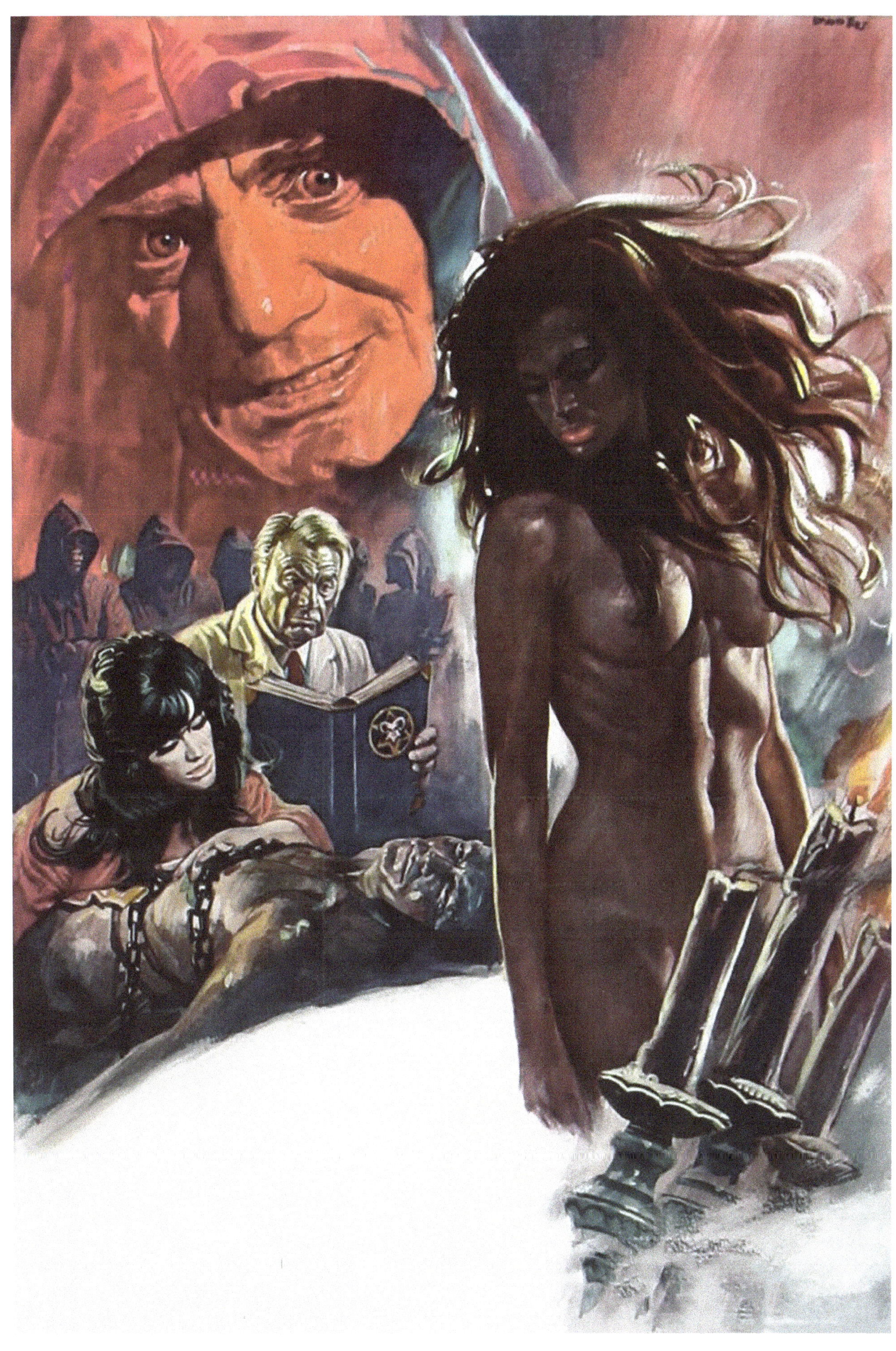

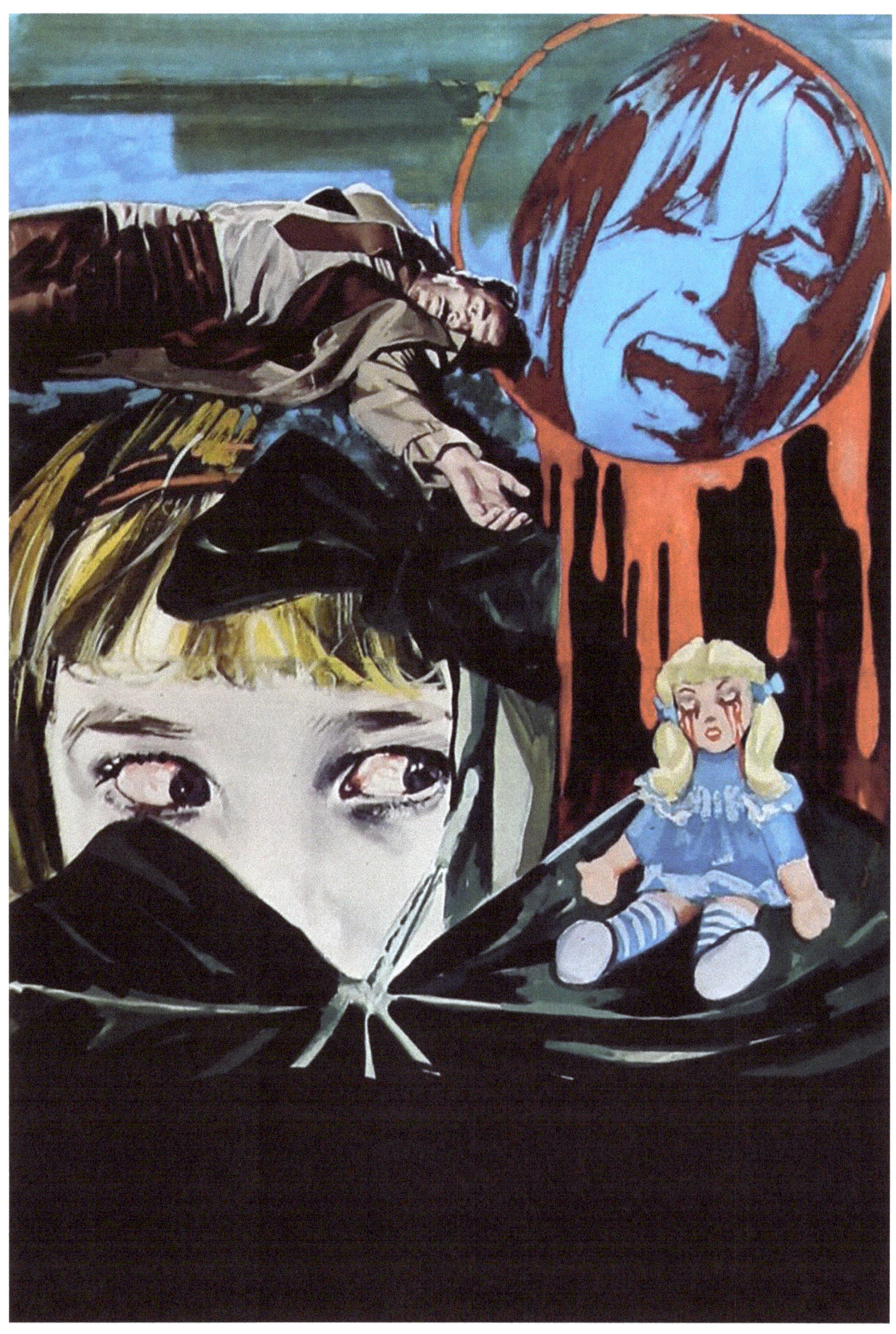

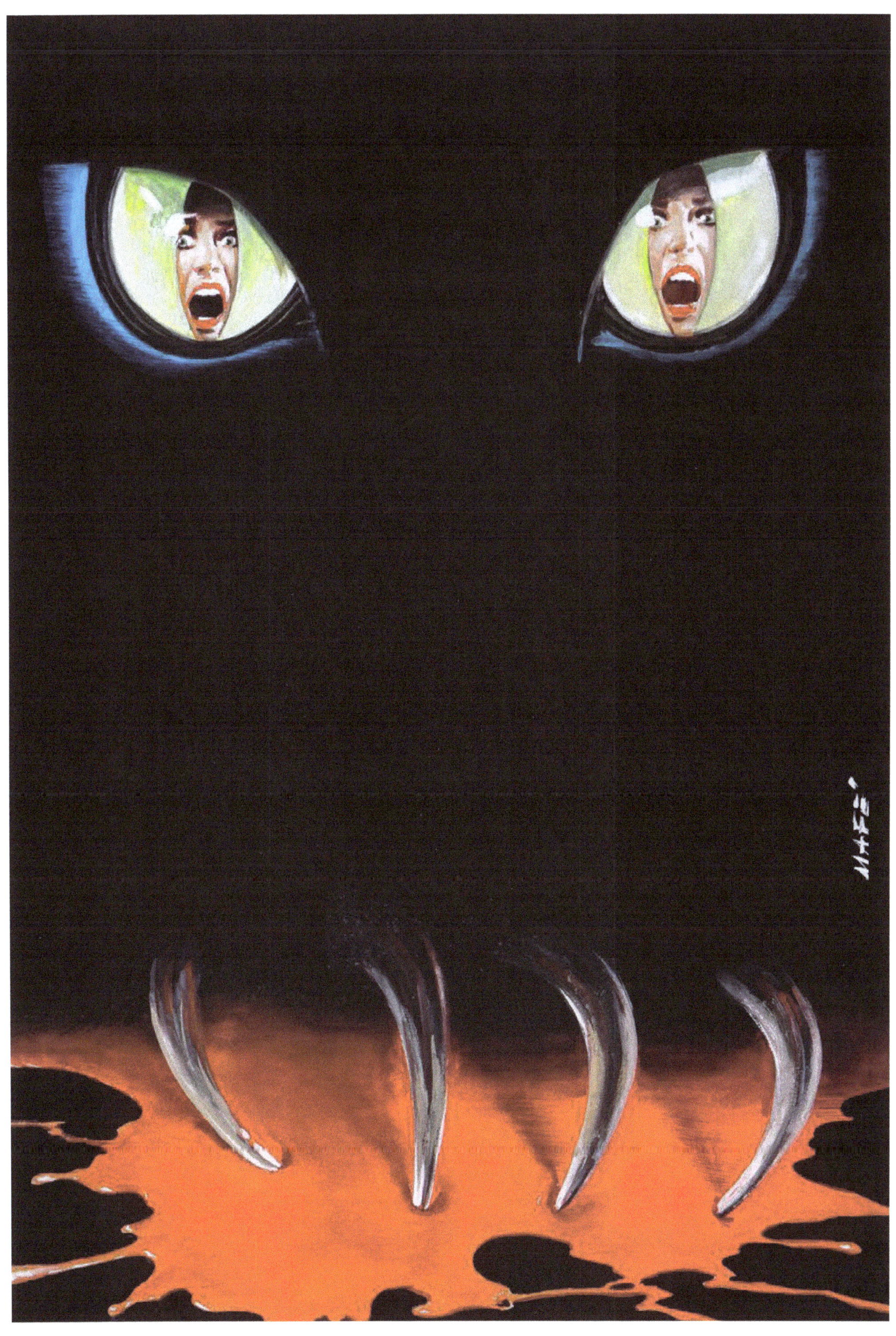

ARTIGLI (1977). Artist: Mafé.

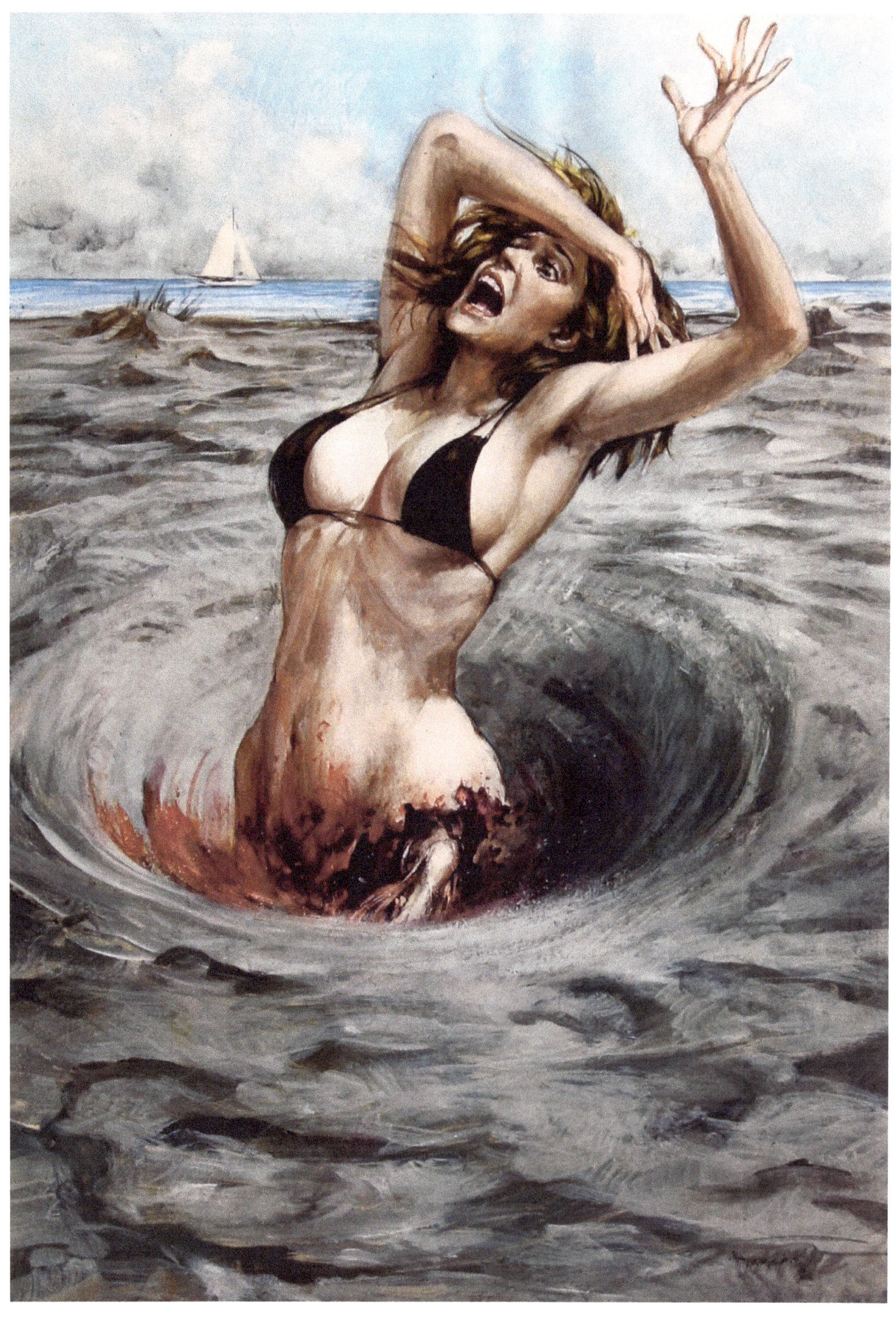

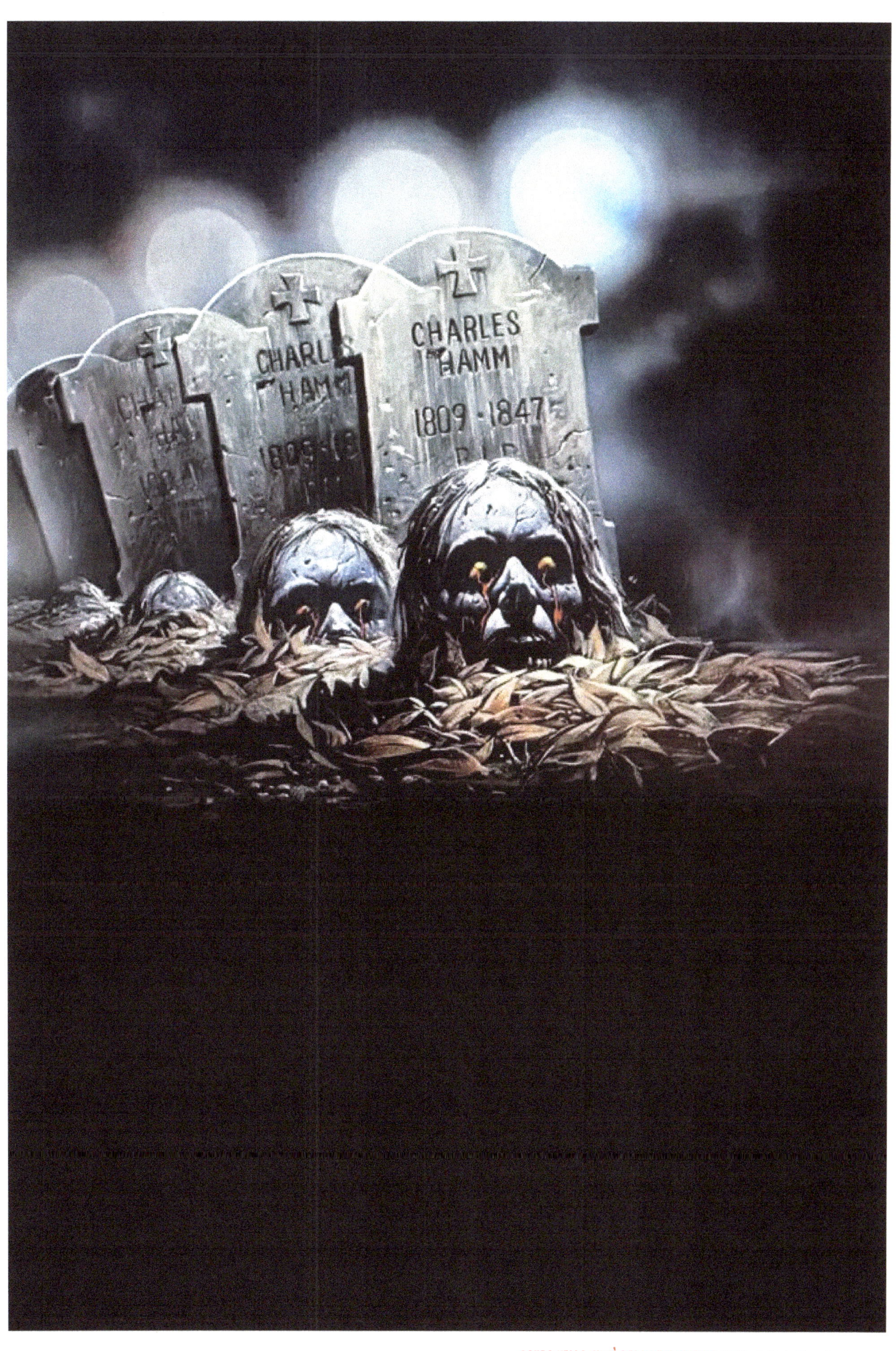

CHARLES
HAMM
1809 - 1847
CHARLES
HAMM
1809

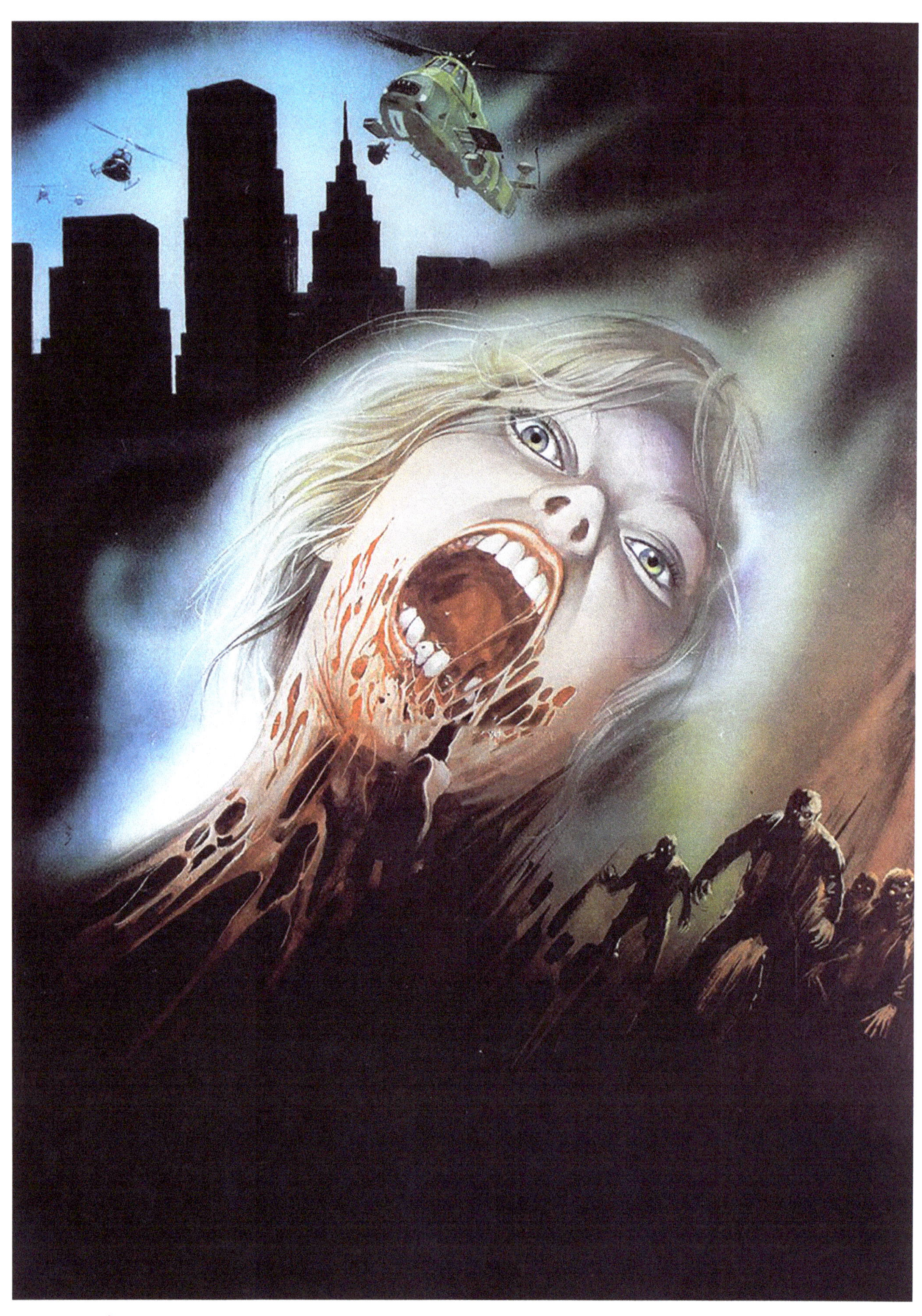

INCUBO SULLA CITTÀ CONTAMINATA (1980). Artist: unsigned.

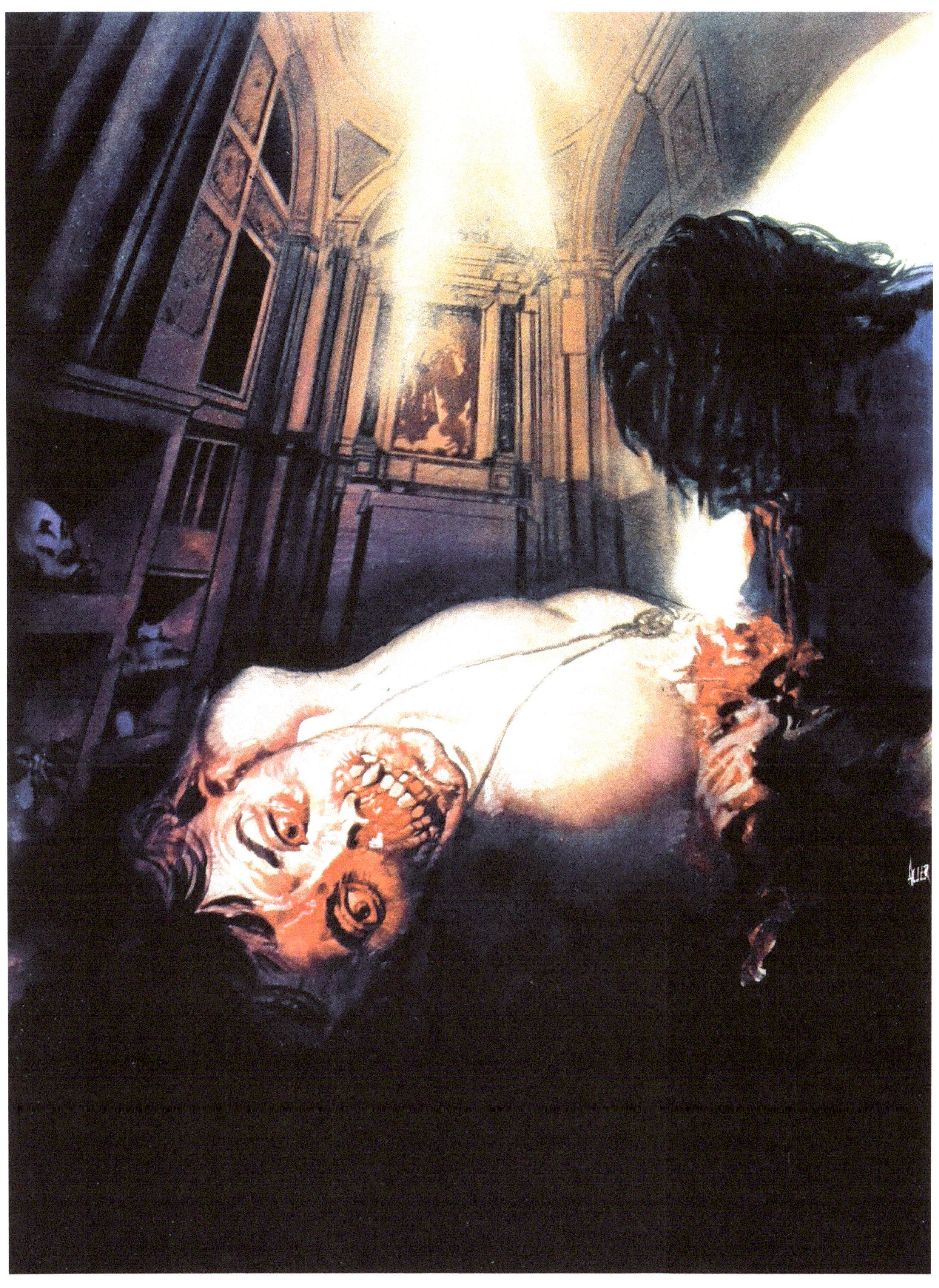

ANTHROPOPHAGUS (1980). Artist: Carlo Alessandrini.

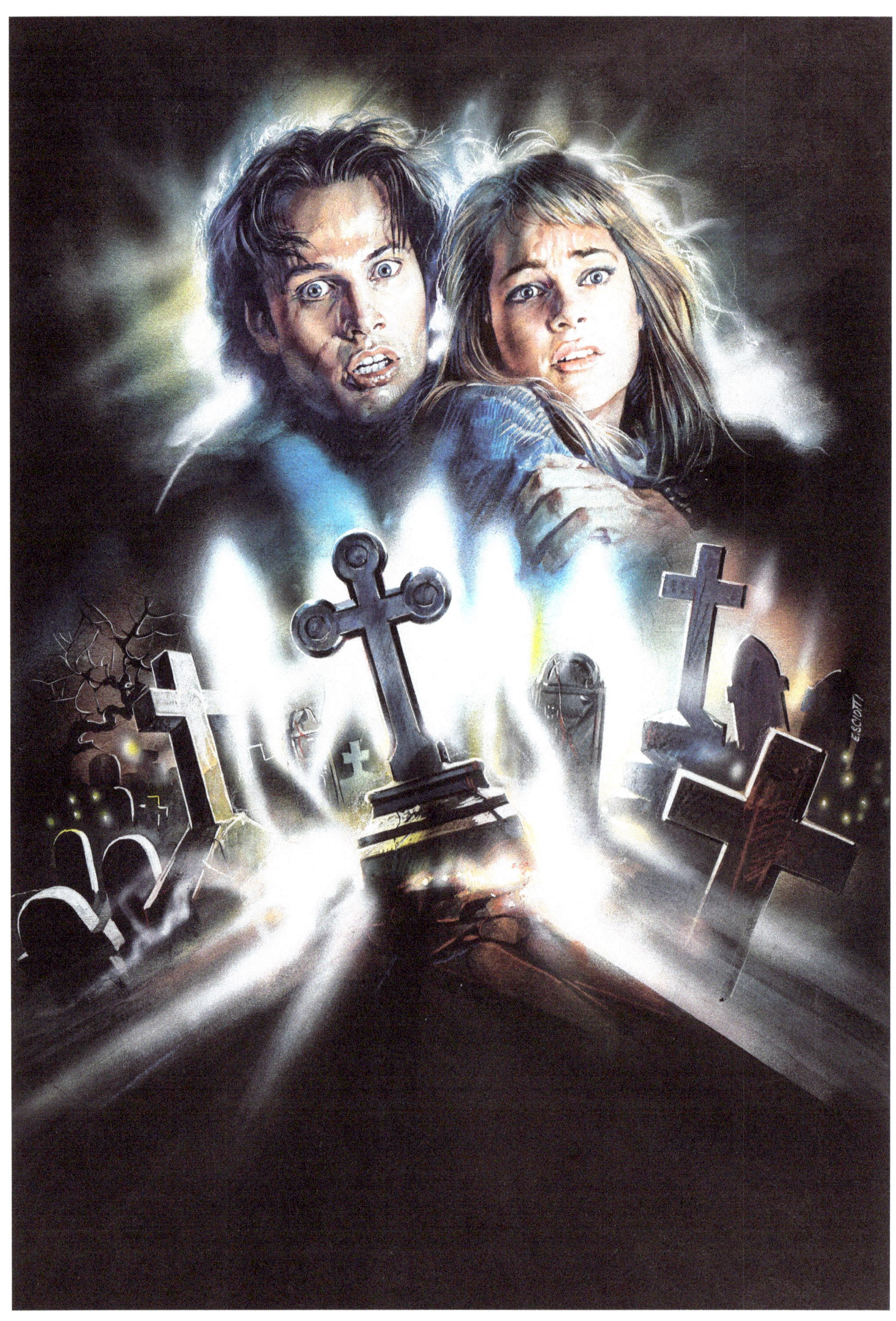

PHANTASM II (1988). Artist: Enzo Sciotti.

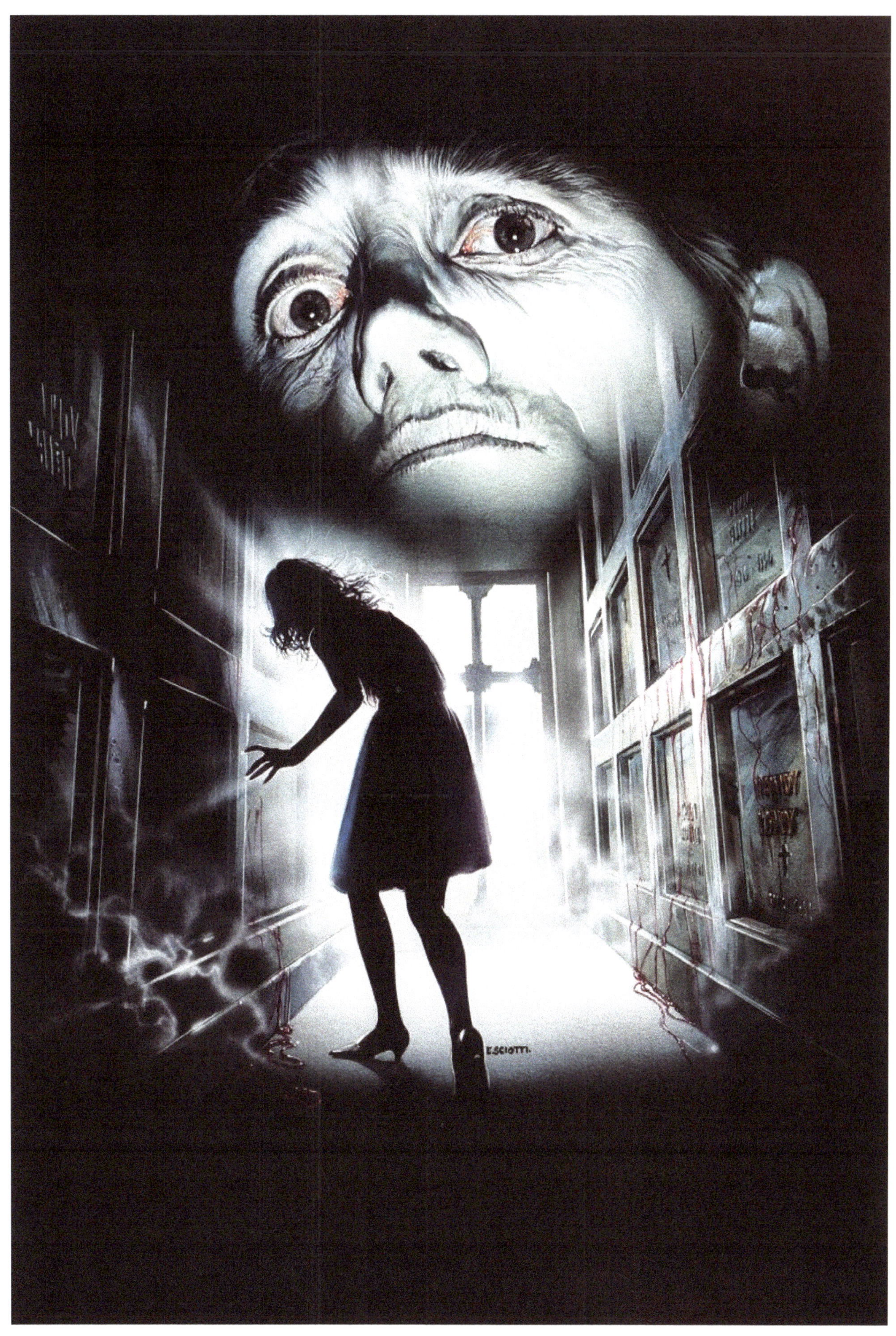

VOCI DAL PROFONDO (1991). Artist: Enzo Sciotti.

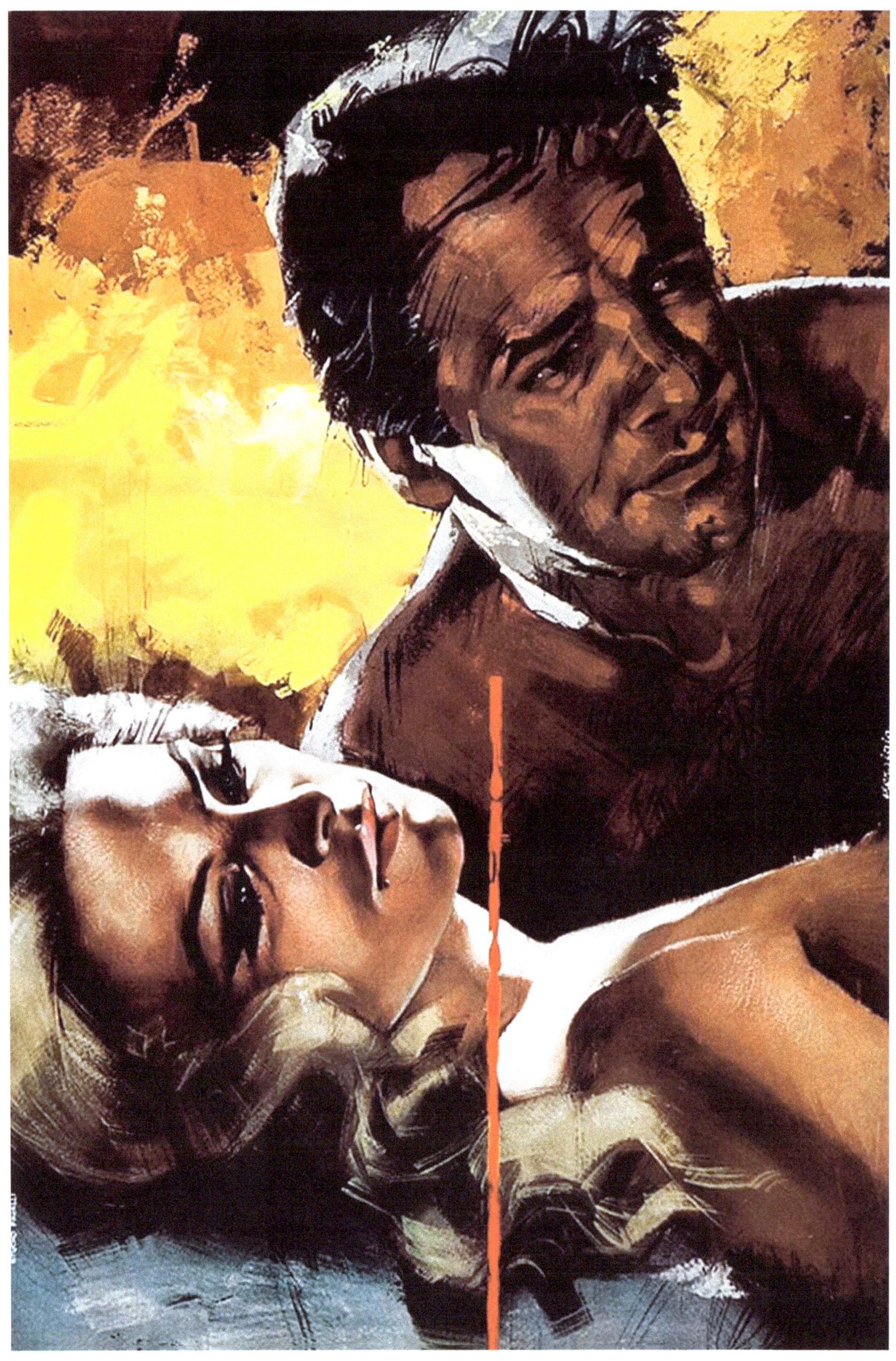

LA DONNA DEL LAGO (1965). Artist: Studio Favalli/Piero Ermanno Iaia.

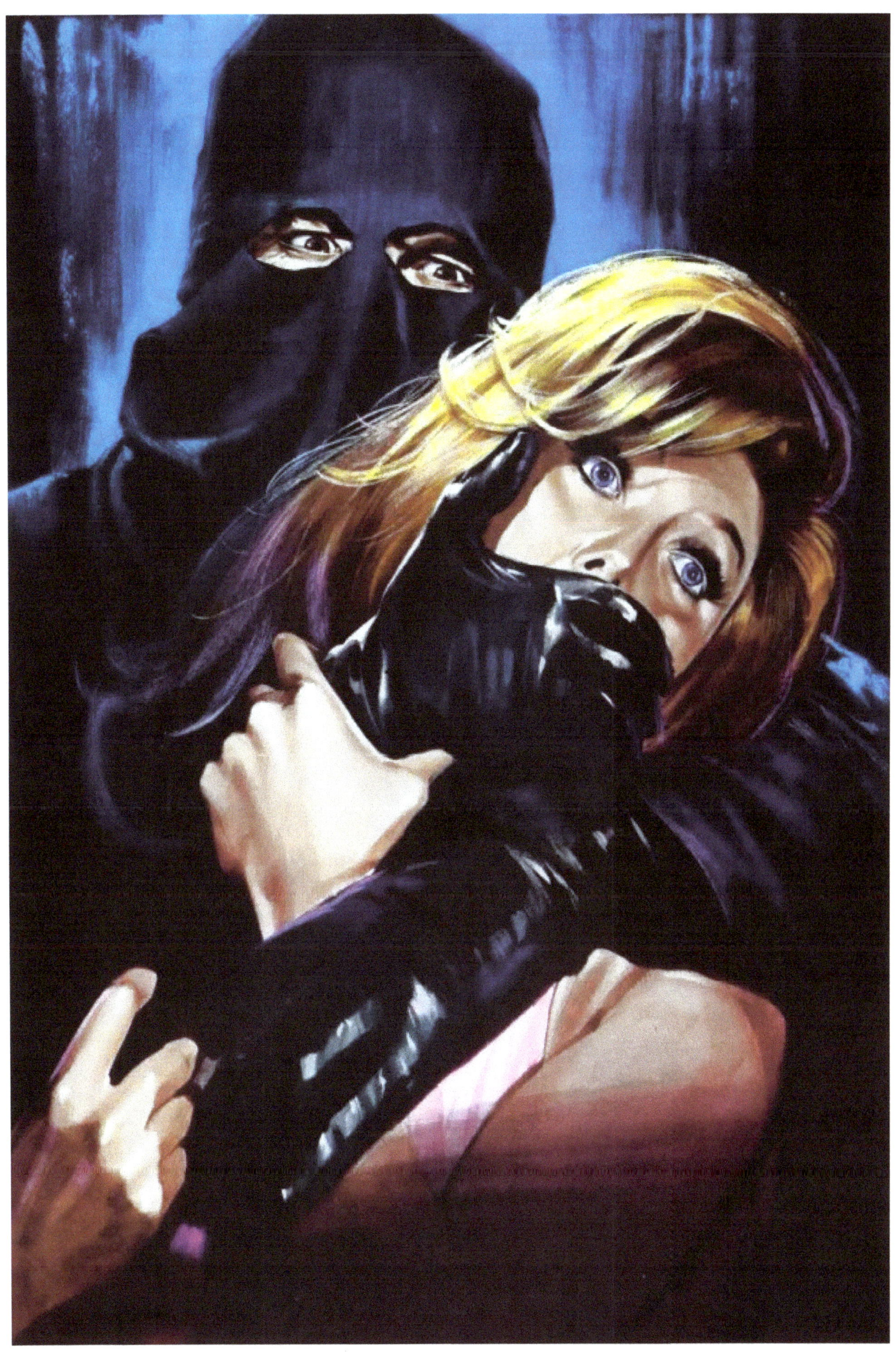

LA BAMBOLA DI SATANA (1969). Artist: Mario Piovano.

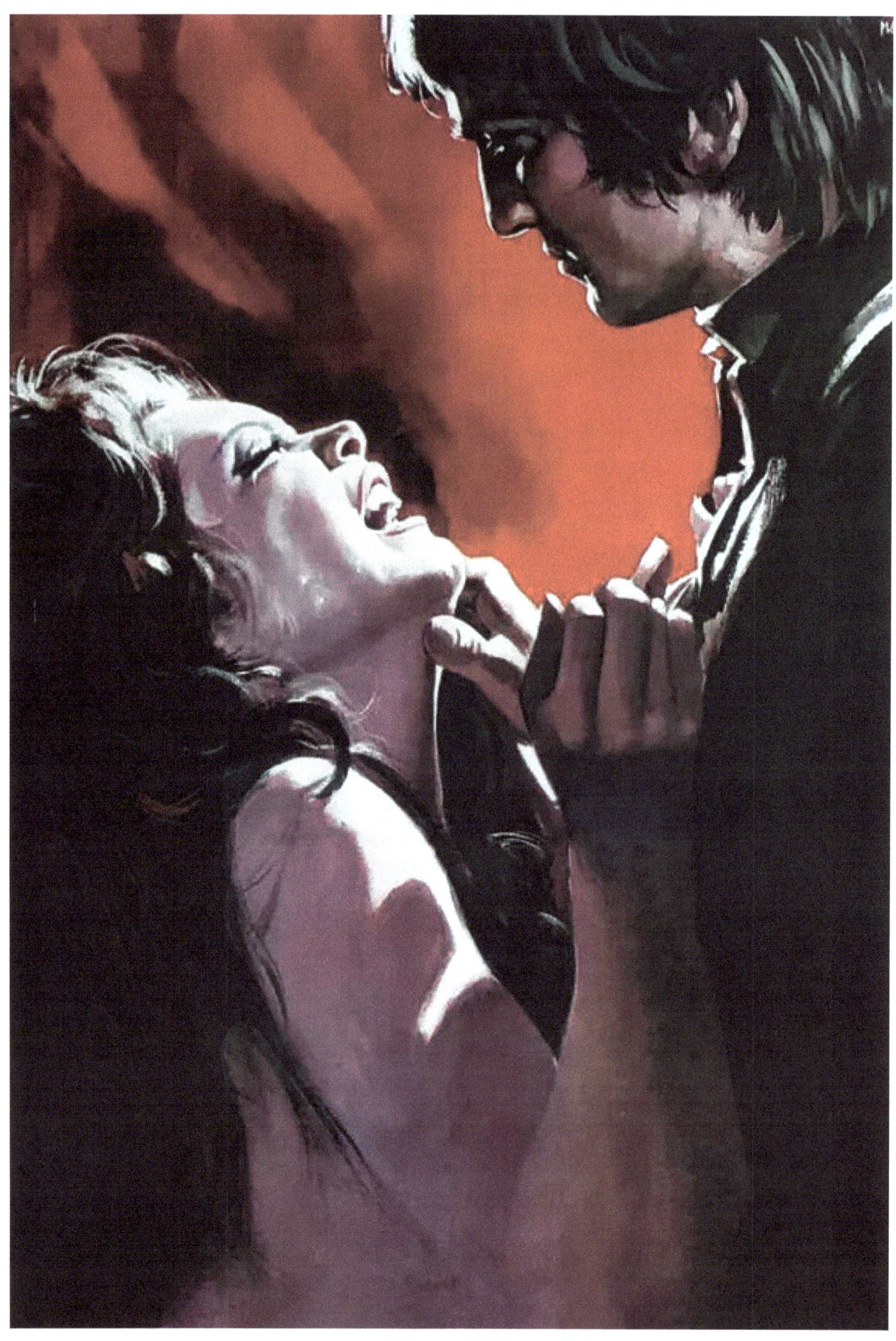

YELLOW LE CUGINE (1969). Artist: Mario De Berardinis.

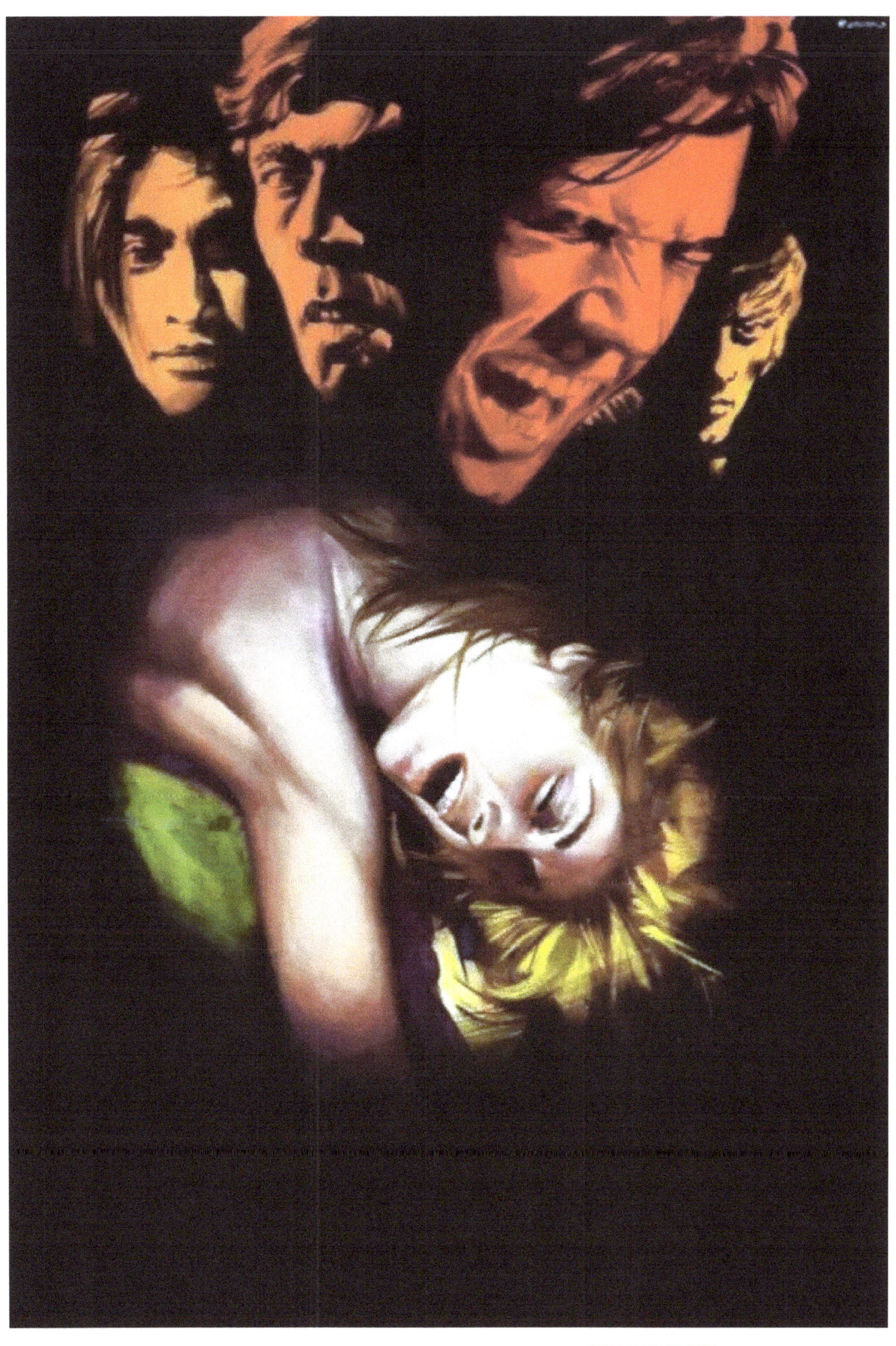

I RAGAZZI DEL MASSACRO (1969). Artist: Renato Casaro.

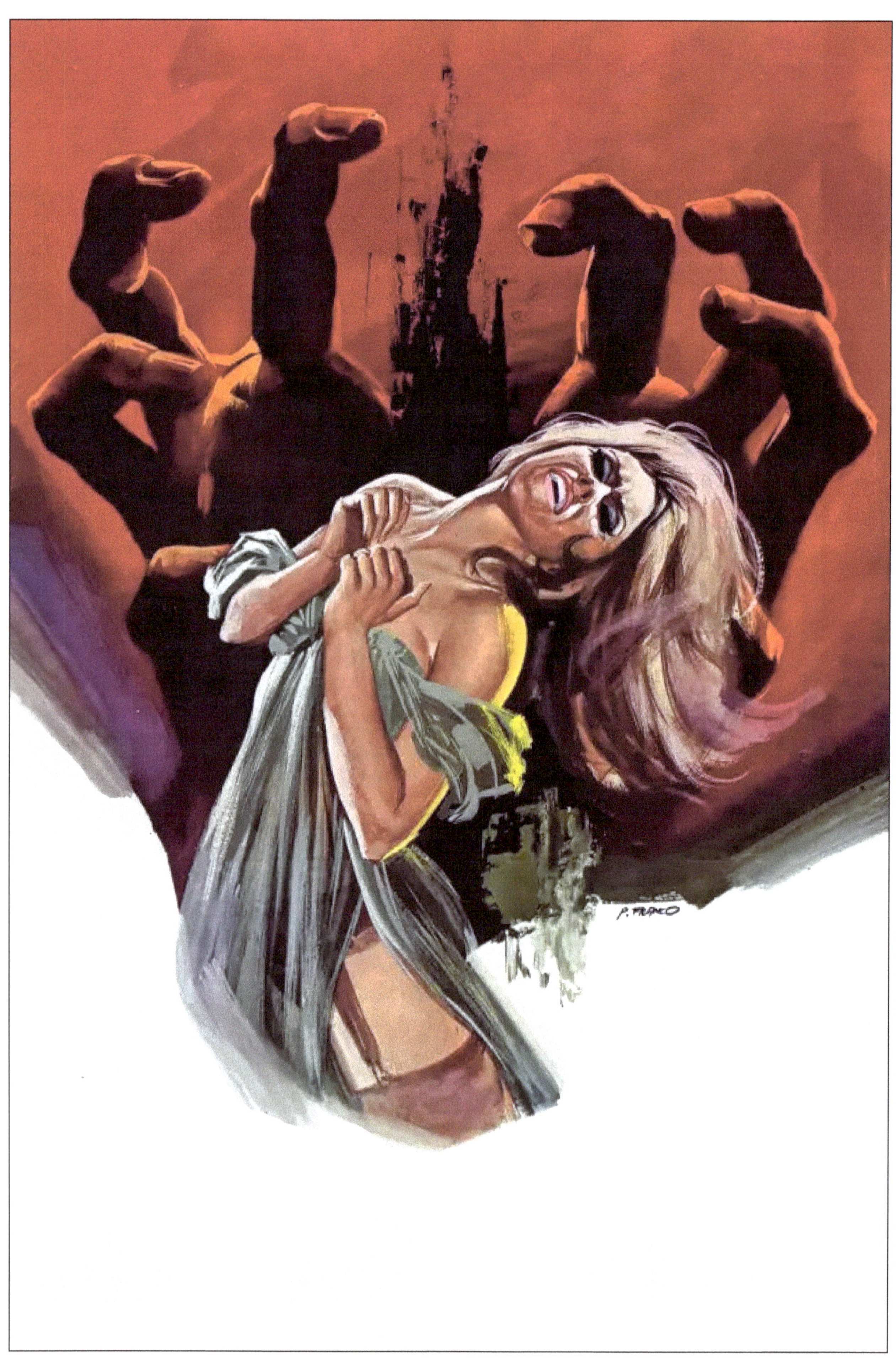

IL TUO DOLCE CORPO DA UCCIDERE (1970). Artist: Franco Picchioni.

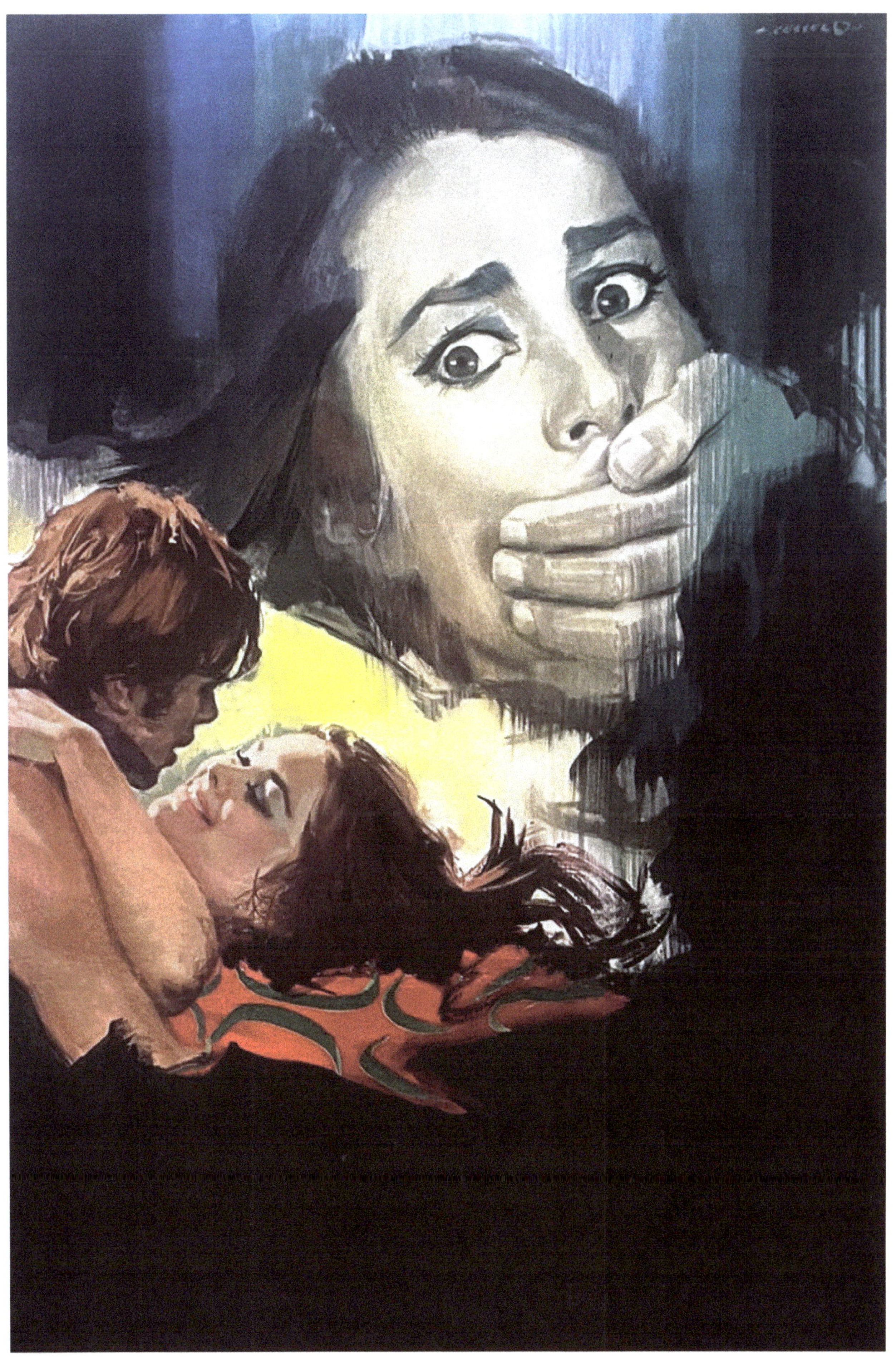

UN POSTO IDEALE PER UCCIDERE (1971). Artist:Angelo Cesselon.

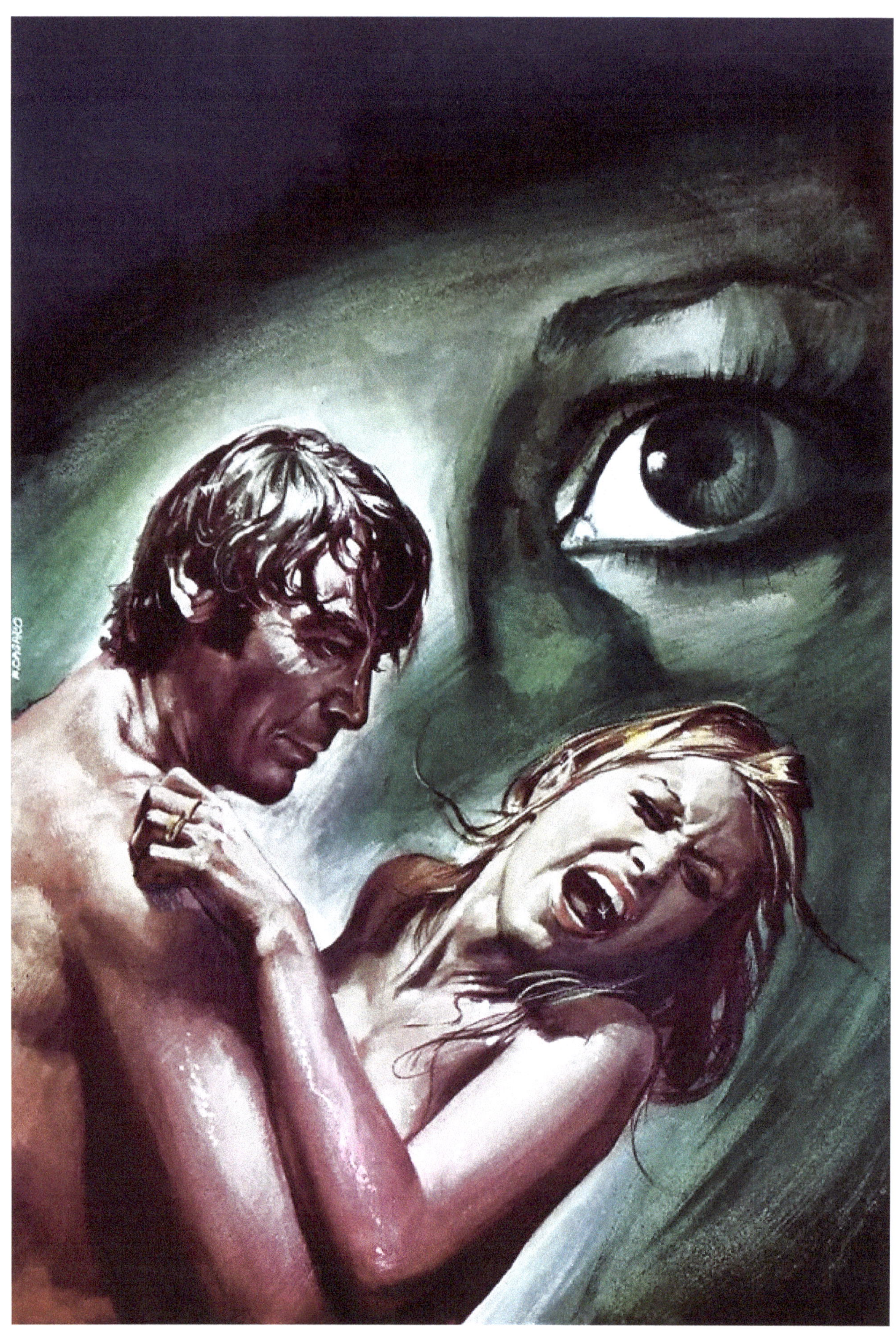

LA MORTE SCENDE LEGGERA (1972). Artist: Renato Casaro.

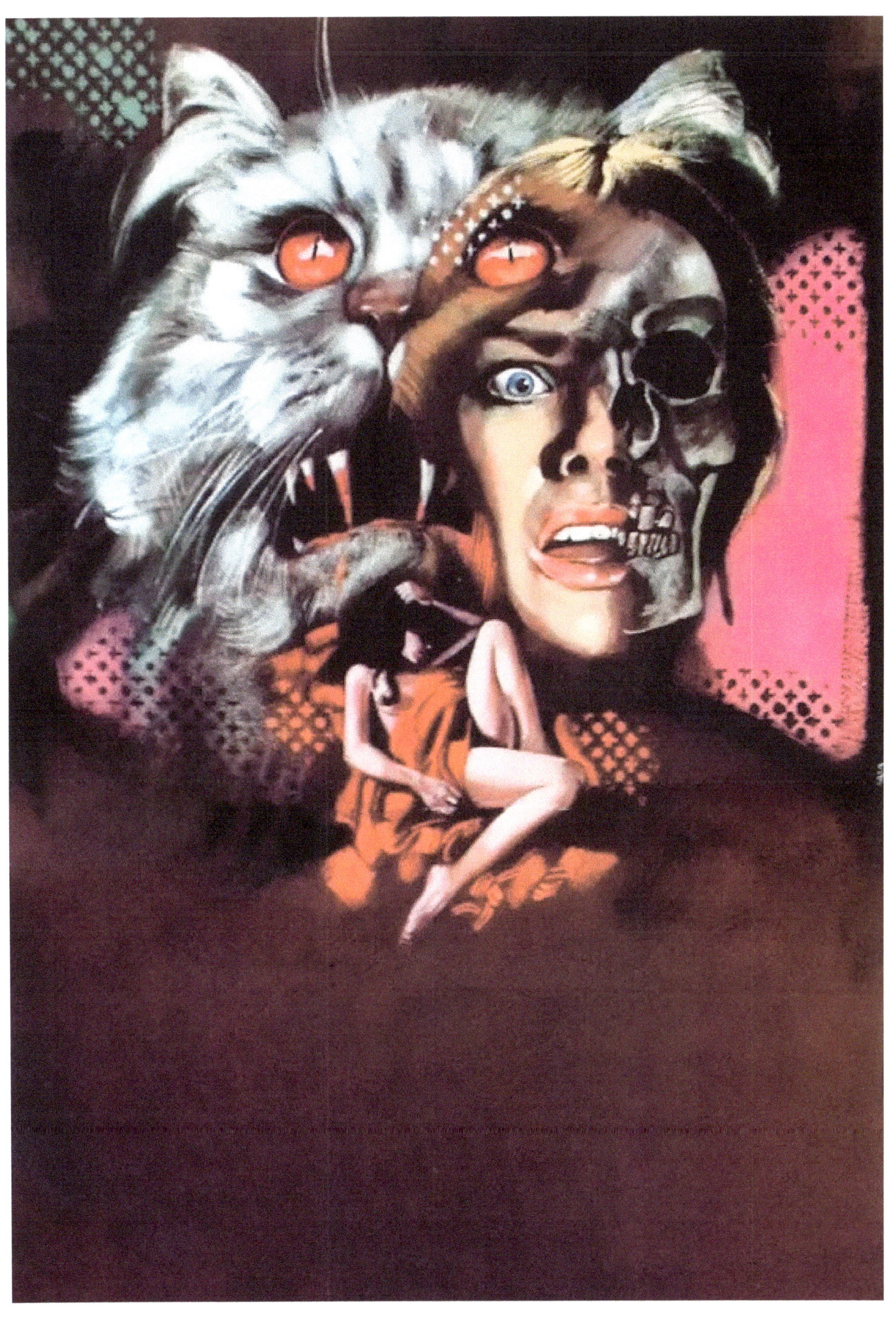

LA MORTE NEGLI OCCHI DEL GATTO (1973). Artist: Piero Ermanno Iaia.

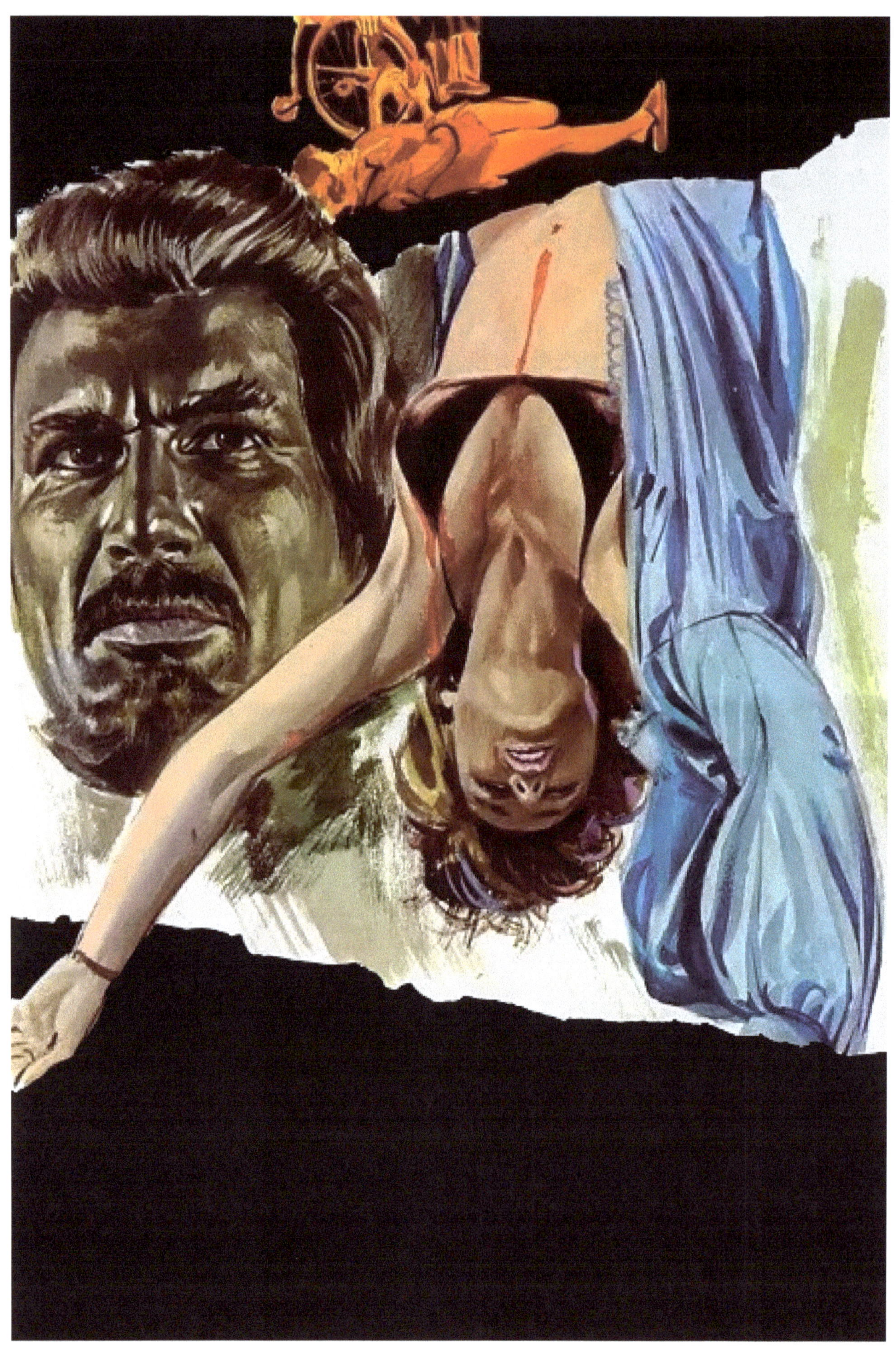

MANIA (1974). Artist: unsigned.

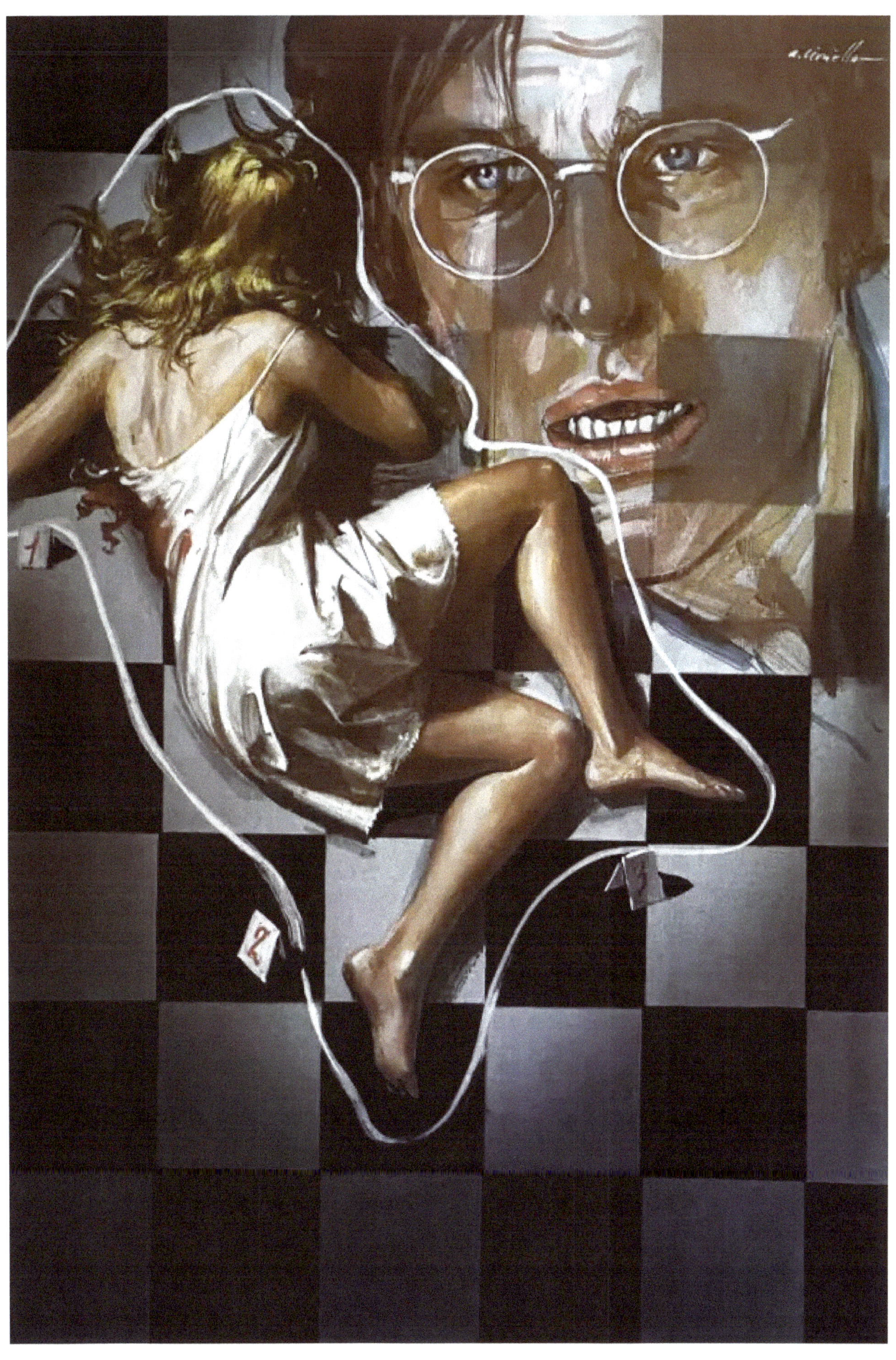

MORTE SOSPETTA DI UNA MINORENNE (1975). Artist: Averardo Ciriello.

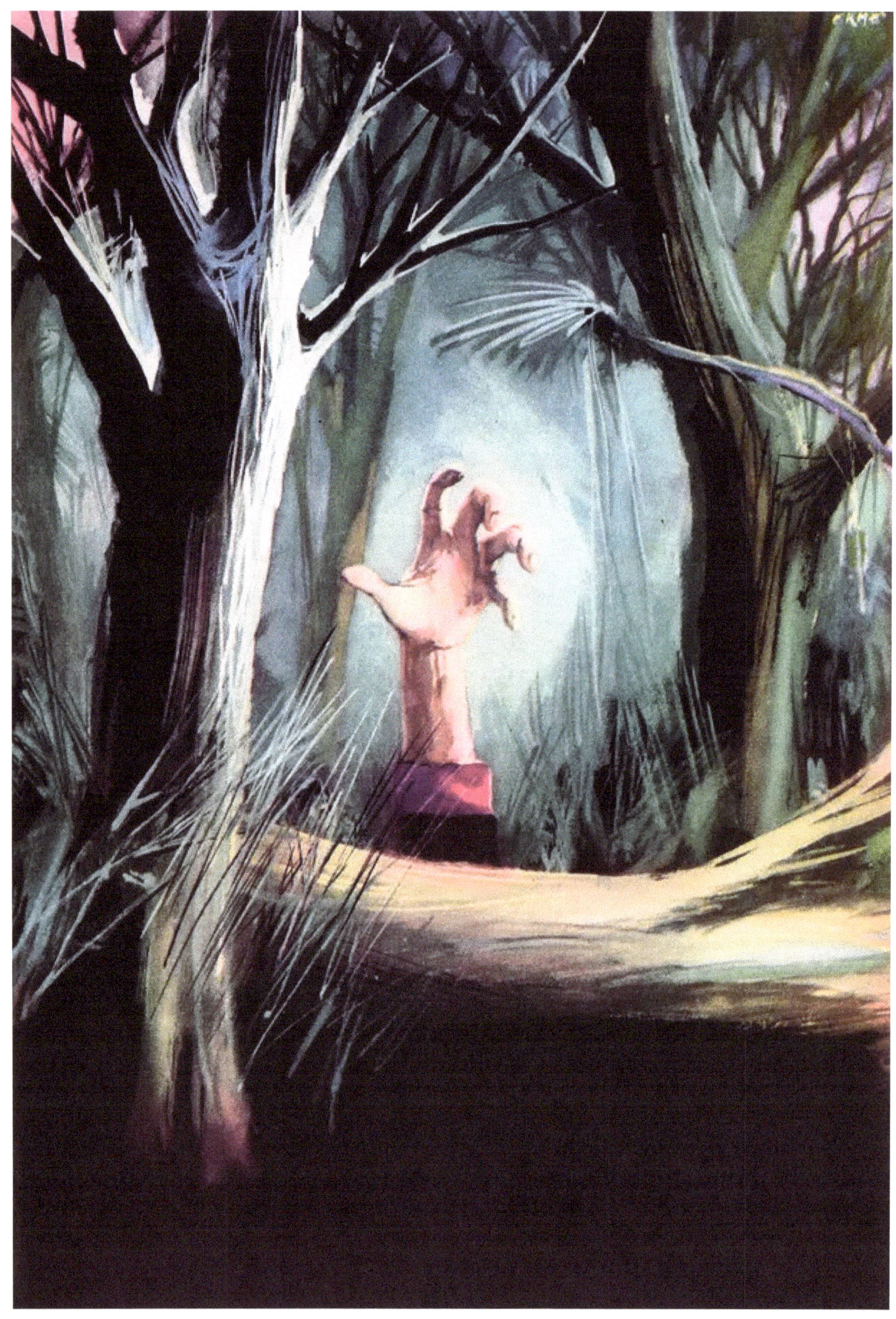

LA BANDA DEL TERRORE (1960). Artist: Ermé.

74

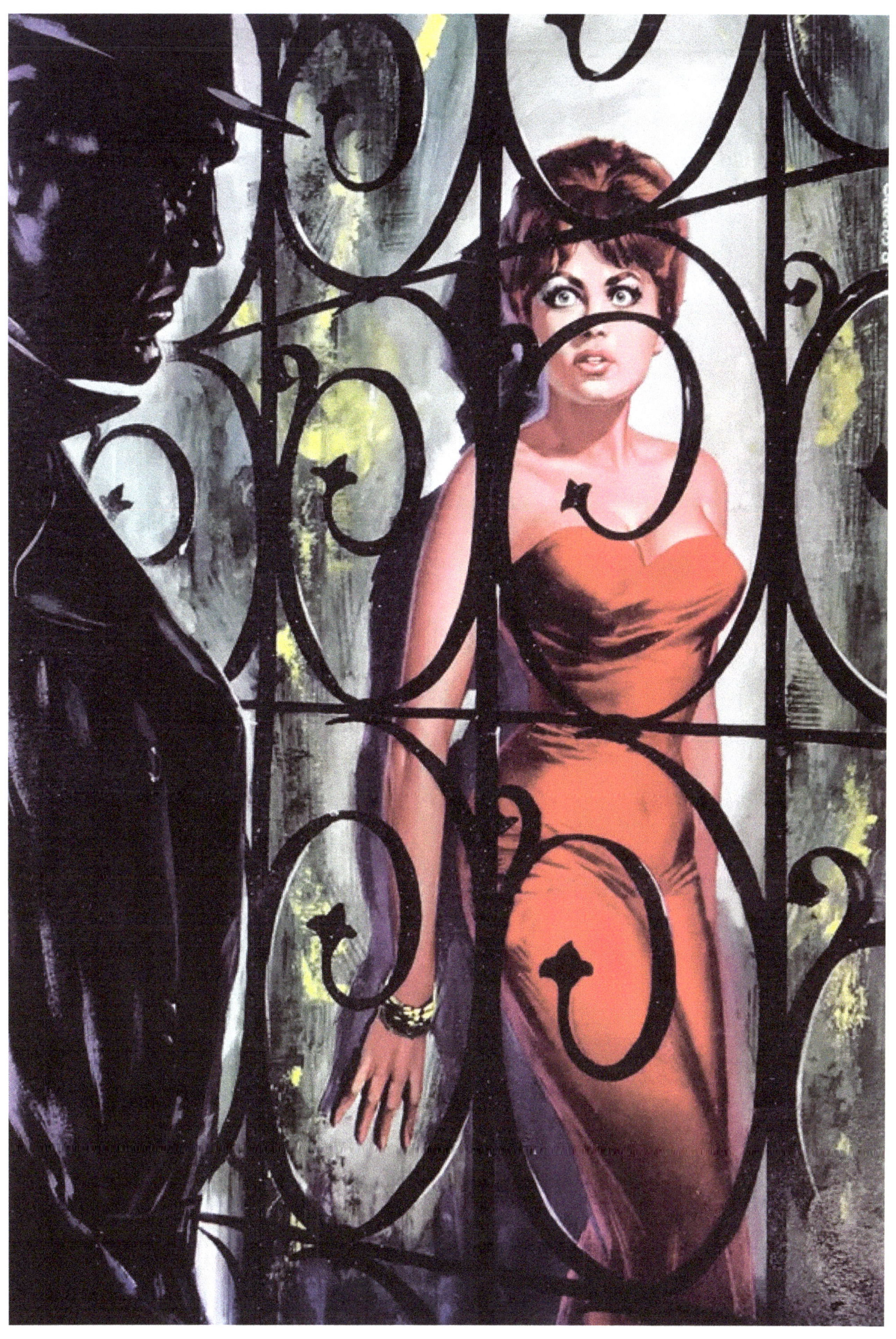

IL VOLTO DELL'ASSASSINO (1962). Artist: Renato Casaro.

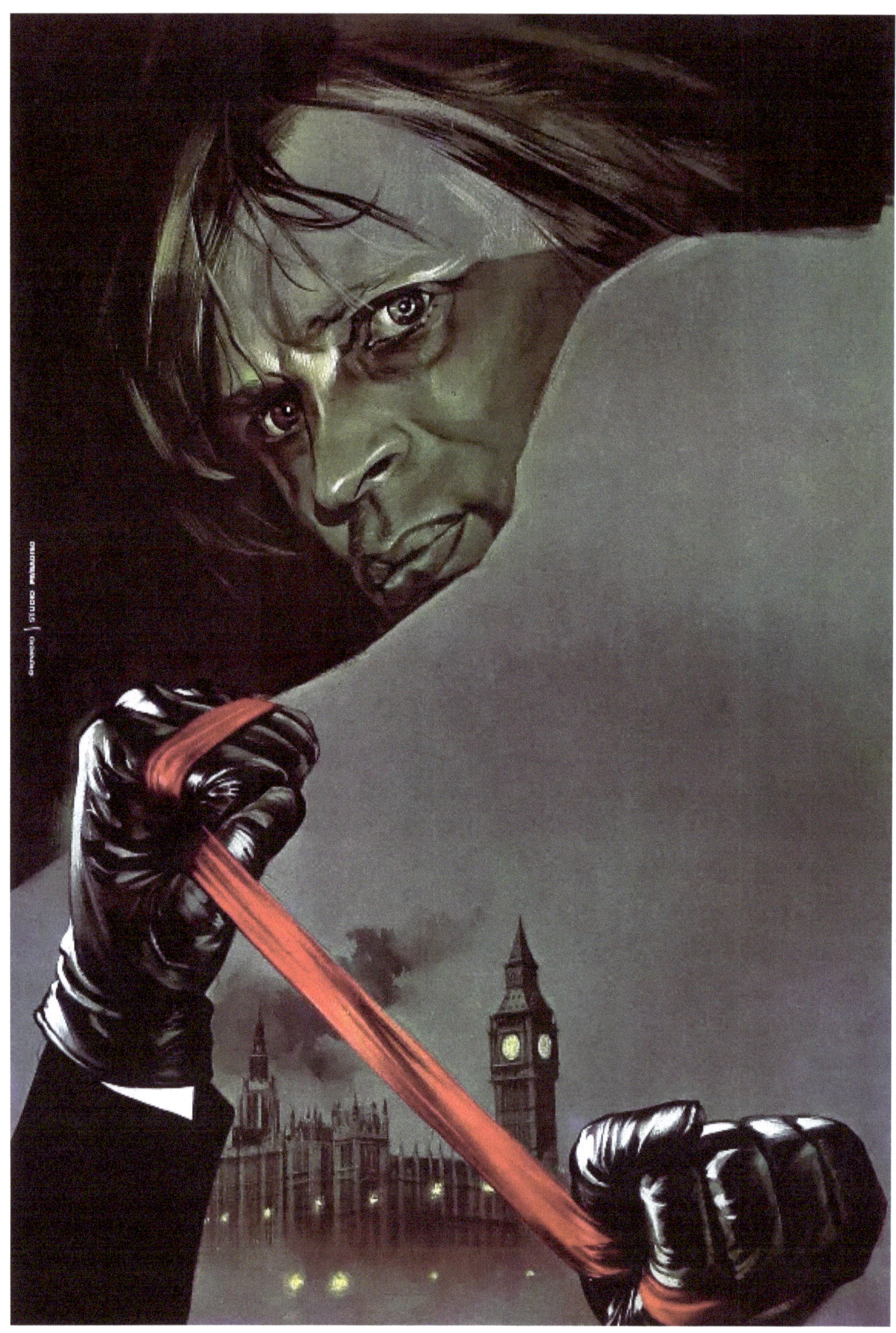

IL LACCIO ROSSO (1963). Artist: Mario Piovano.

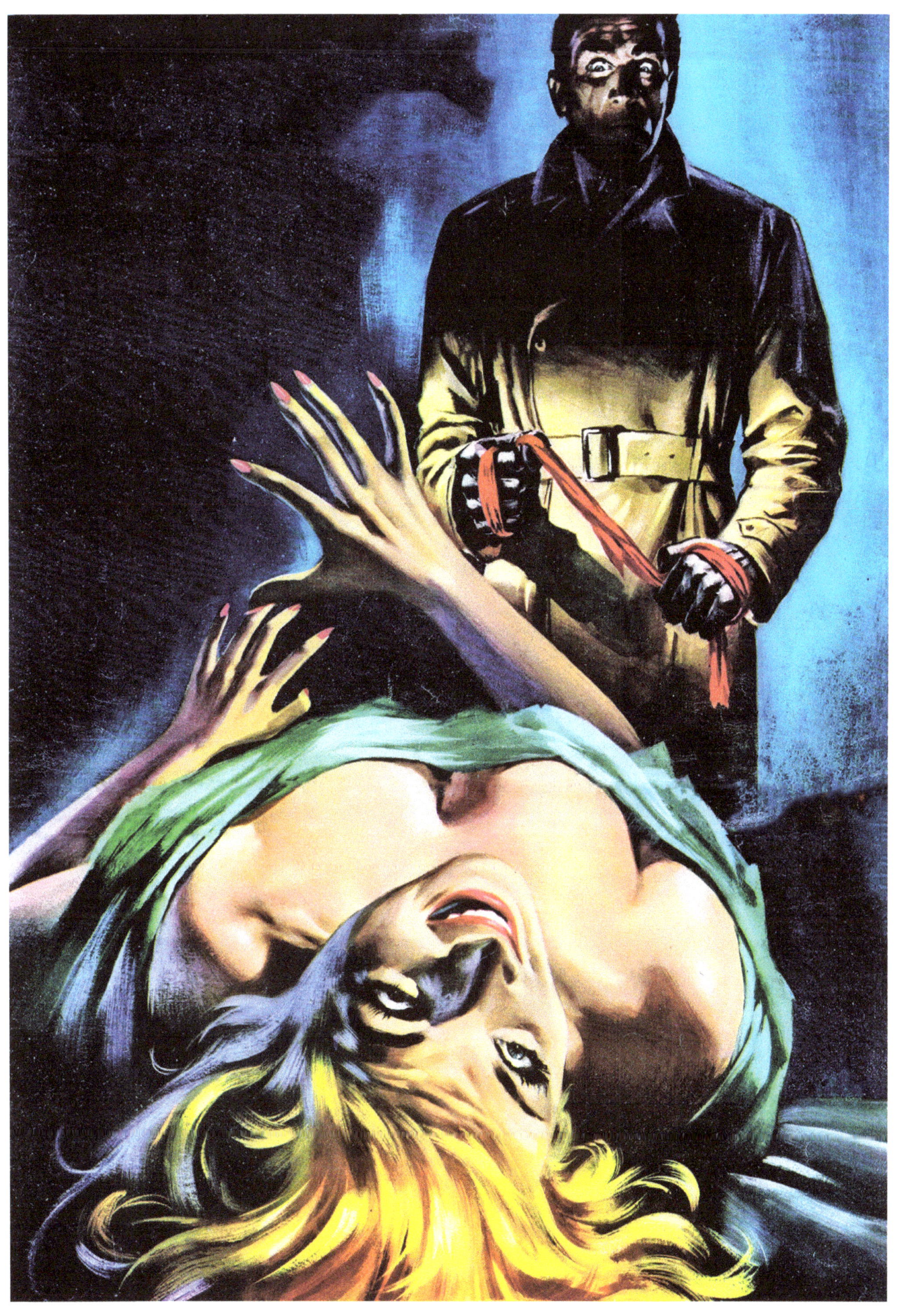

IL LACCIO ROSSO (1963). Artist: Renato Casaro.

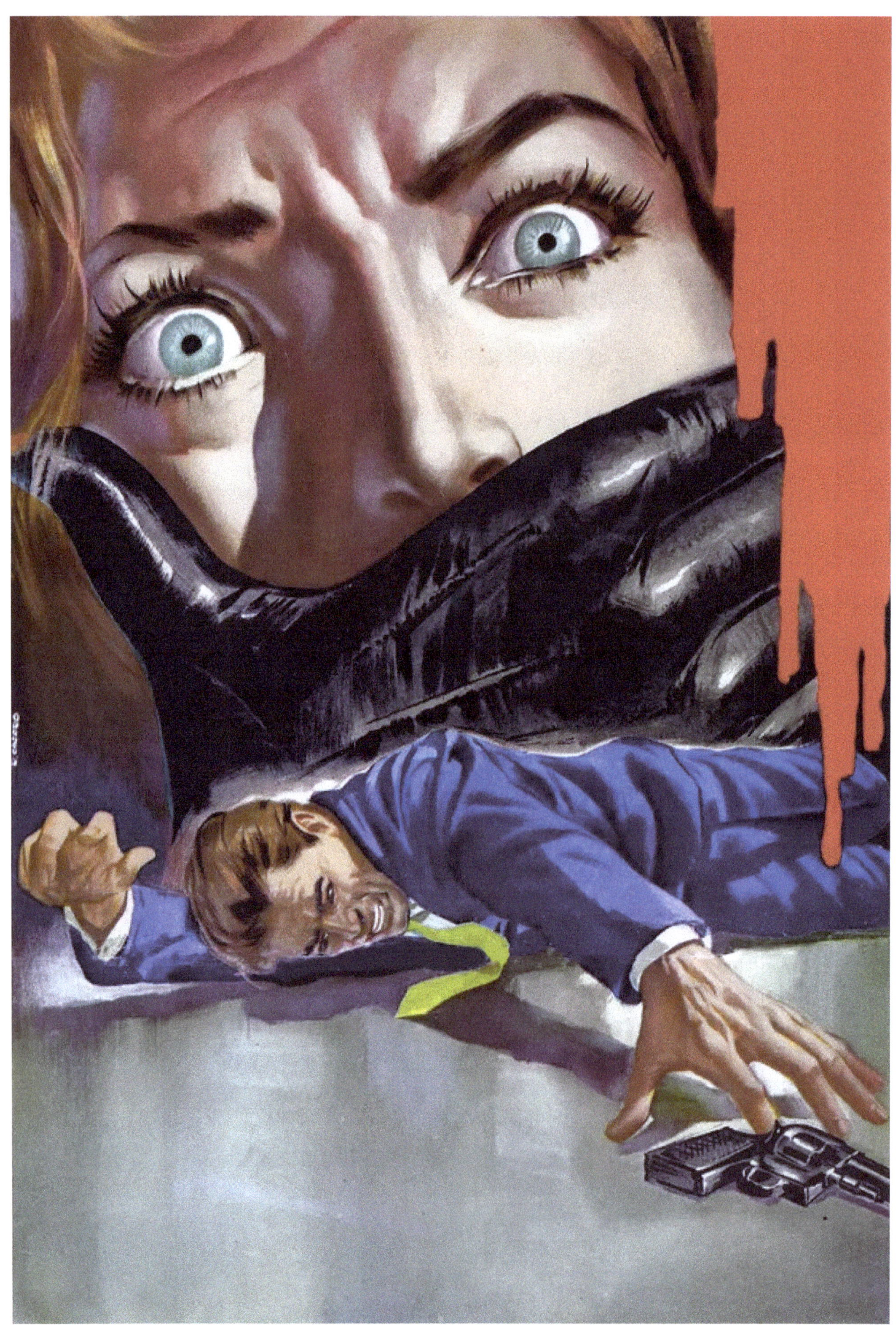

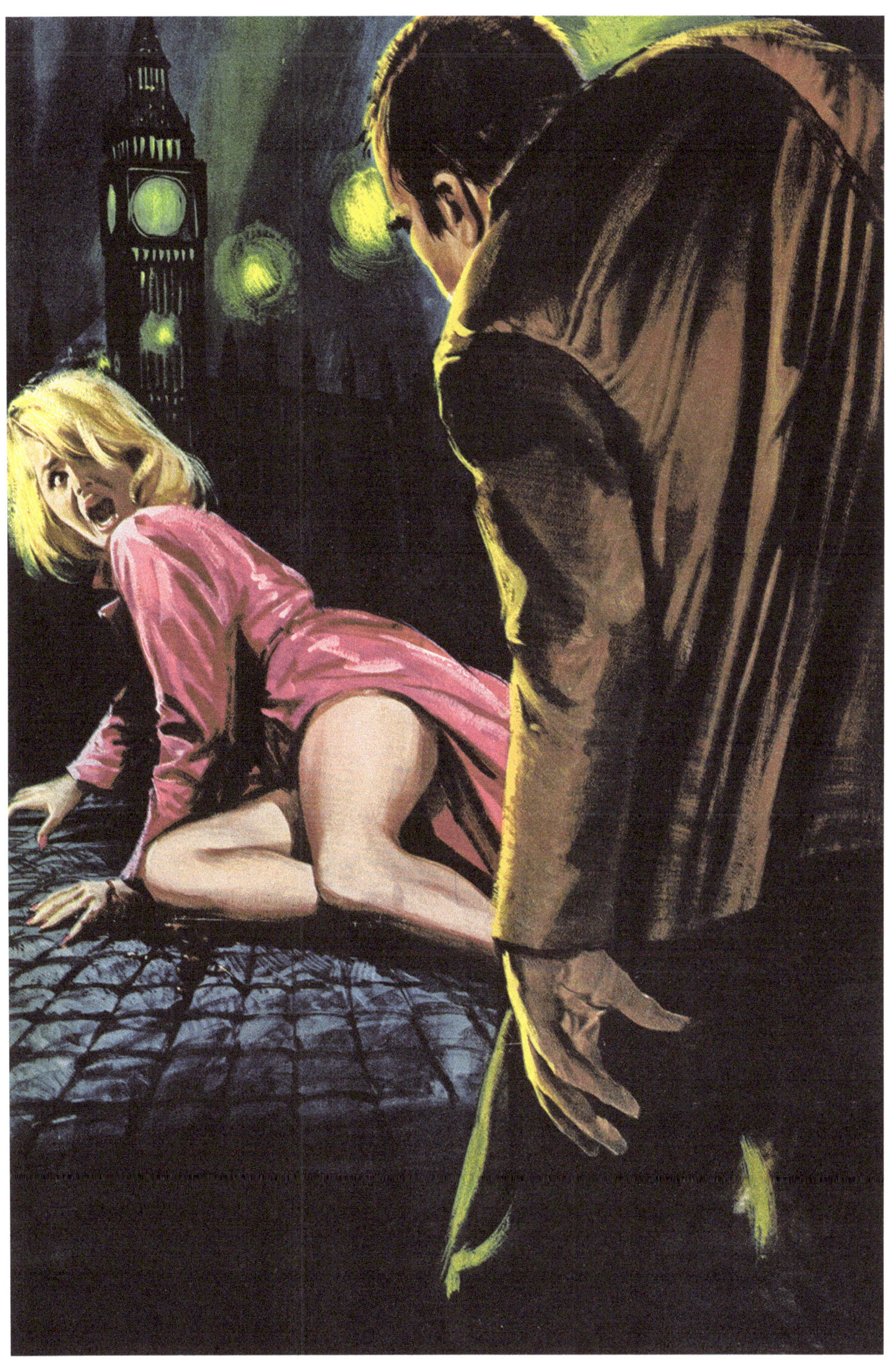

IL GOBBO DI LONDRA (1966). Artist: unsigned.

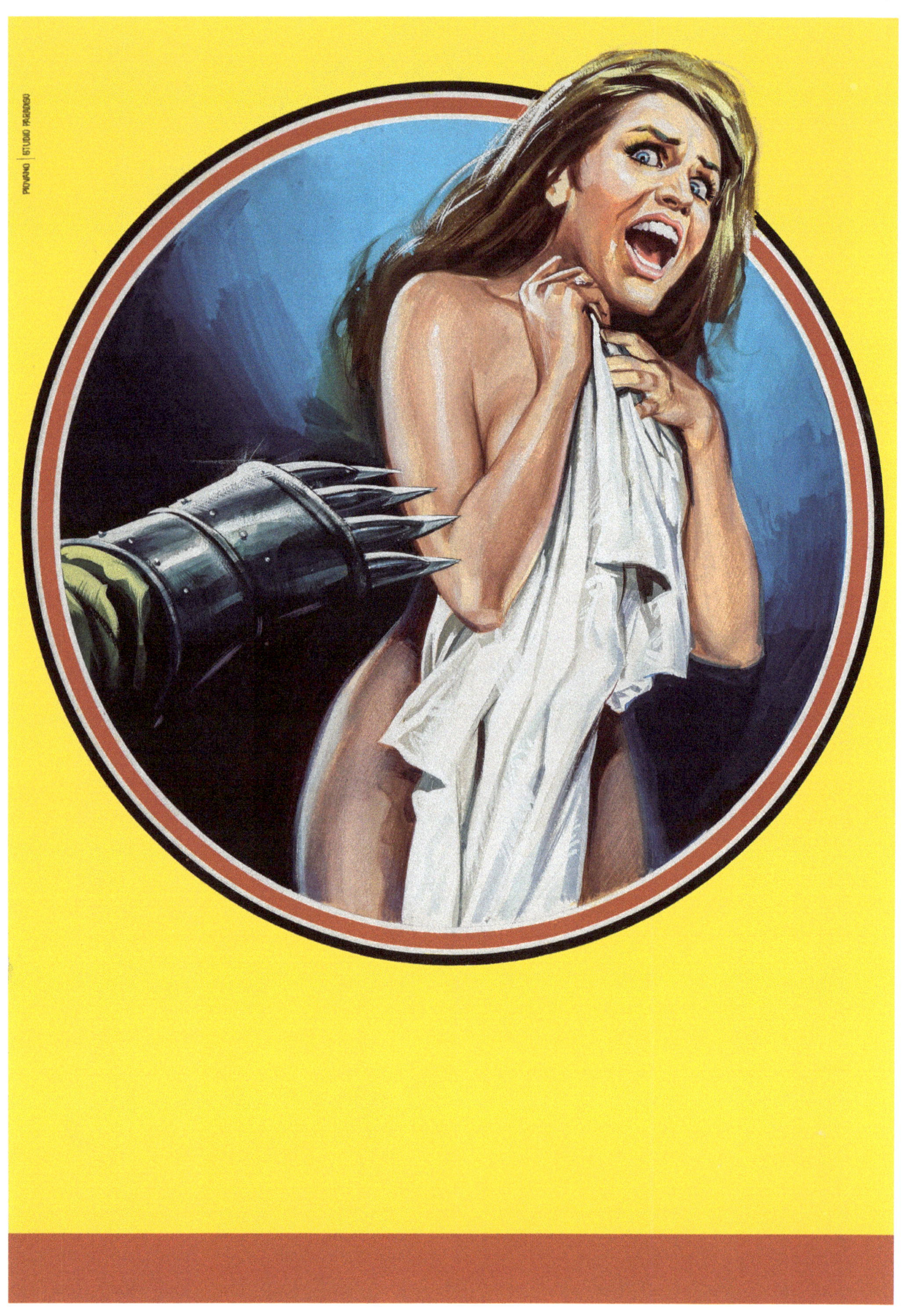

L'ARTIGLIO BLU (1967). Artist: Mario Piovano.

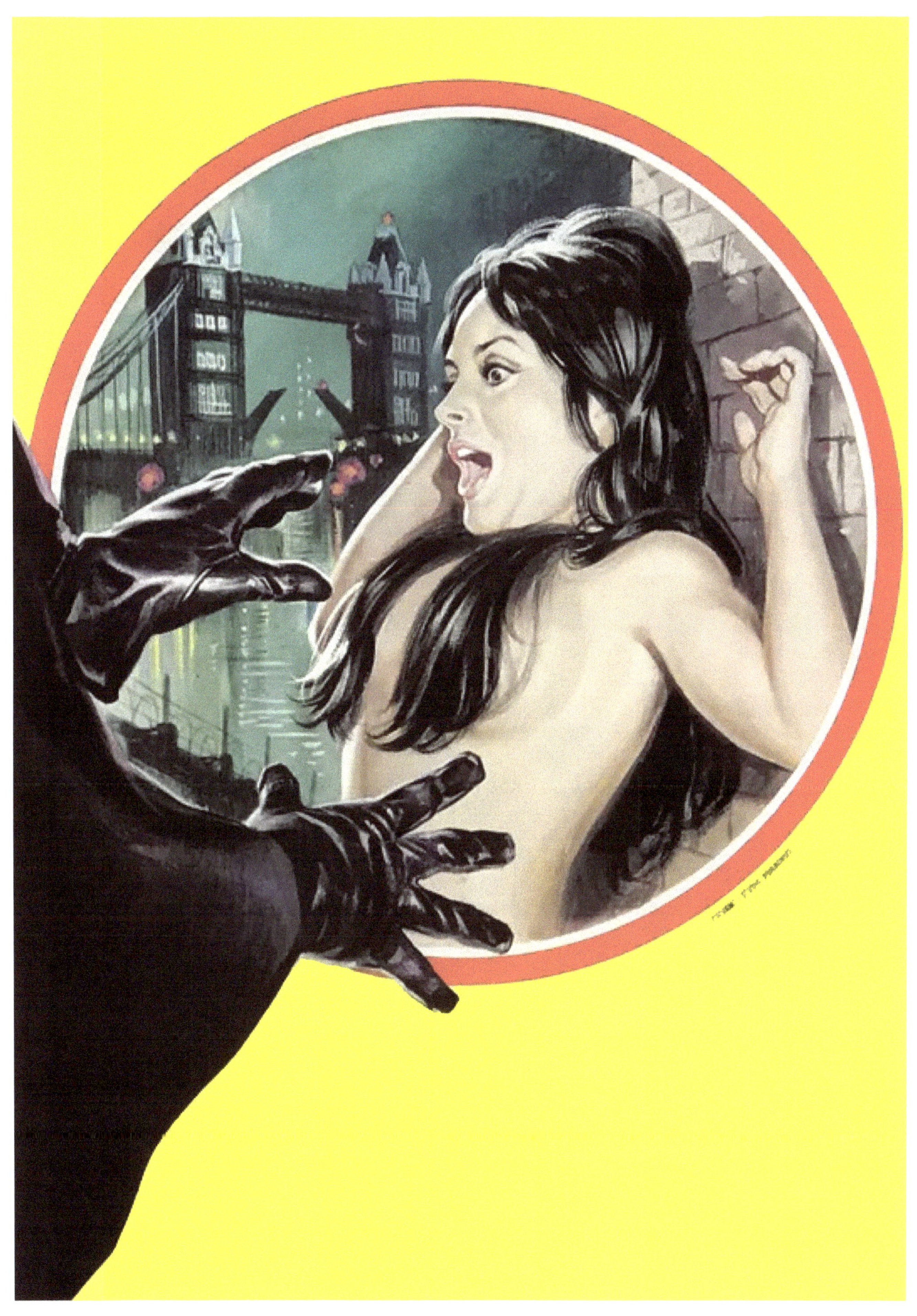

ALLARME A SCOTLAND YARD 6 OMICIDI SENZA ASSASINO! (1972). Artist: Mario Piovano.

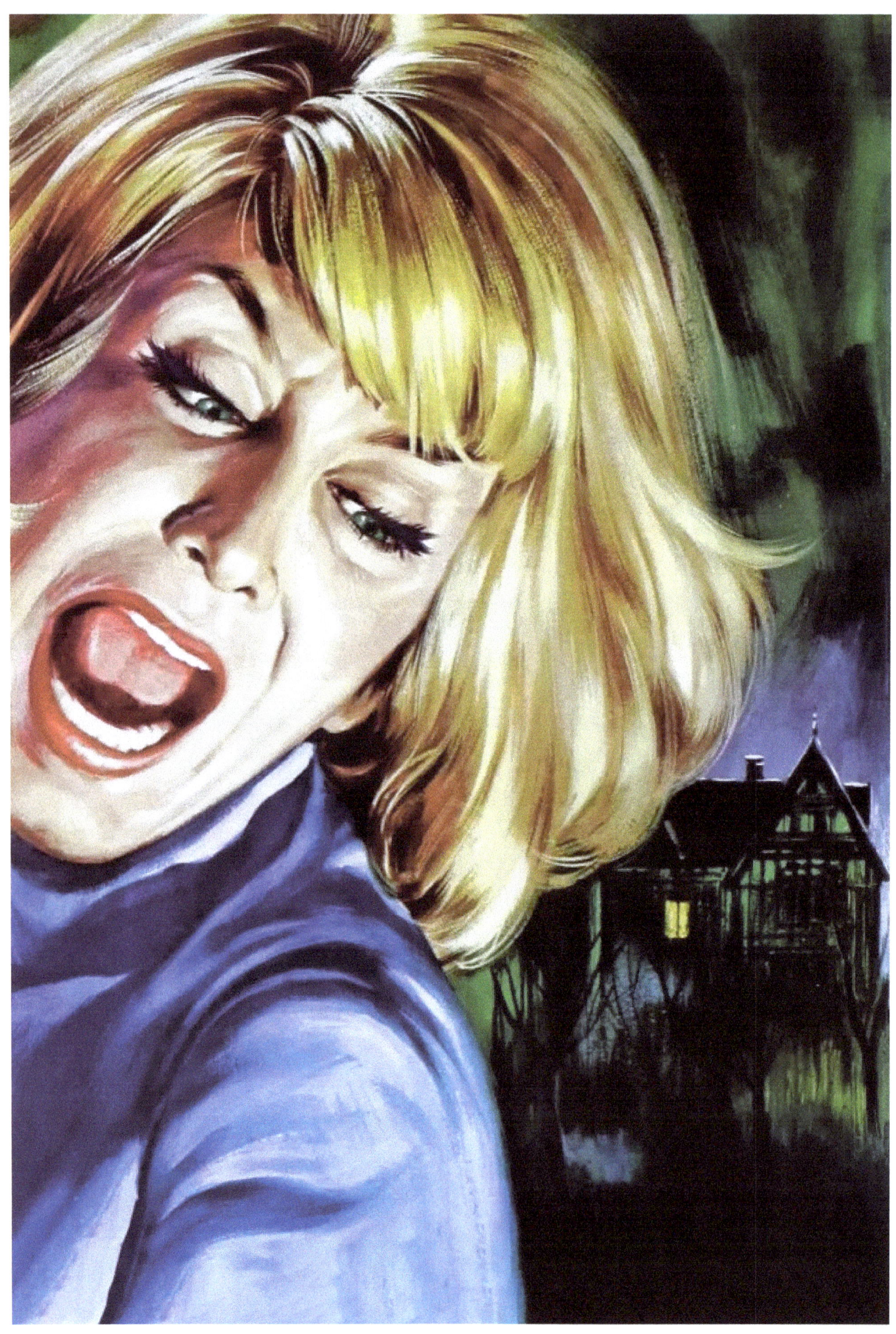

GIALLO COBRA (1968). Artist: unsigned.

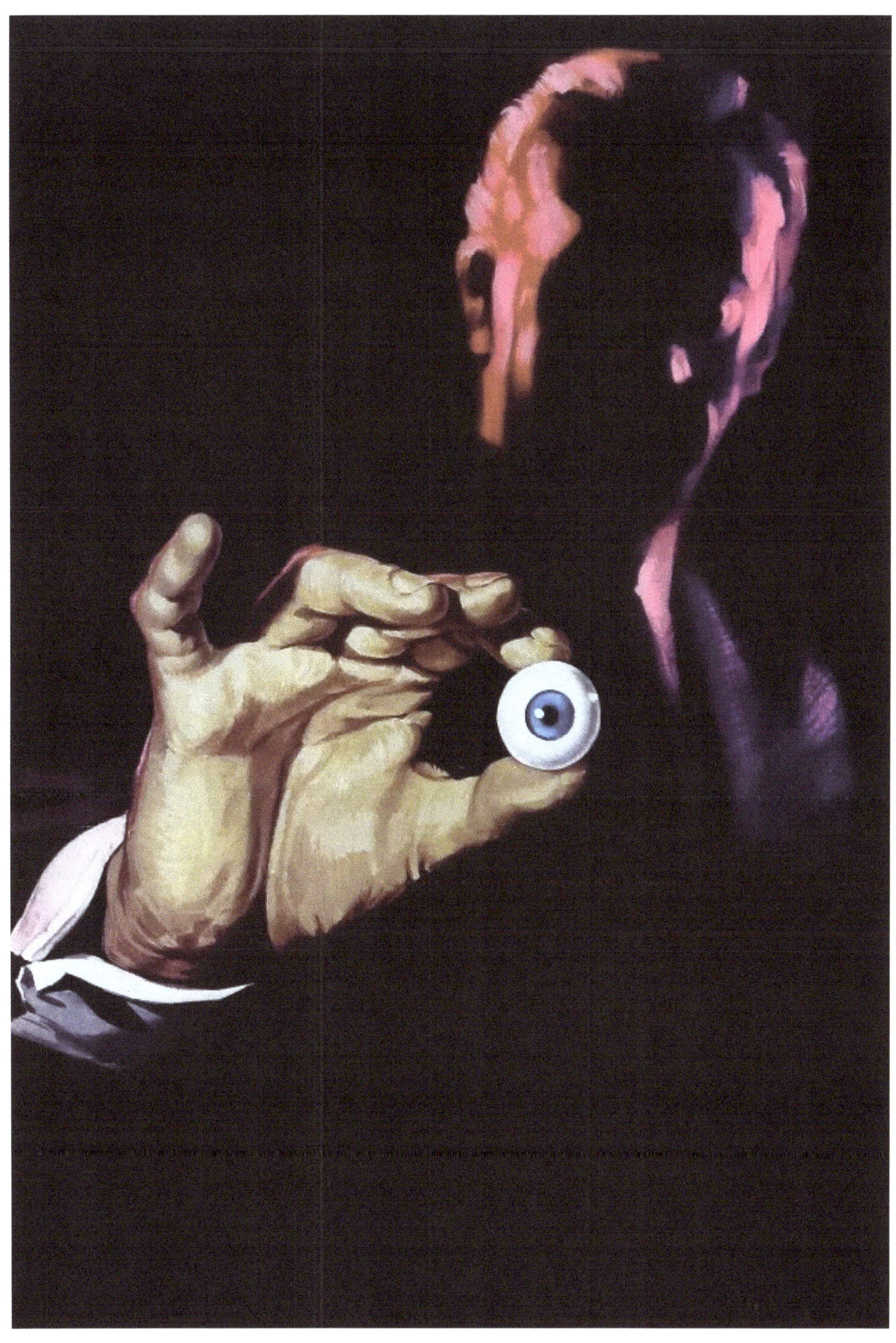

L'UOMO DALL'OCCHIO DI VETRO (1969). Artist: unsigned.

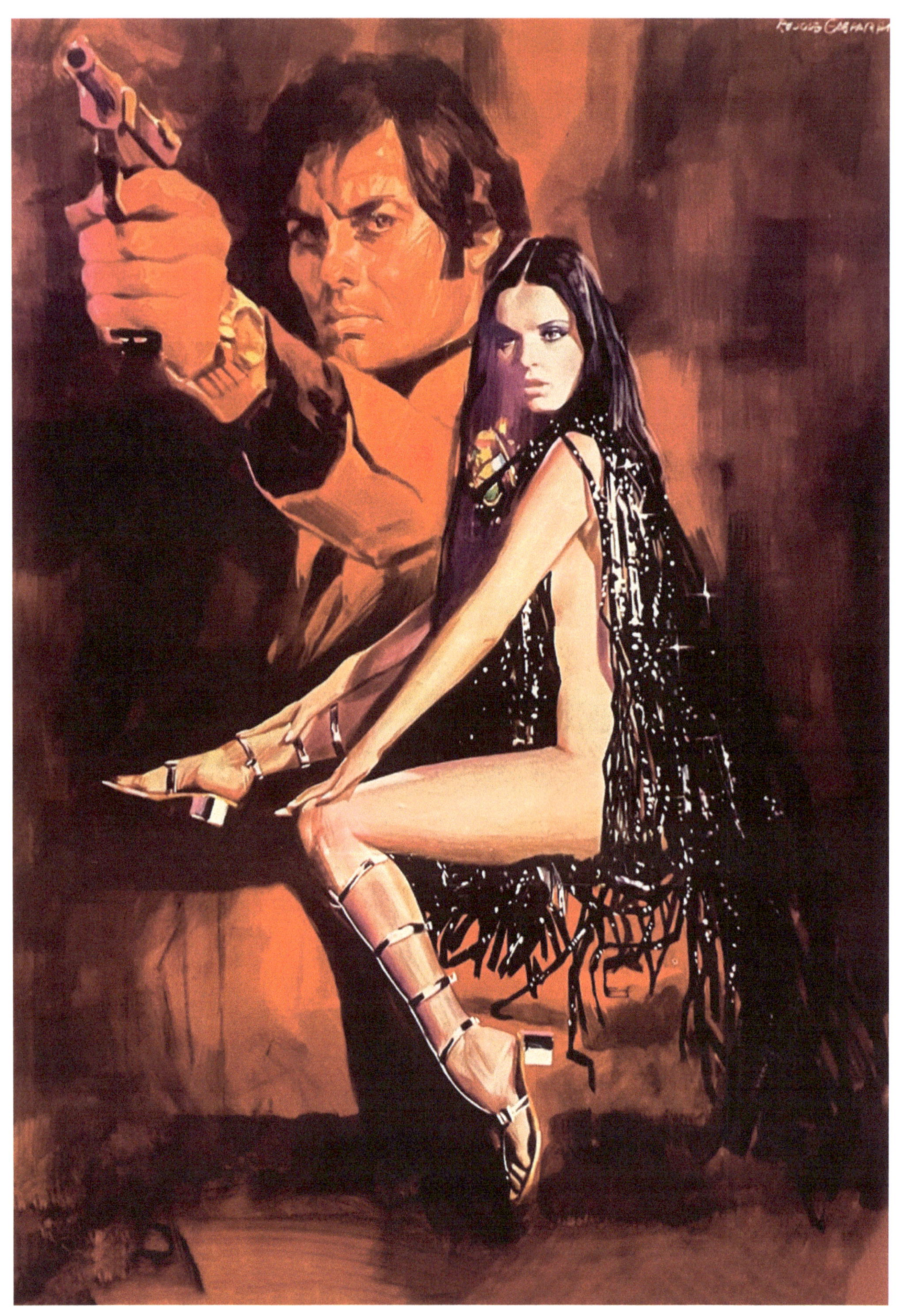

UNA VENERE SENZA NOME PER L'ISPETTORE FORRESTER (1971). Artist: Rodolfo Gasparri.

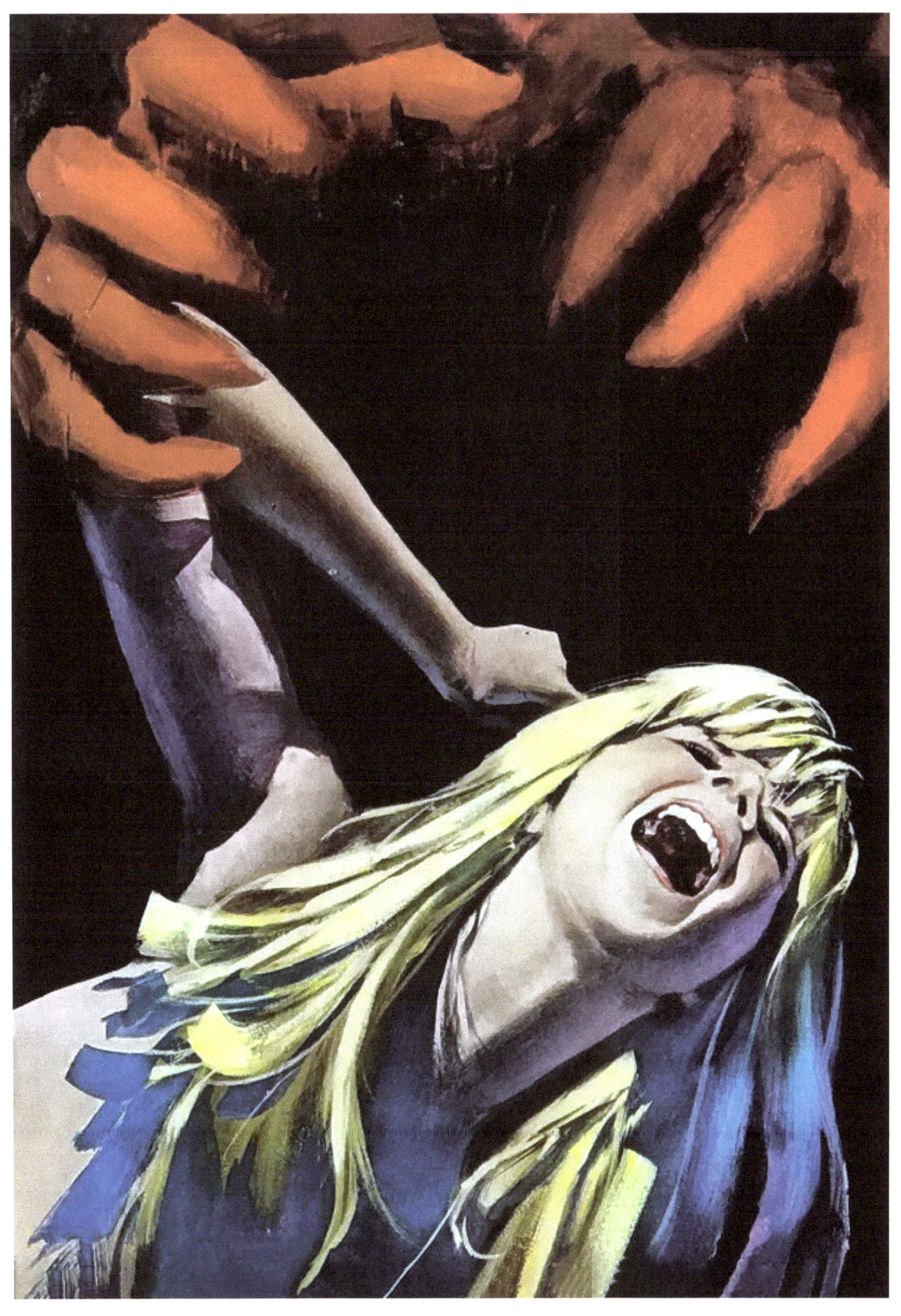

IL CIGNO DAGLI ARTIGLI DI FUOCO (1970). Artist: unsigned.

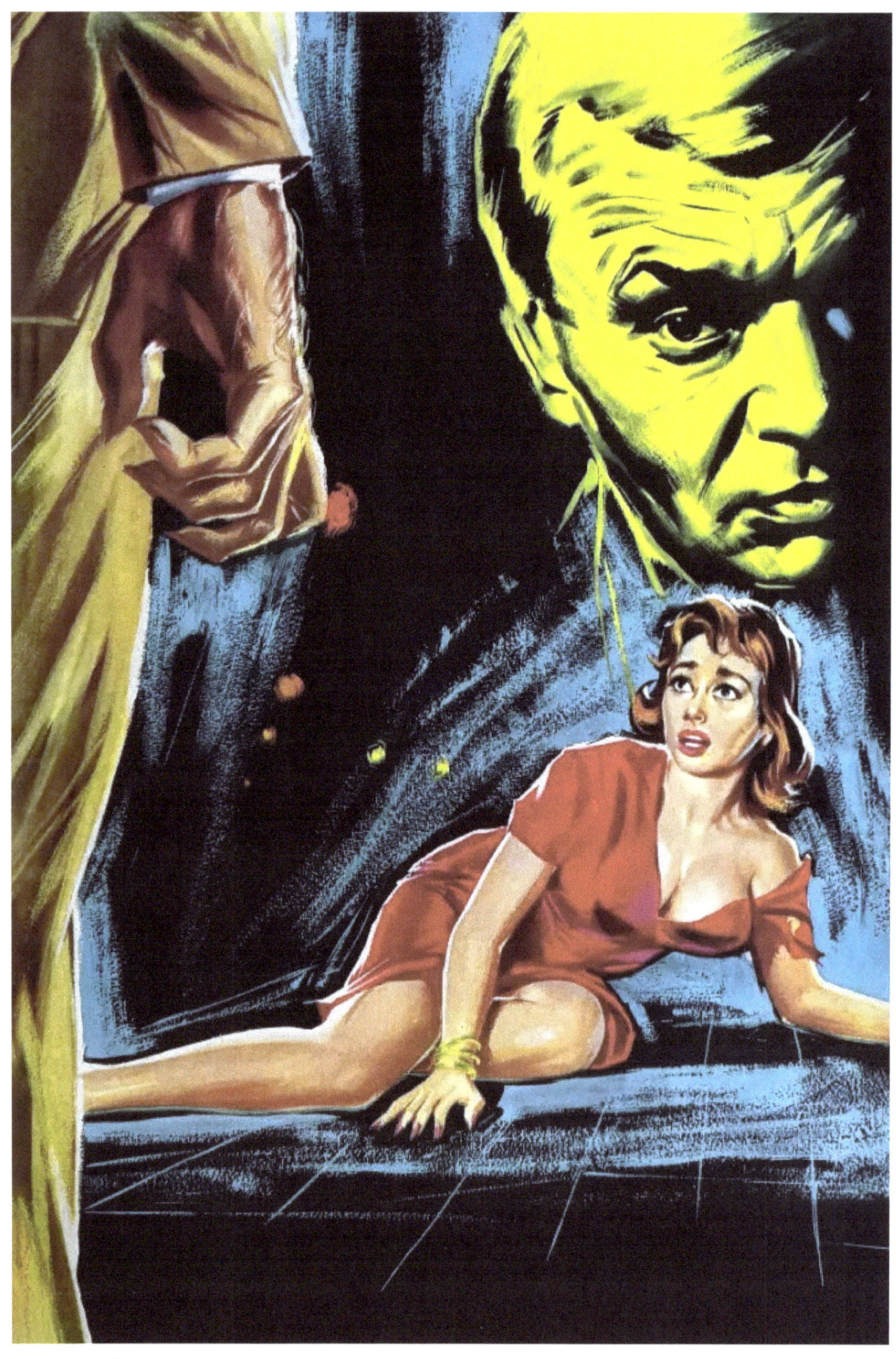

IL DOTTOR CRIPPEN È VIVO! (1958). Artist: unsigned.

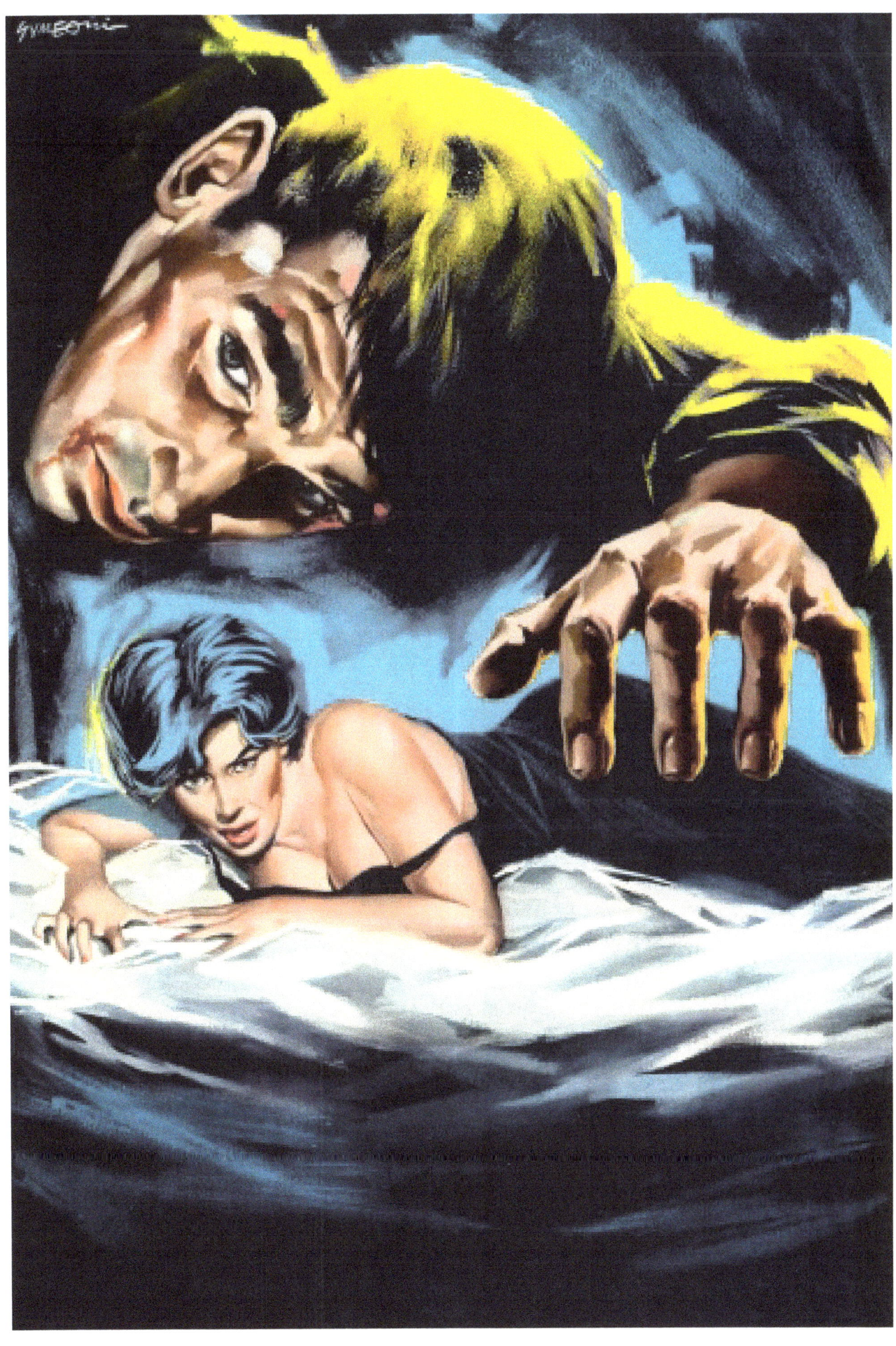

I VAMPIRI DEL SESSO (1959). Artist: Sandro Symeoni.

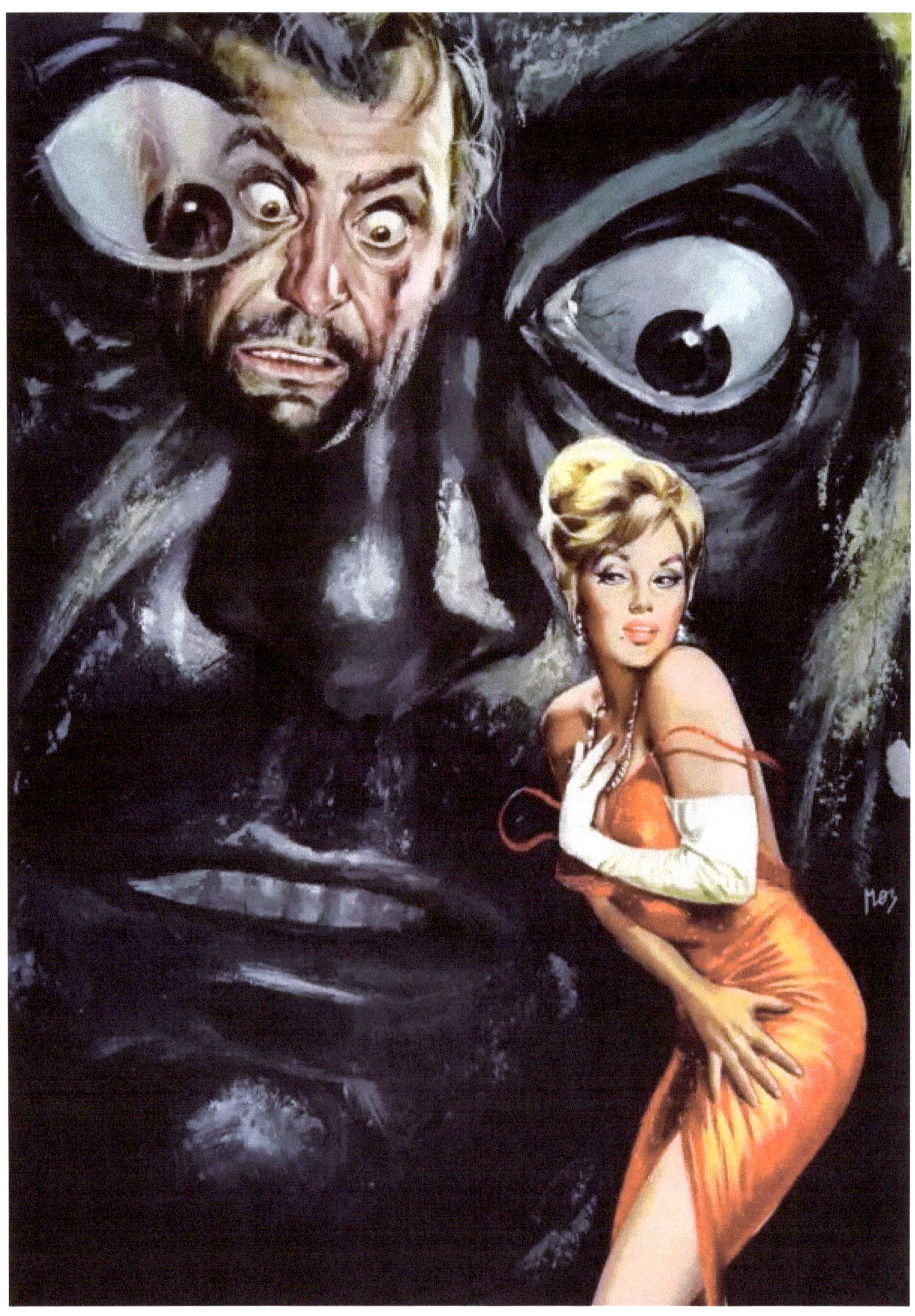

SESSO E VIOLENZA (1963). Artist: Mario De Berardinis.

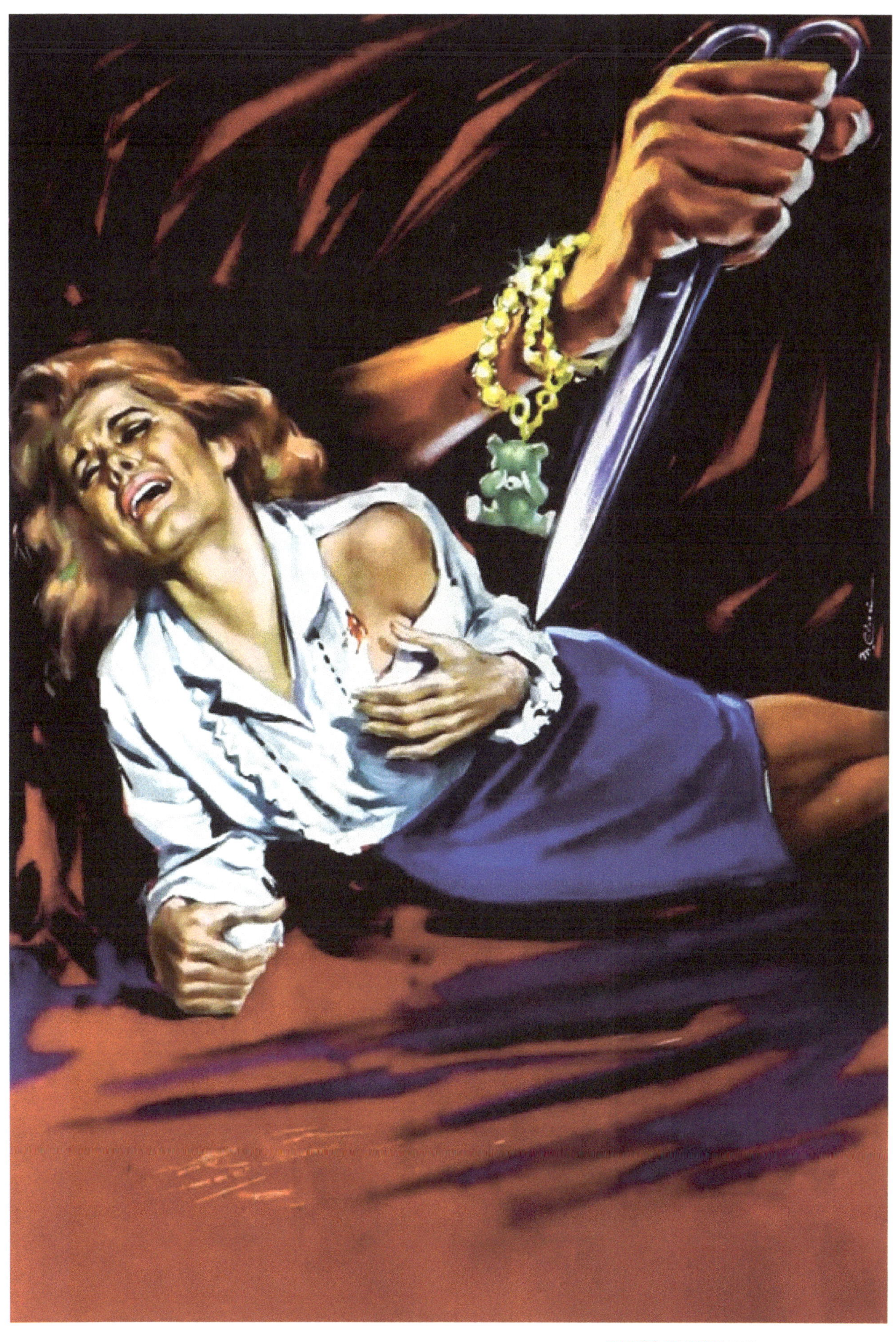

UNA NOTTE PER MORIRE (1965). Artist: Mauro Colizzi.

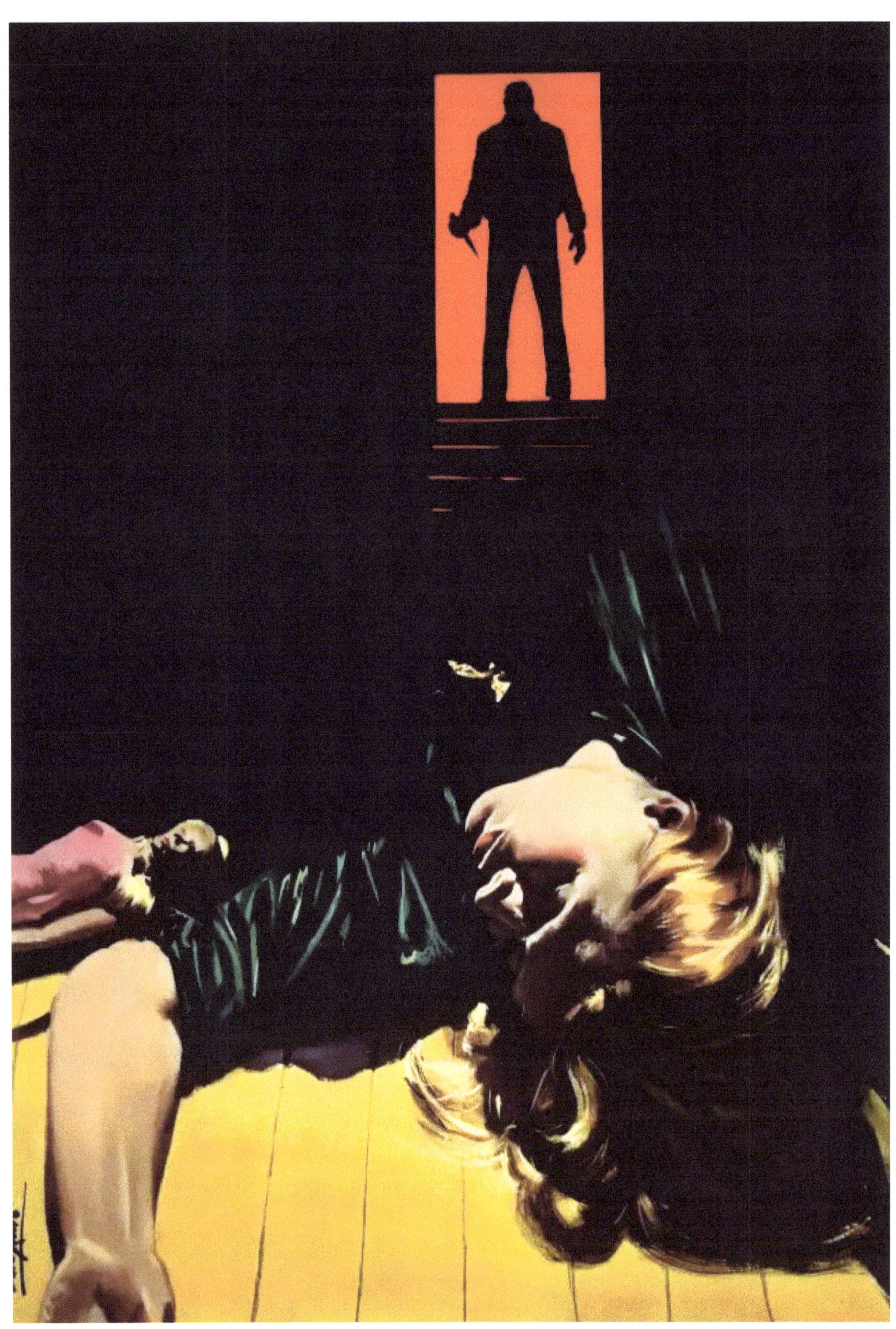

LA BAMBOLA DI CERA (1966). Artist: Enzo Nistri.

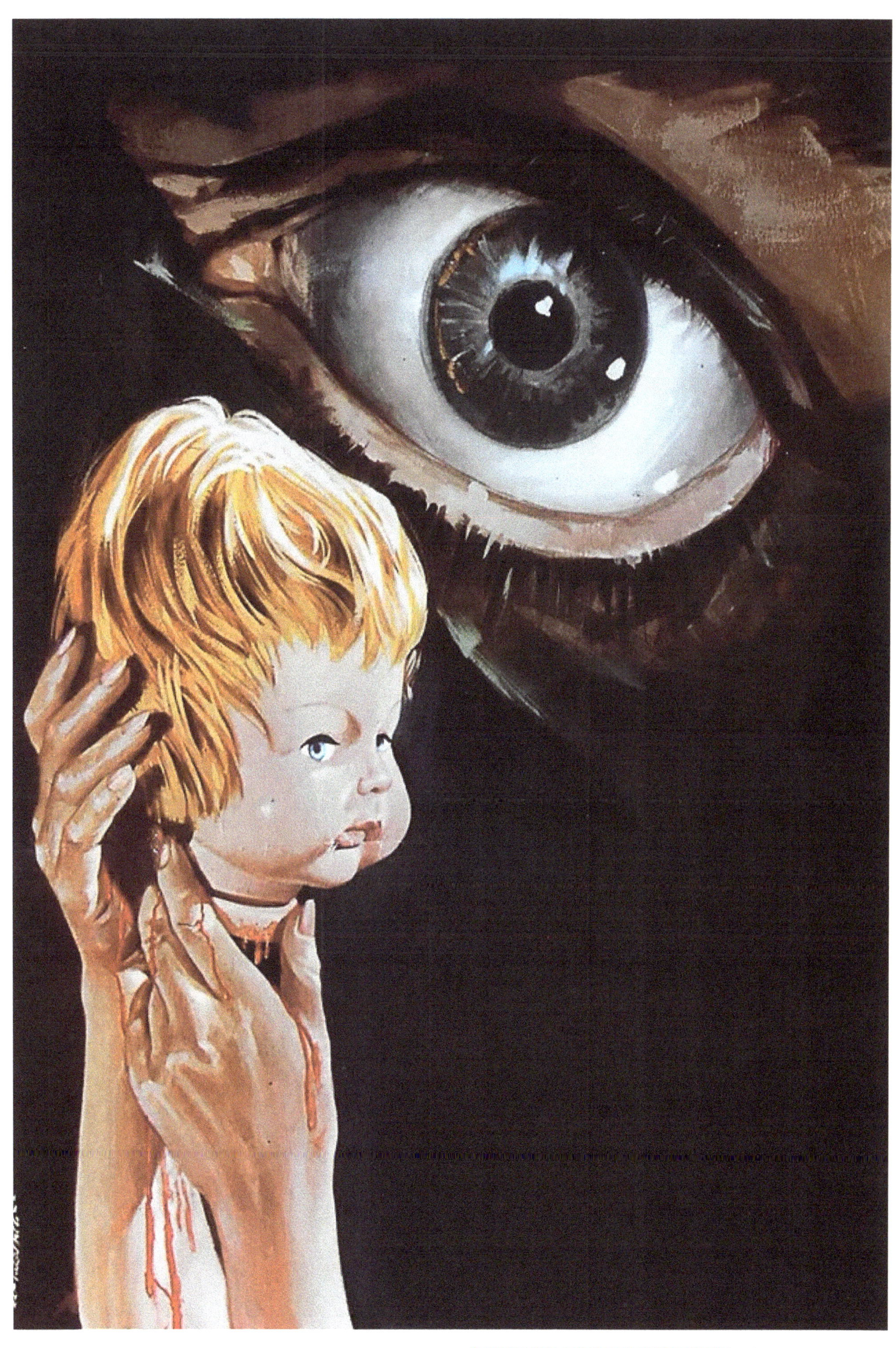

IL MISTERO DELLA BAMBOLA DALLA TESTA MOZZATA **(1968)**. Artist: Ezio Tarantelli.

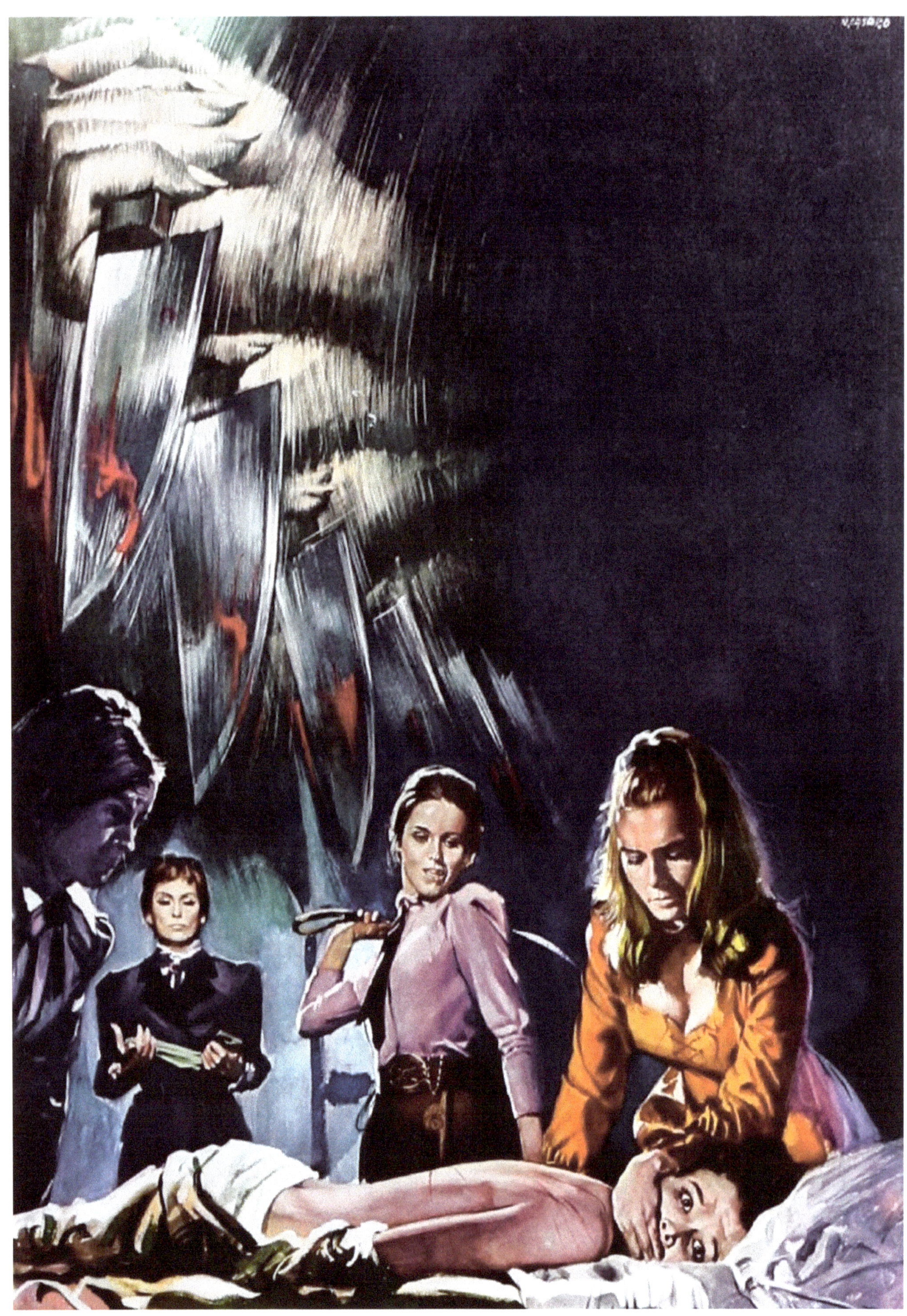

GLI ORRORI DEL LICEO FEMMINILE (1969). Artist: Renato Casaro.

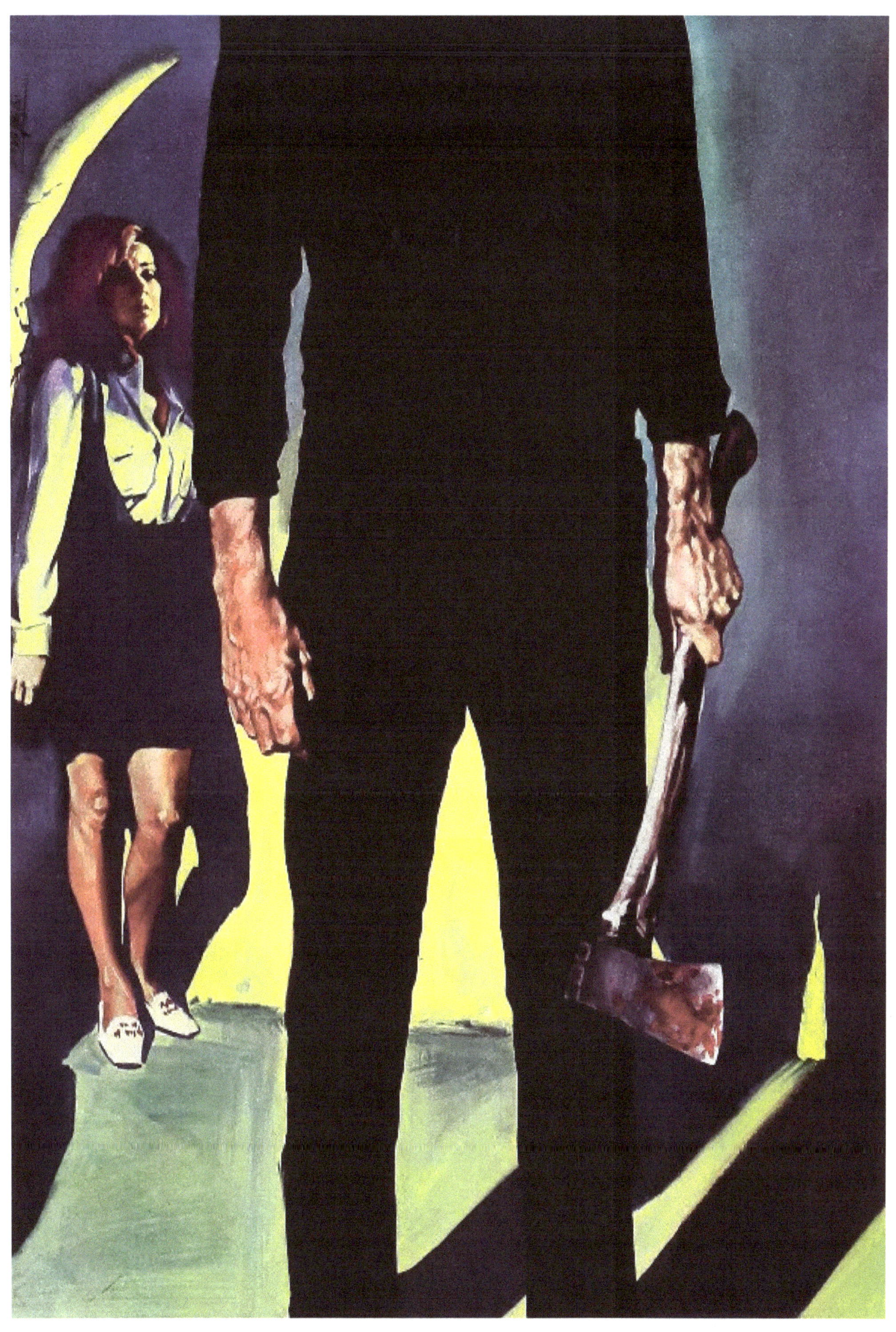

93

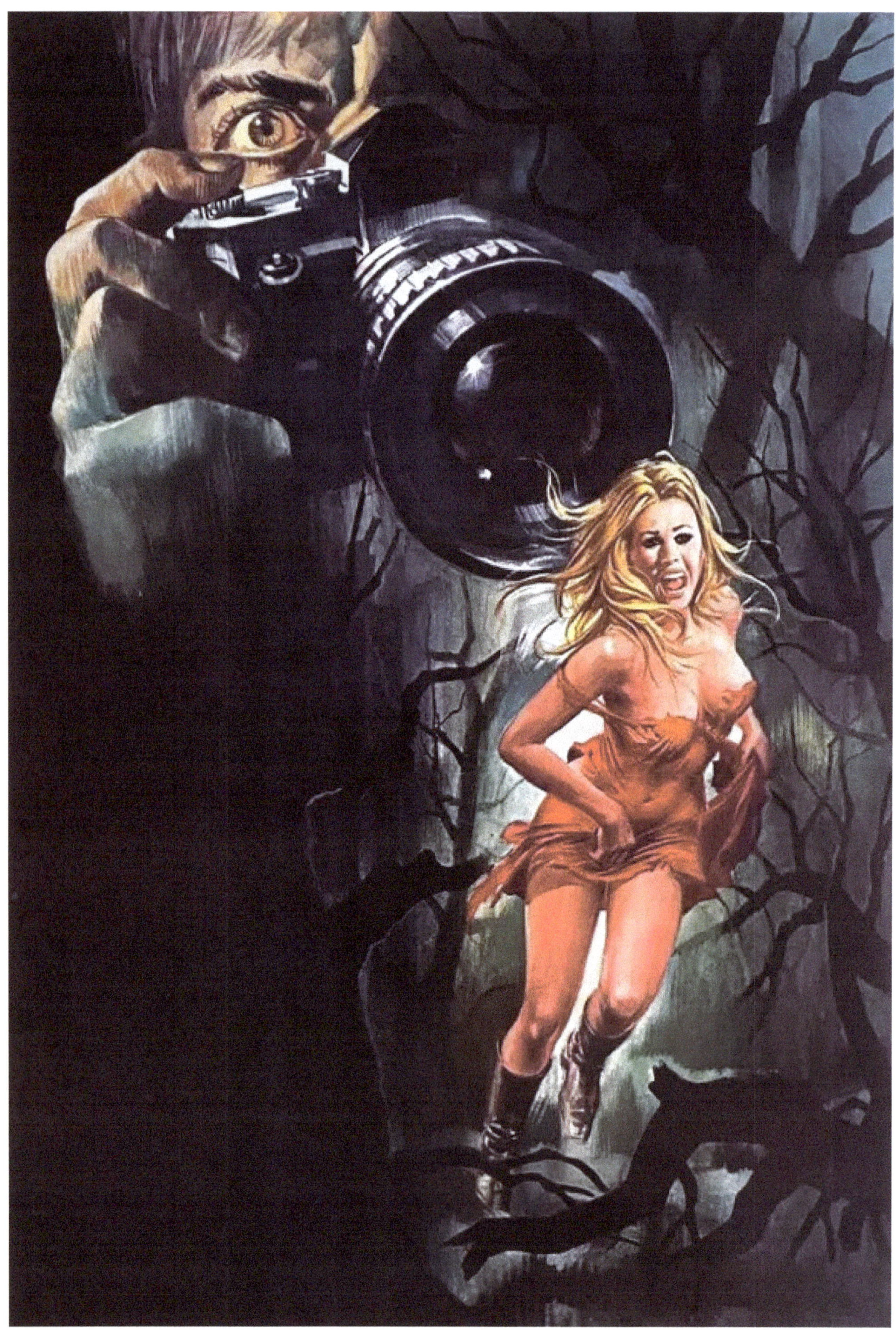

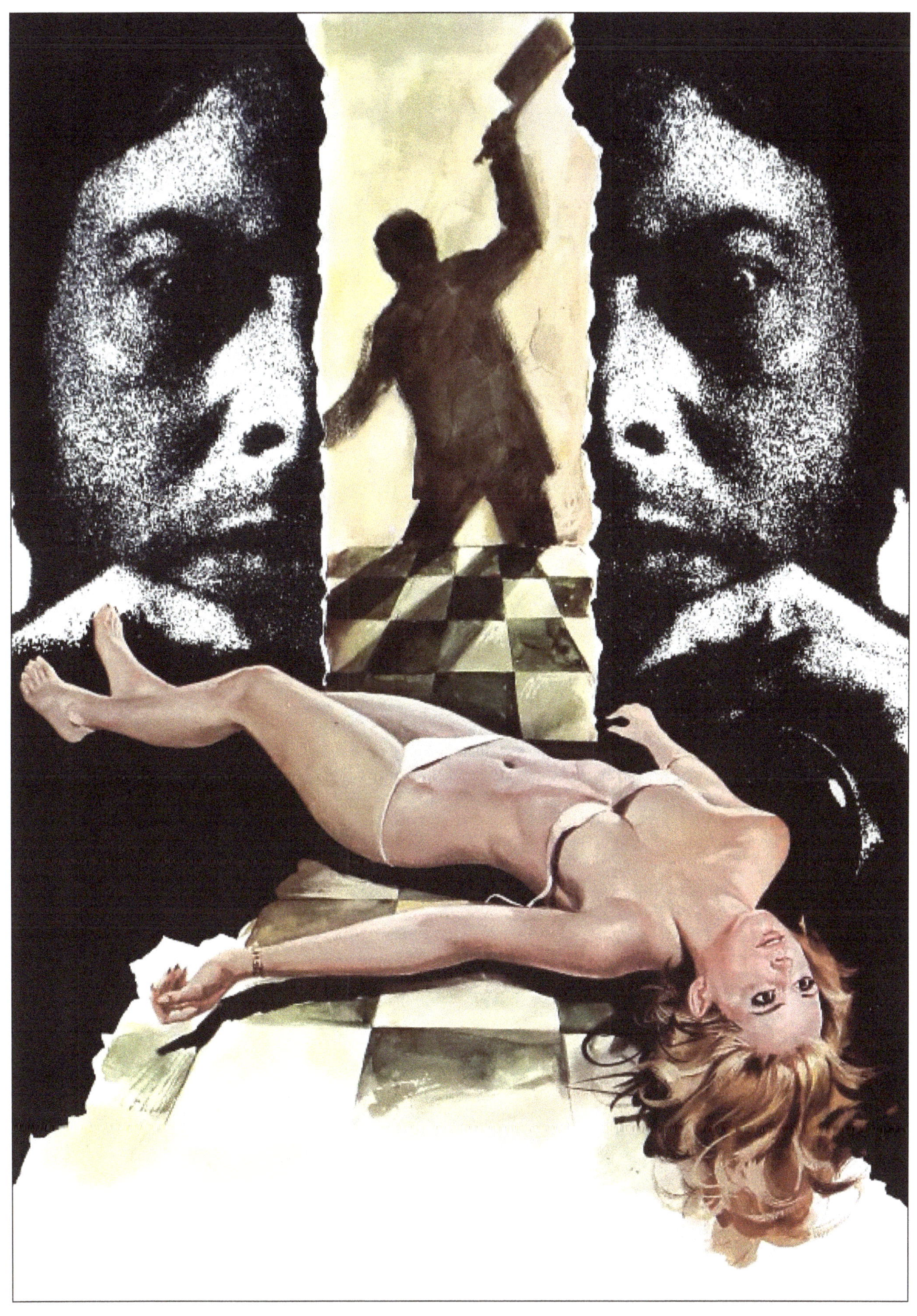

L'APPARTAMENTO DEL 13° PIANO (1973). Artist: unsigned.

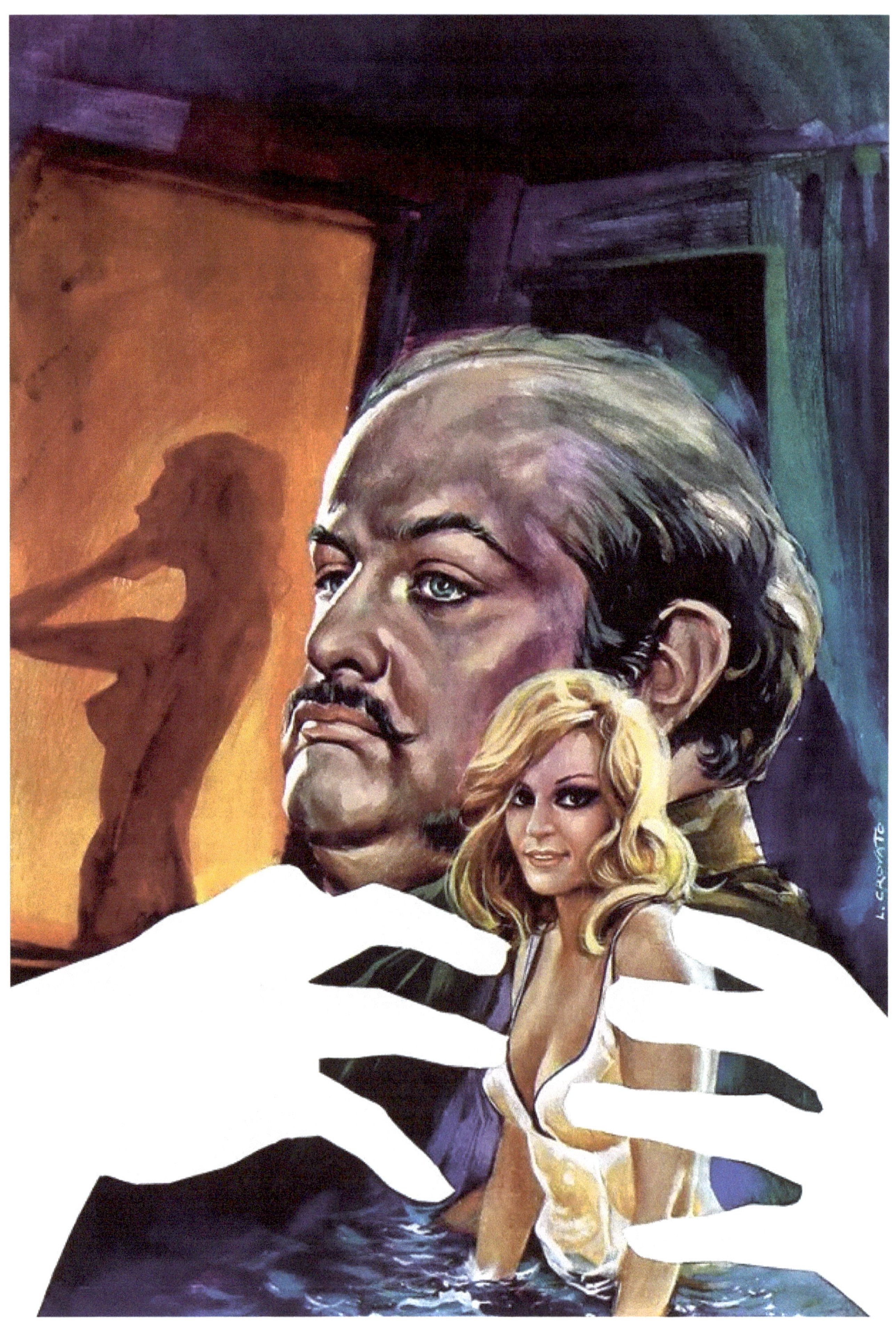

LO STRANGOLATORE DI VIENNA (1971). Artist: Luca Crovato.

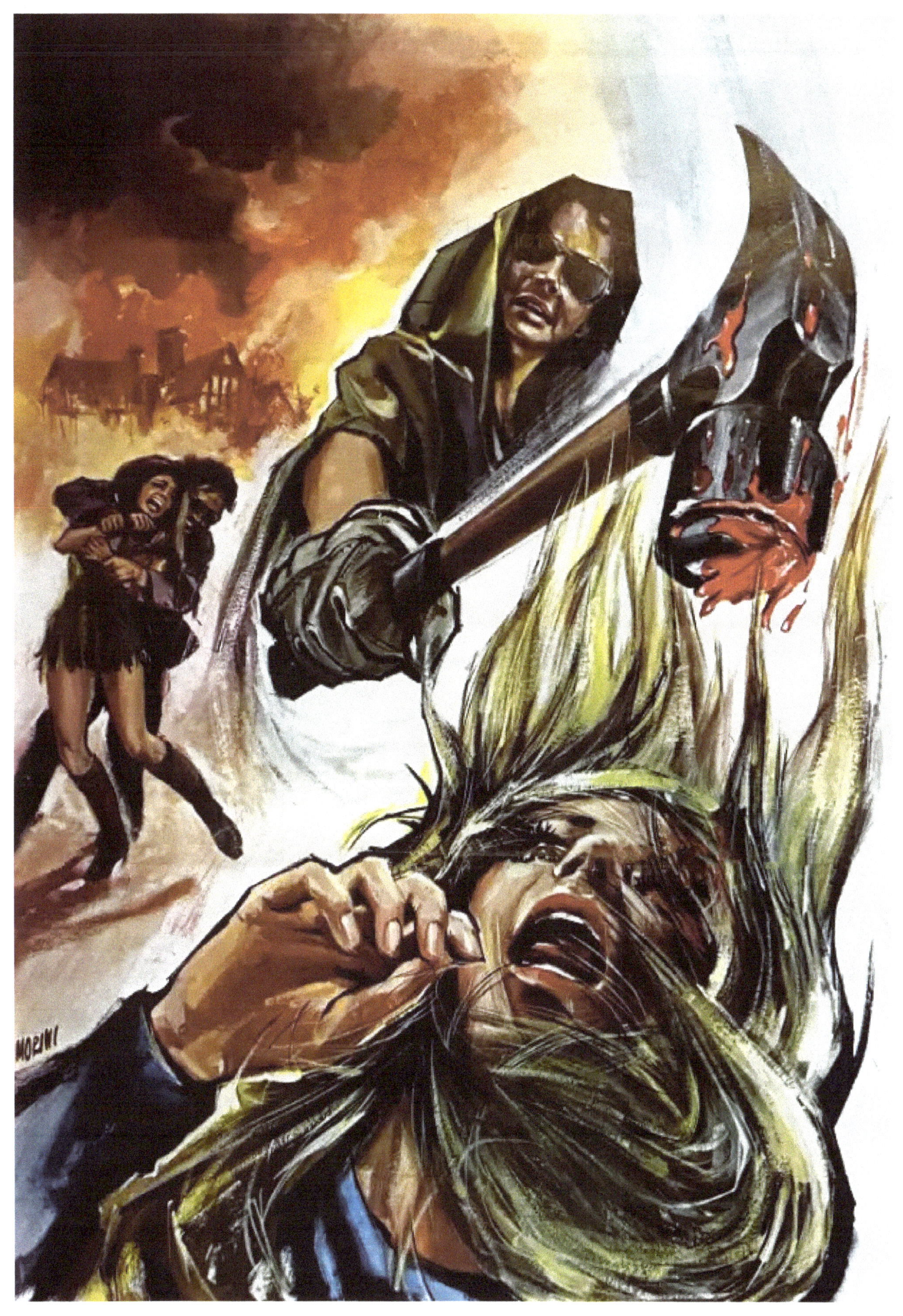

IL MARTELLO MACCHIATO DI SANGUE (1971). Artist: Morini.

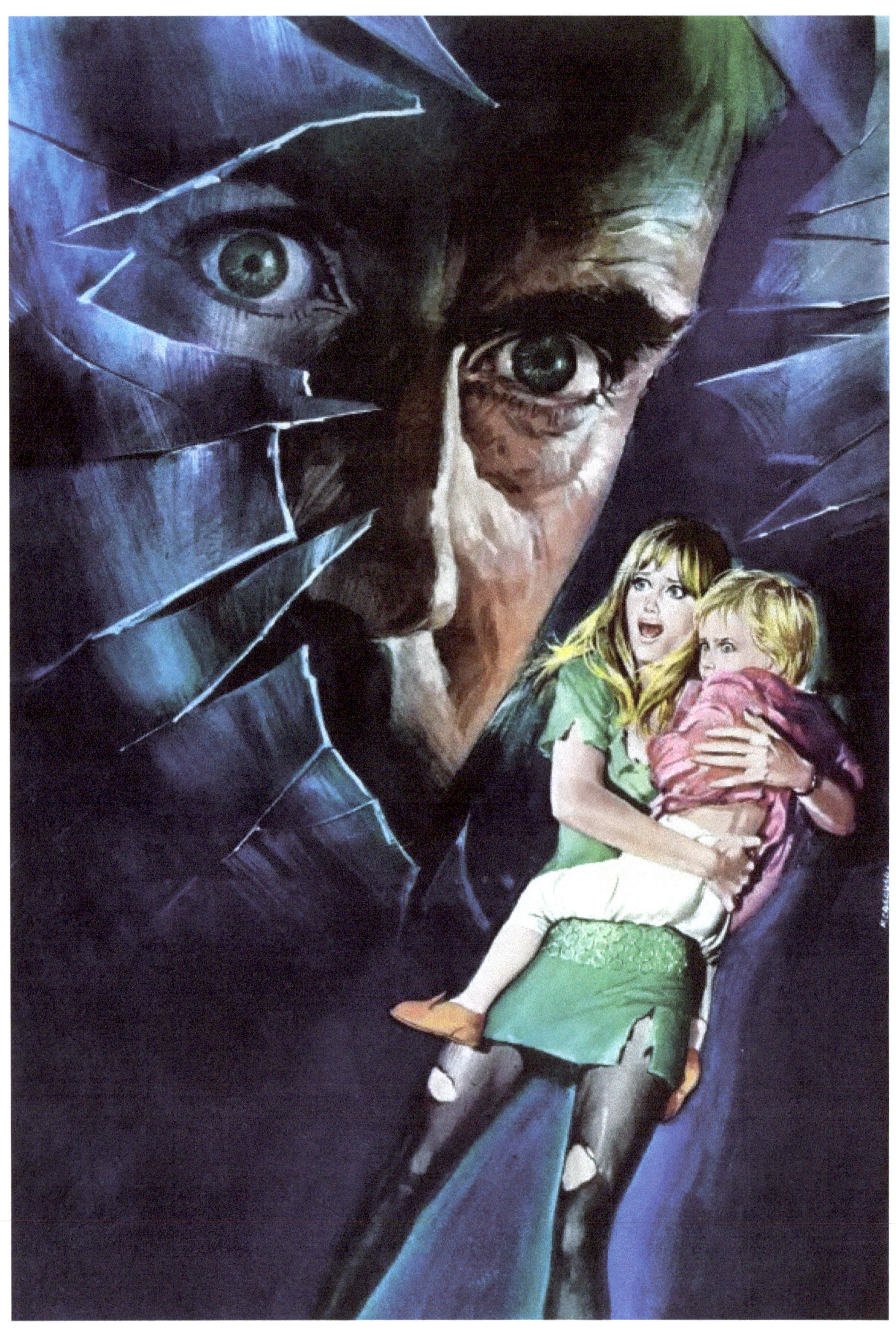

VIOLENZA A UNA BABY SITTER (1971). Artist: Renato Casaro.

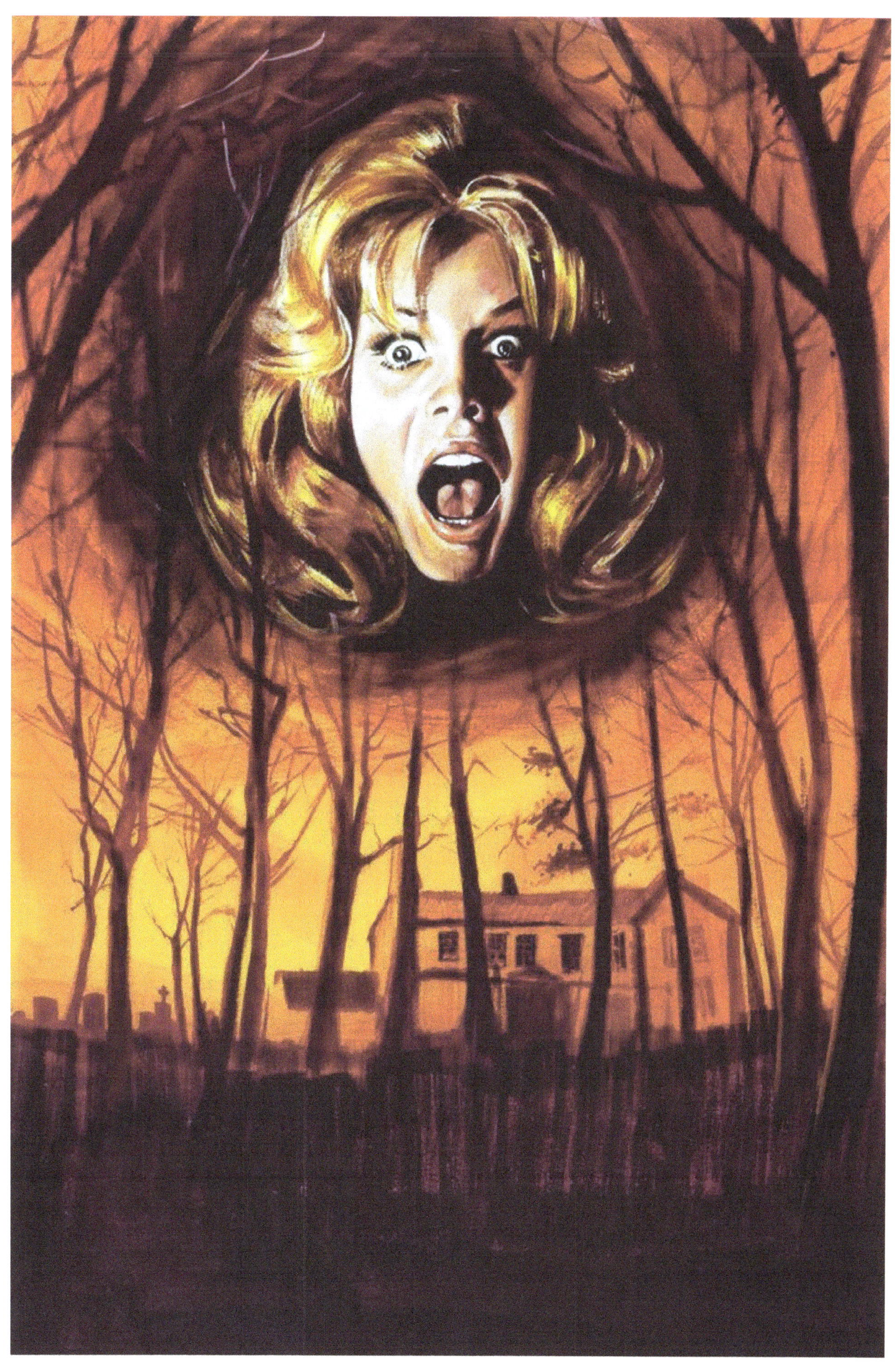

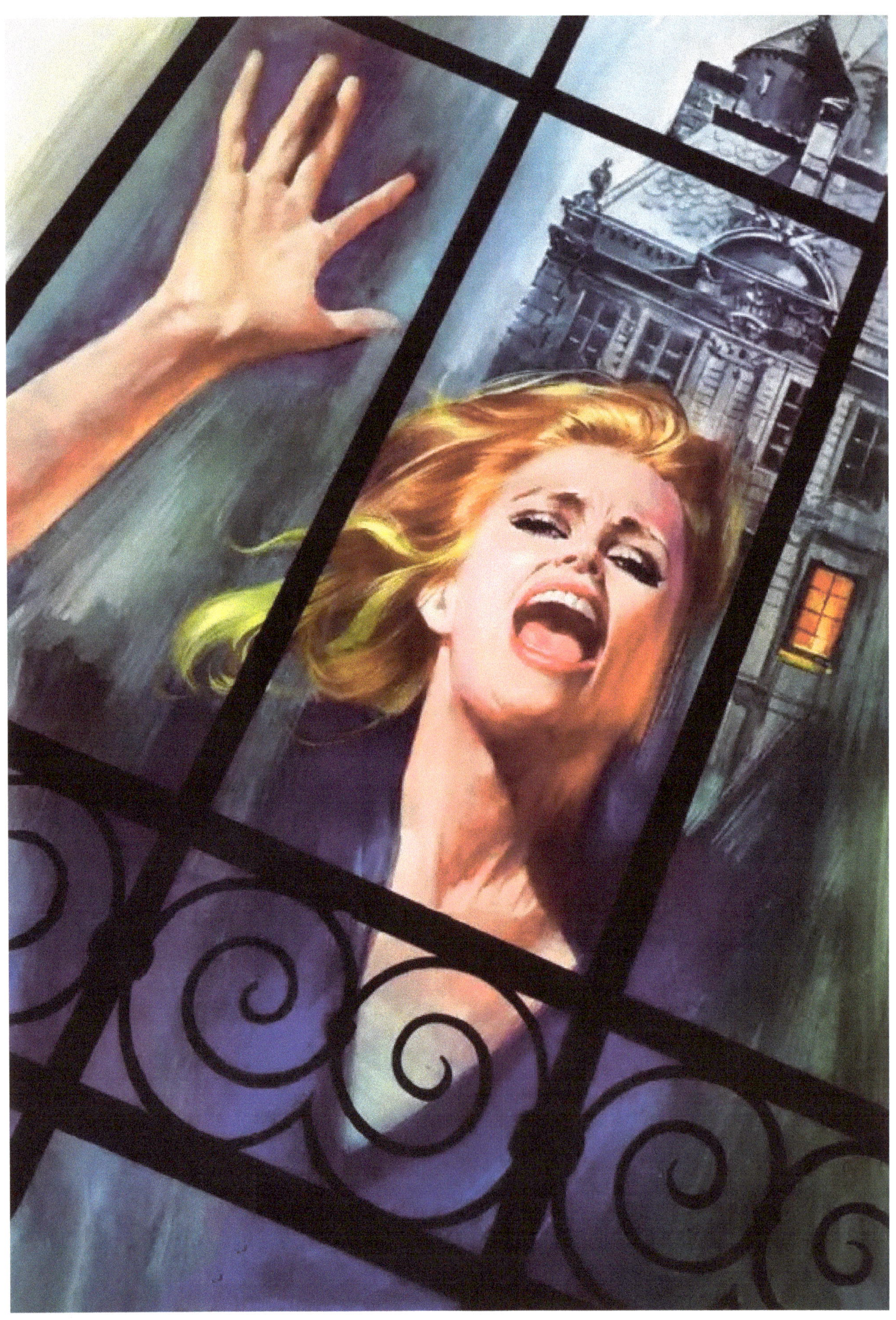

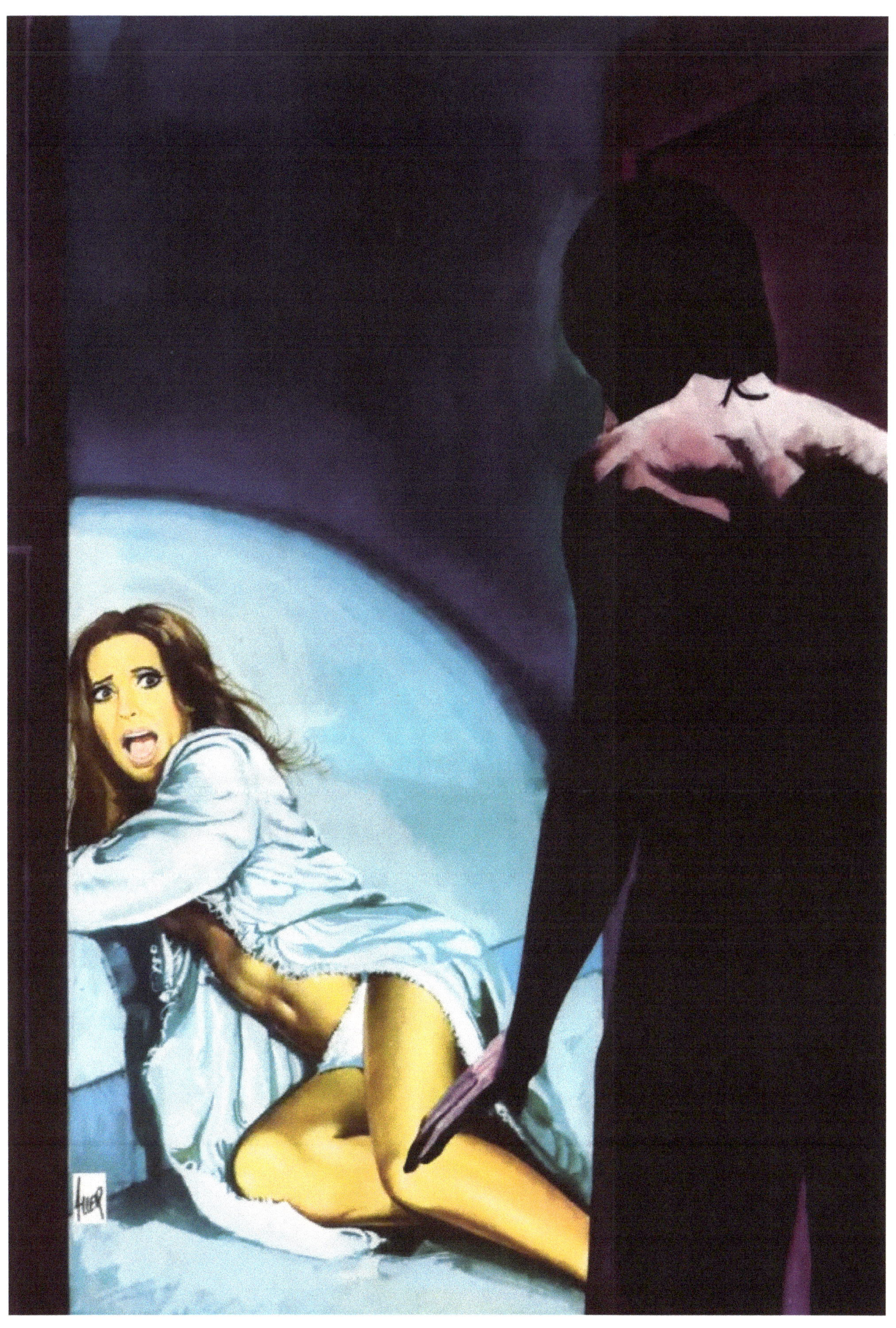

LA CASA DELLA PAURA (1973). Artist: Carlo Alessandrini.

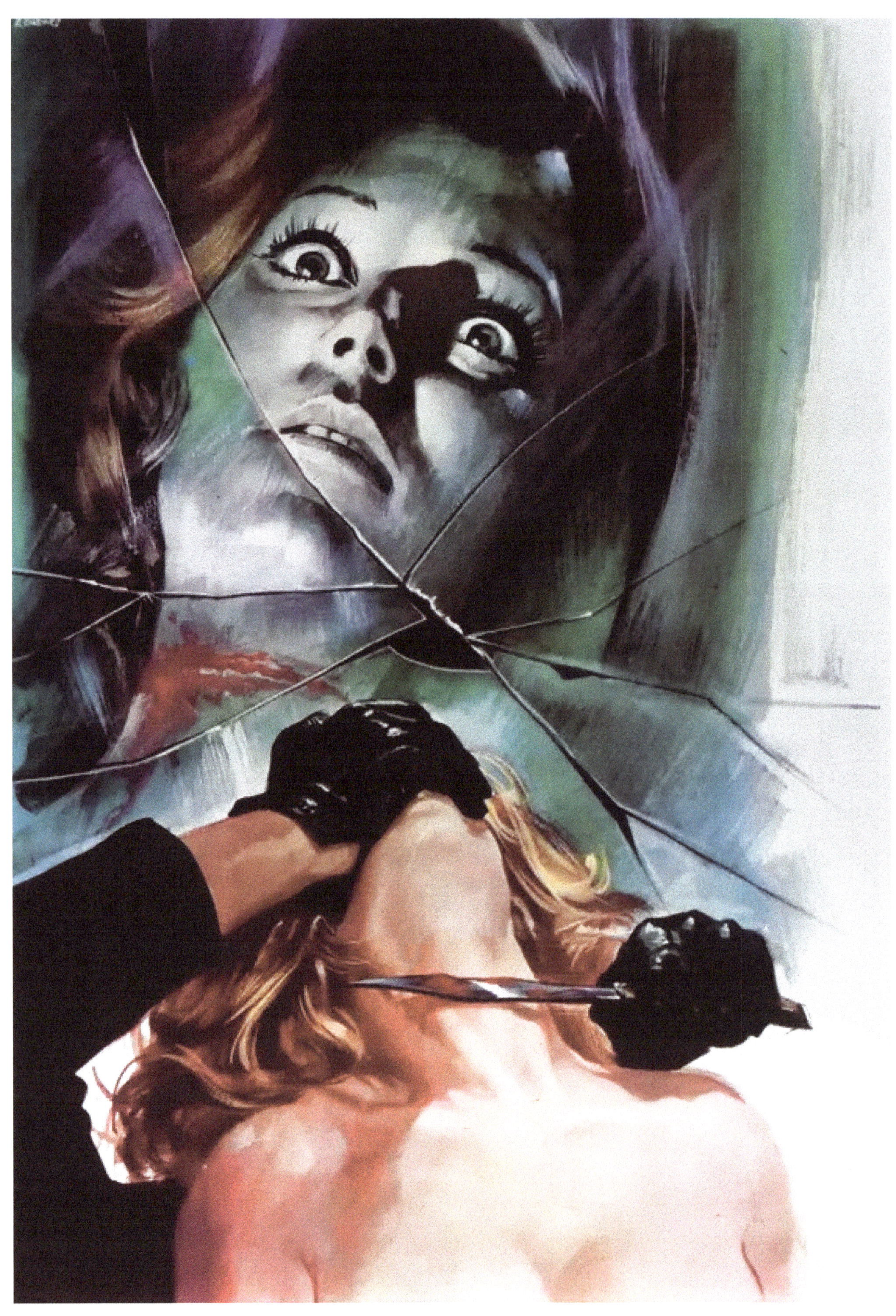

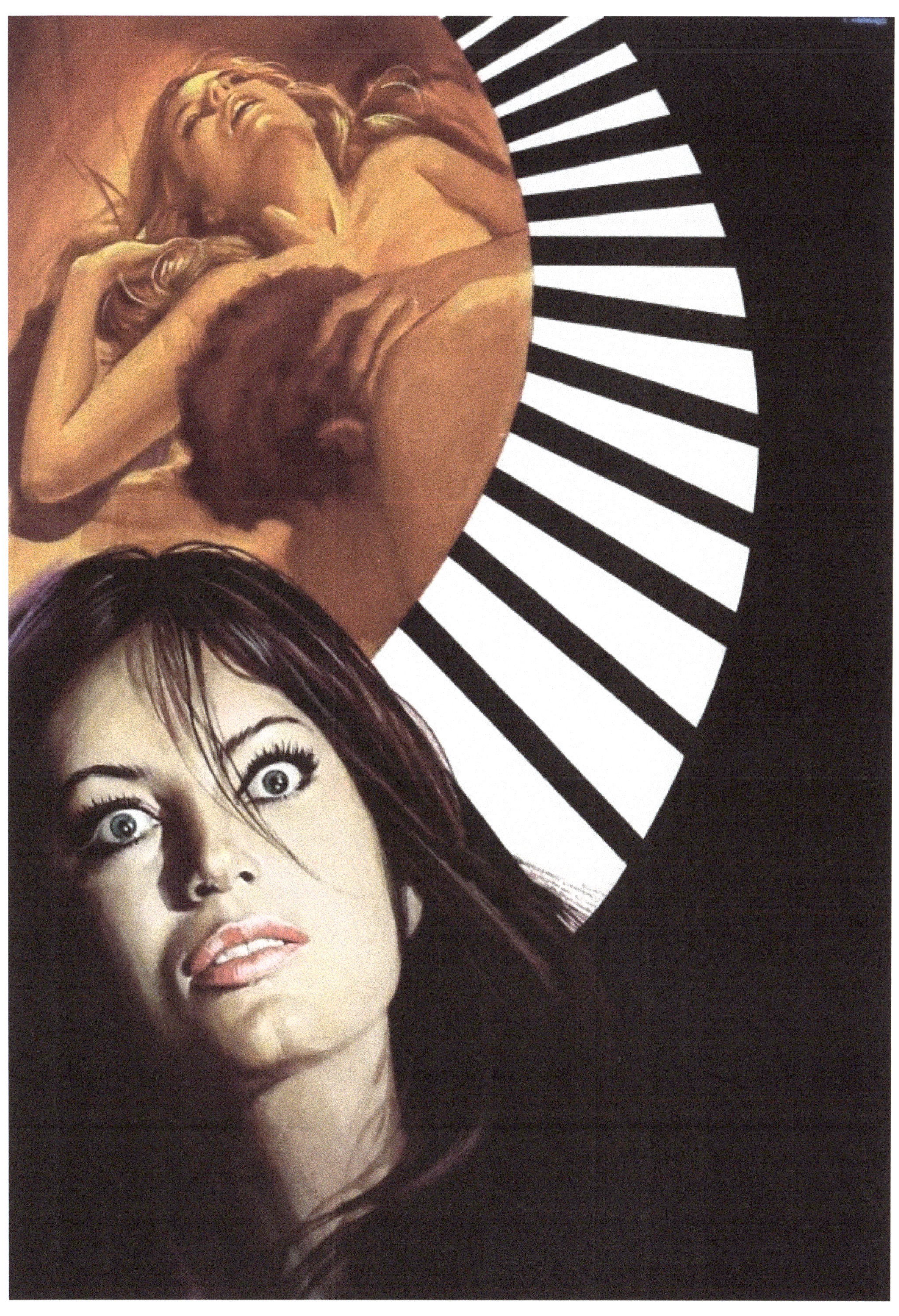

PERVERSIONE (1973). Artist: Renato Casaro.

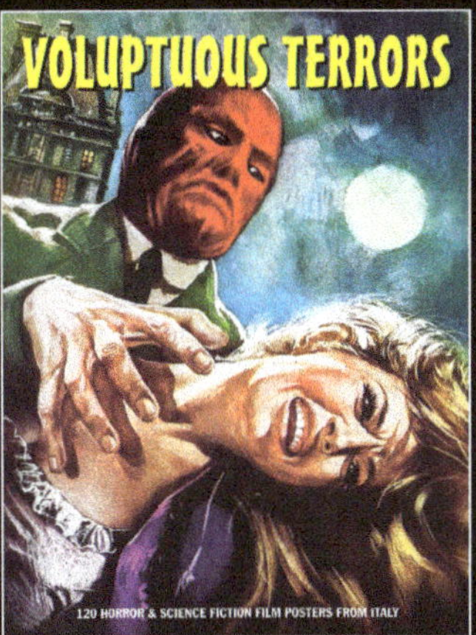
VOLUPTUOUS TERRORS
120 HORROR & SCIENCE FICTION FILM POSTERS FROM ITALY

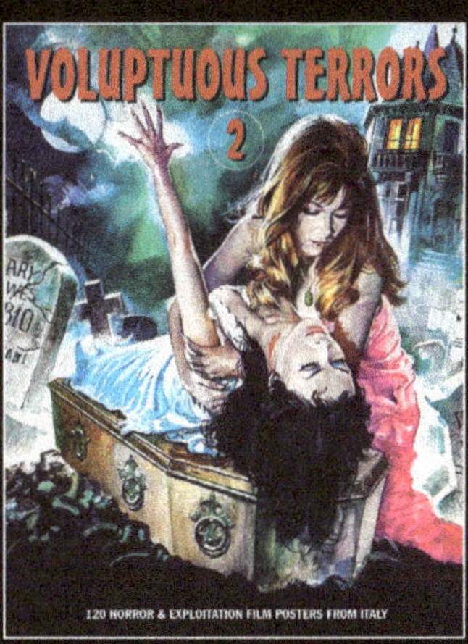
VOLUPTUOUS TERRORS
2
120 HORROR & EXPLOITATION FILM POSTERS FROM ITALY

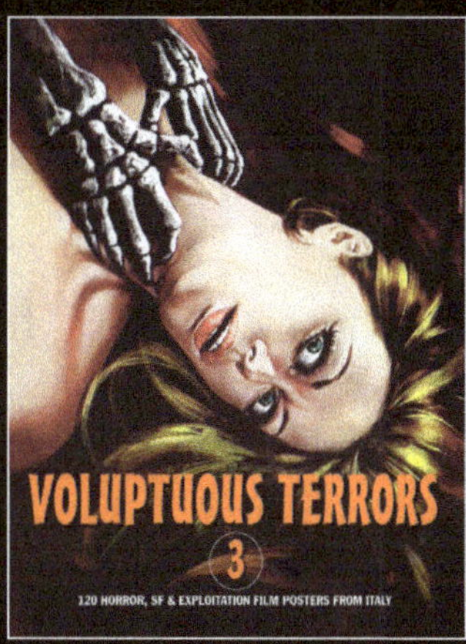
VOLUPTUOUS TERRORS
3
120 HORROR, SF & EXPLOITATION FILM POSTERS FROM ITALY

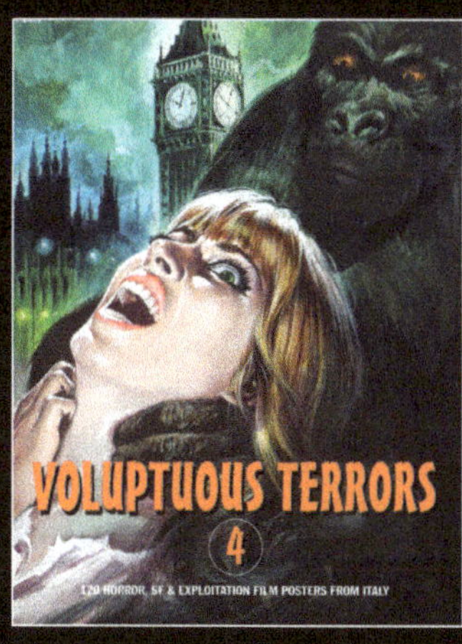
VOLUPTUOUS TERRORS
4
120 HORROR, SF & EXPLOITATION FILM POSTERS FROM ITALY

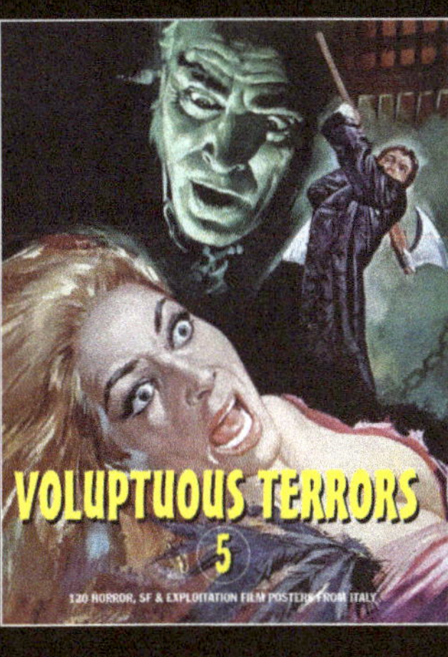
VOLUPTUOUS TERRORS
5
120 HORROR, SF & EXPLOITATION FILM POSTERS FROM ITALY

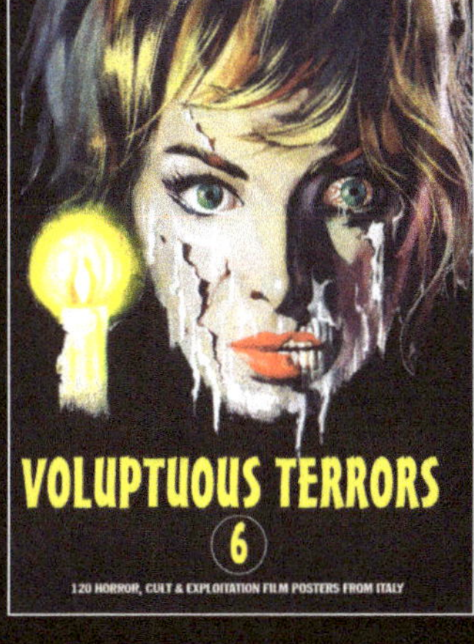
VOLUPTUOUS TERRORS
6
120 HORROR, CULT & EXPLOITATION FILM POSTERS FROM ITALY

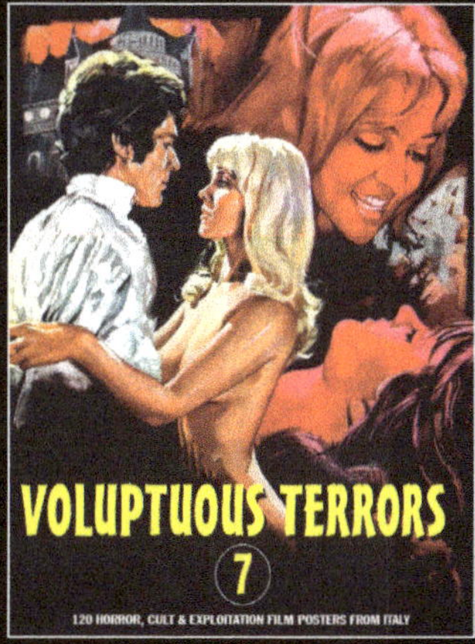
VOLUPTUOUS TERRORS
7
120 HORROR, CULT & EXPLOITATION FILM POSTERS FROM ITALY

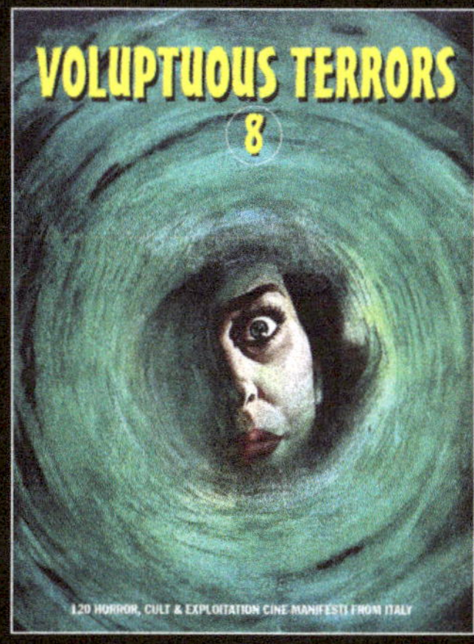
VOLUPTUOUS TERRORS
8
120 HORROR, CULT & EXPLOITATION CINE-MANIFESTI FROM ITALY

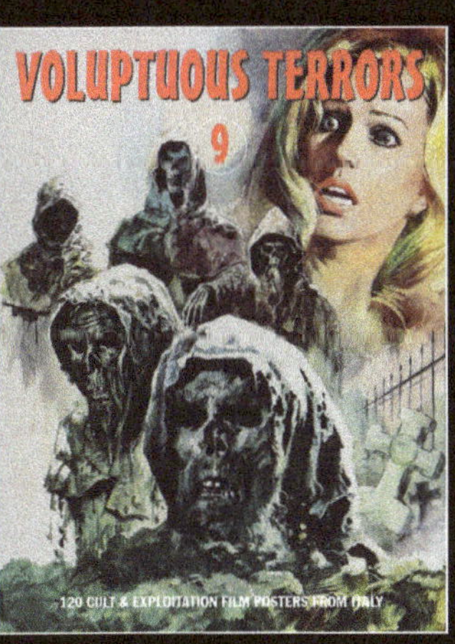
VOLUPTUOUS TERRORS
9
120 CULT & EXPLOITATION FILM POSTERS FROM ITALY

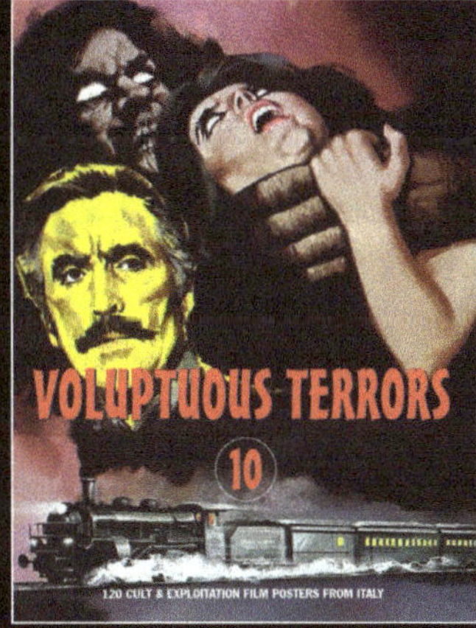
VOLUPTUOUS TERRORS
10
120 CULT & EXPLOITATION FILM POSTERS FROM ITALY

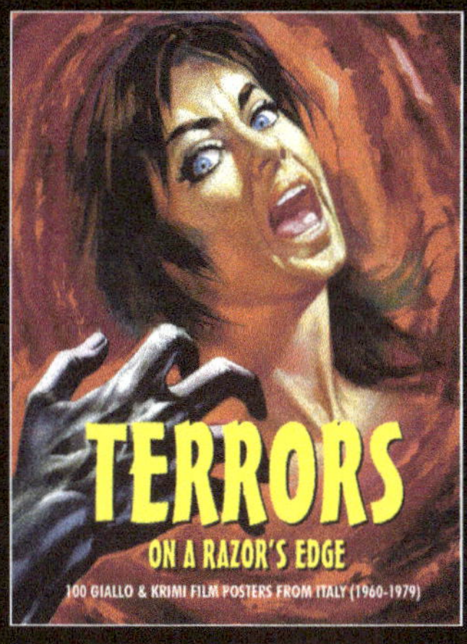
TERRORS
ON A RAZOR'S EDGE
100 GIALLO & KRIMI FILM POSTERS FROM ITALY (1960-1979)

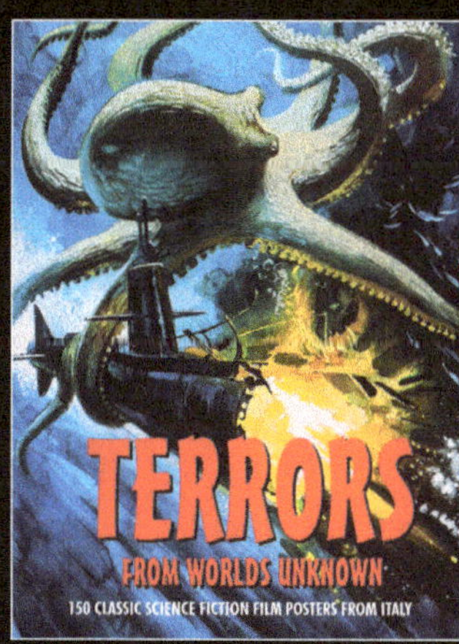
TERRORS
FROM WORLDS UNKNOWN
150 CLASSIC SCIENCE FICTION FILM POSTERS FROM ITALY

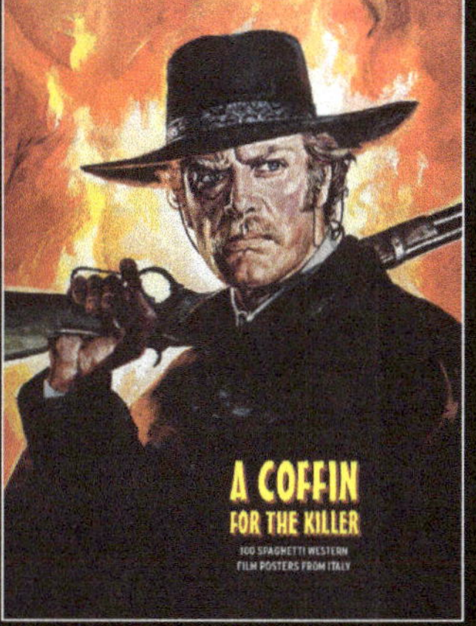
A COFFIN
FOR THE KILLER
100 SPAGHETTI WESTERN
FILM POSTERS FROM ITALY

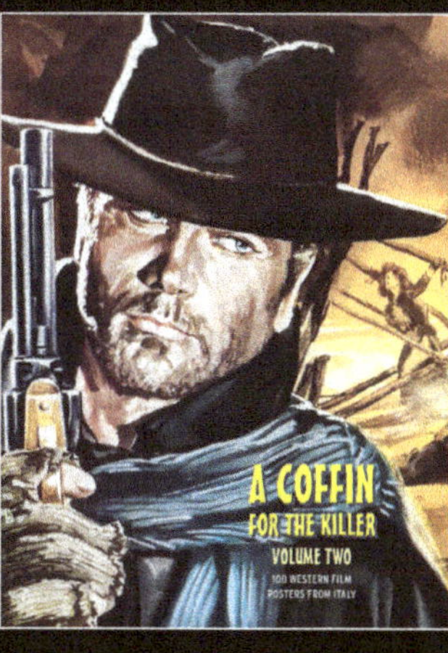
A COFFIN
FOR THE KILLER
VOLUME TWO
100 WESTERN FILM
POSTERS FROM ITALY

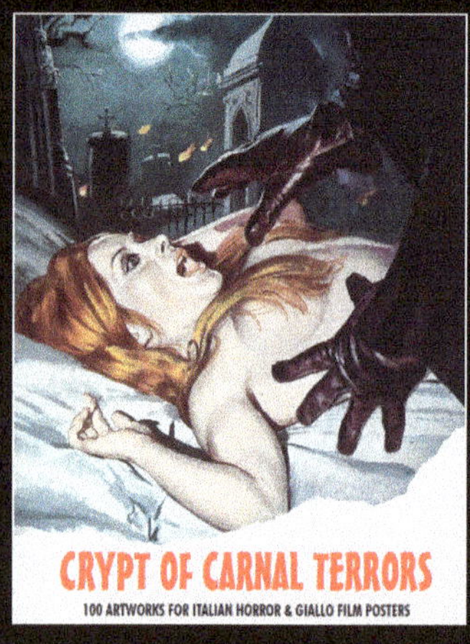
CRYPT OF CARNAL TERRORS
100 ARTWORKS FOR ITALIAN HORROR & GIALLO FILM POSTERS

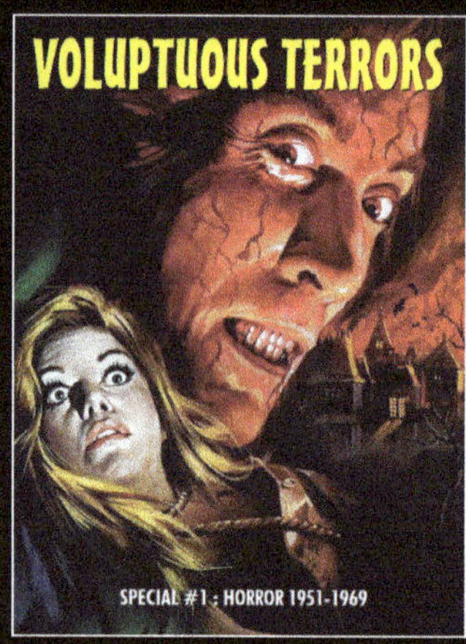
VOLUPTUOUS TERRORS
SPECIAL #1 : HORROR 1951-1969

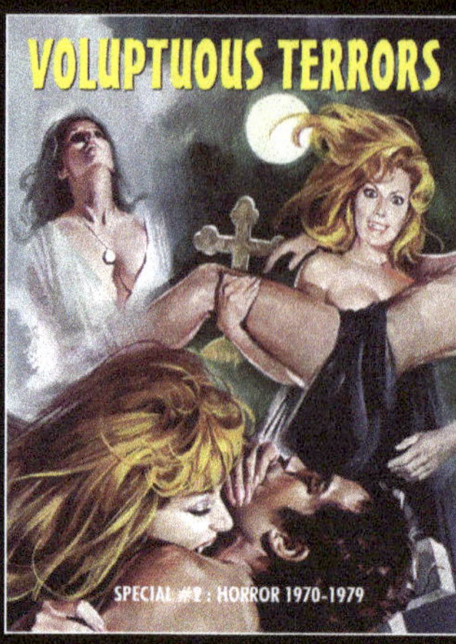
VOLUPTUOUS TERRORS
SPECIAL #2 : HORROR 1970-1979

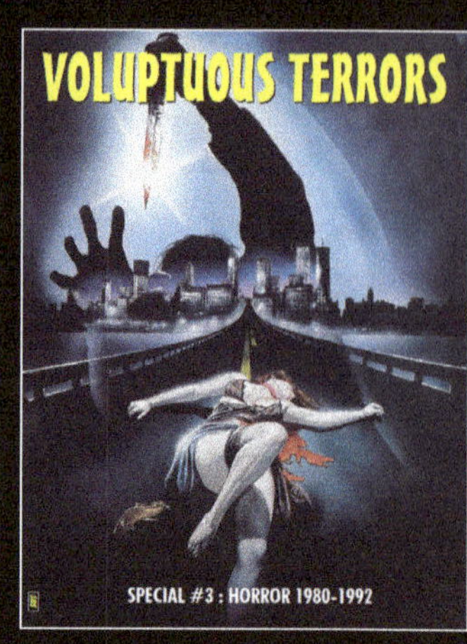
VOLUPTUOUS TERRORS
SPECIAL #3 : HORROR 1980-1992

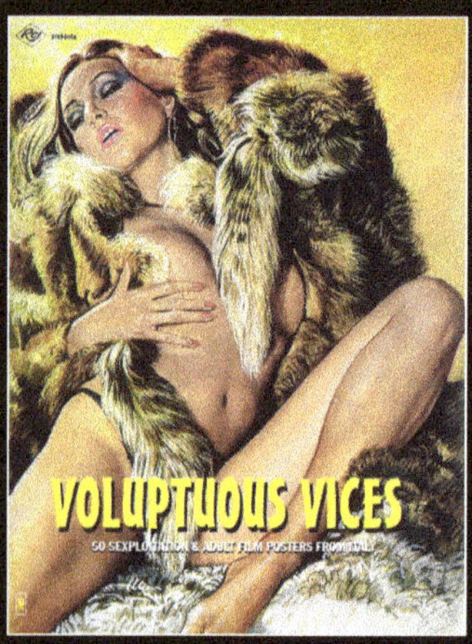
VOLUPTUOUS VICES
50 SEXPLOITATION & ADULT FILM POSTERS FROM ITALY

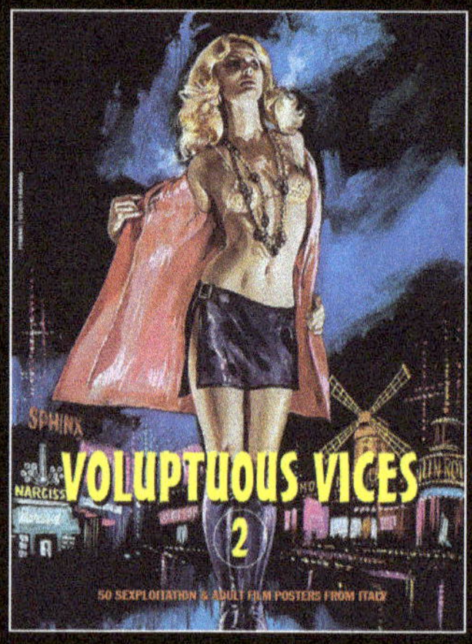
VOLUPTUOUS VICES
2
50 SEXPLOITATION & ADULT FILM POSTERS FROM ITALY

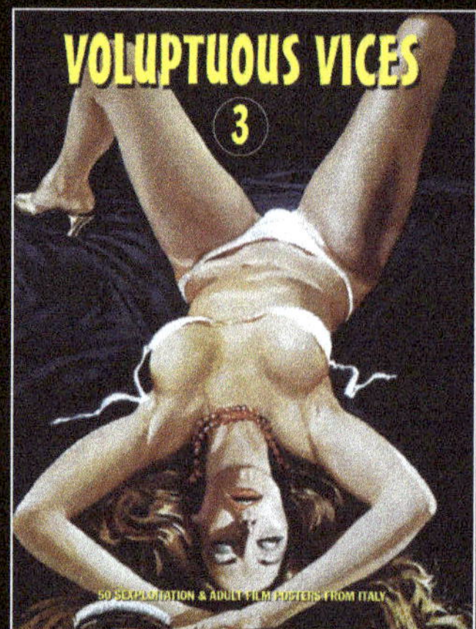
VOLUPTUOUS VICES
3
50 SEXPLOITATION & ADULT FILM POSTERS FROM ITALY

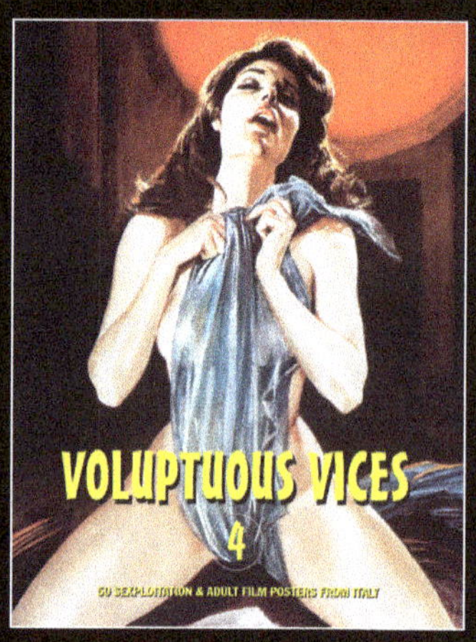
VOLUPTUOUS VICES
4
50 SEXPLOITATION & ADULT FILM POSTERS FROM ITALY

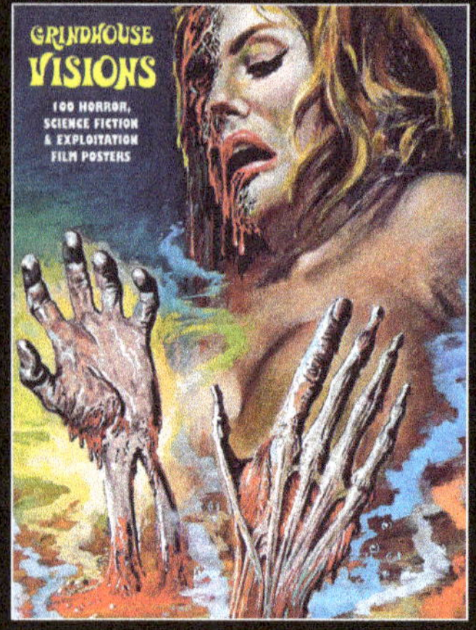
GRINDHOUSE
VISIONS
100 HORROR,
SCIENCE FICTION
& EXPLOITATION
FILM POSTERS

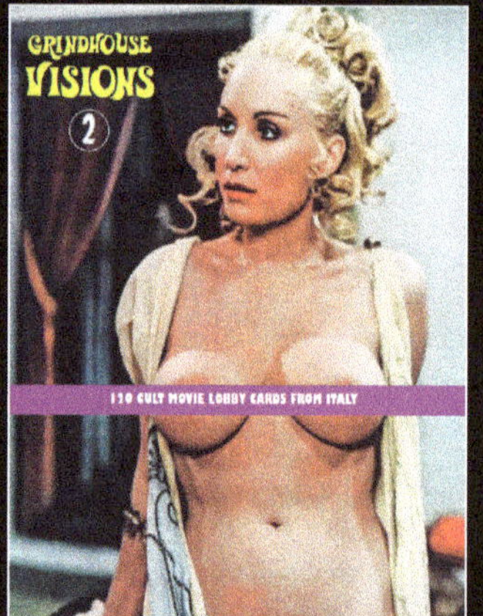
GRINDHOUSE
VISIONS
2
110 CULT MOVIE LOBBY CARDS FROM ITALY

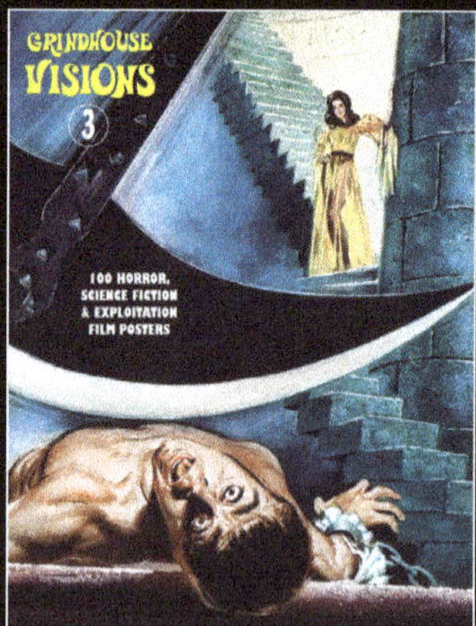
GRINDHOUSE
VISIONS
3
100 HORROR,
SCIENCE FICTION
& EXPLOITATION
FILM POSTERS

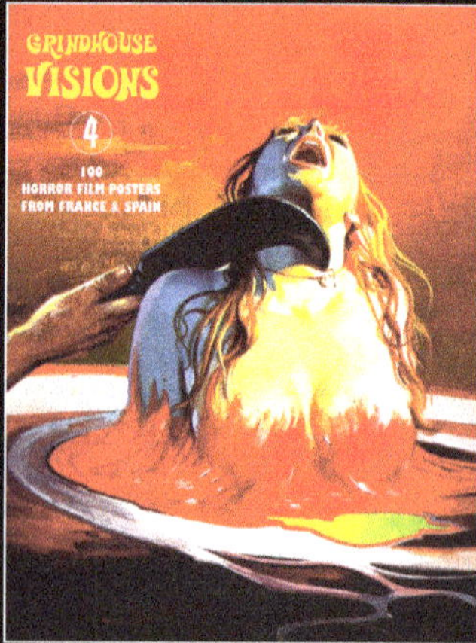
GRINDHOUSE
VISIONS
4
100
HORROR FILM POSTERS
FROM FRANCE & SPAIN

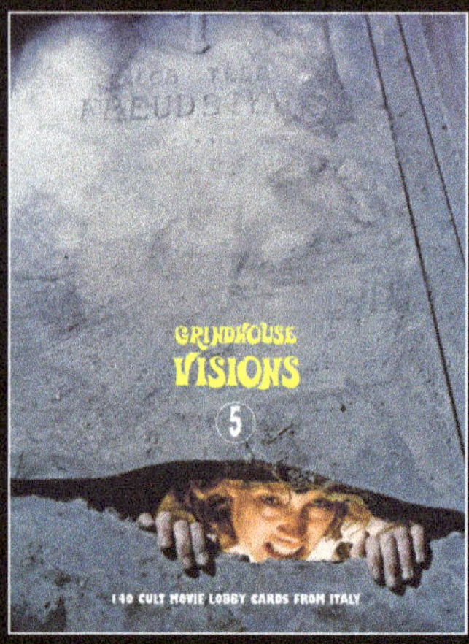
GRINDHOUSE
VISIONS
5
140 CULT MOVIE LOBBY CARDS FROM ITALY

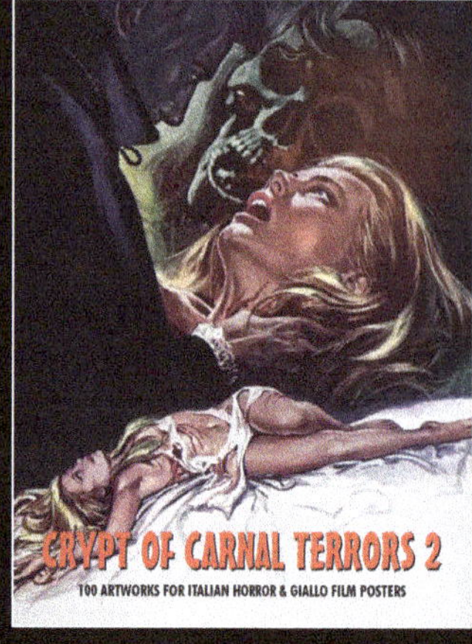
CRYPT OF CARNAL TERRORS 2
100 ARTWORKS FOR ITALIAN HORROR & GIALLO FILM POSTERS